The Honoured Society

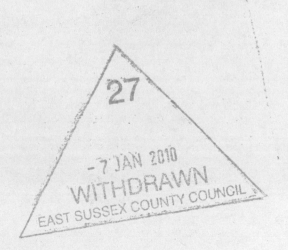

THE HONOURED SOCIETY

My Journey to the Heart of the Mafia

Petra Reski

Translated by Shaun Whiteside

Atlantic Books

LONDON

First published in Germany in 2008 by
Droemersche Verlagsanstalt Th. Knaur Nachf. GmbH & Co.

First published in Great Britain in 2012 by Atlantic Books,
an imprint of Atlantic Books Ltd.

This paperback edition published in Great Britain in 2013 by Atlantic Books

10 9 8 7 6 5 4 3 2 1

A CIP catalogue record for this book is available from the British Library.

Paperback ISBN 978 1 84887 136 6
EBook ISBN 978 0 85789 929 3

Designed by Richard Marston
Printed in Great Britain by CPI Group (UK) Ltd, Croydon, CR0 4YY

Atlantic Books
An imprint of Atlantic Books Ltd
Ormond House
26–27 Boswell Street
London WC1N 3JZ

www.atlantic-books.co.uk

For Shobha

Contents

Foreword

The sun is shining, and a light spring breeze stirs the lawyers' robes as we walk to the hearing in the Higher Regional Court. It's an impressive building, with colonnades, broad flights of stairs and high ceilings.

Even before I get the chance to admire the architecture any further, we've reached the courtroom, which has two policemen armed with guns and truncheons standing outside. Which surprises me a little. At the last hearing in a regional court there were no policemen; after all, these weren't criminal trials.

Has police protection become standard in German regional courts? After all, much has changed in Germany since I've been living in Italy. I don't have a chance to ask our lawyer. It's only a few minutes until the hearing's due to start. We step into the courtroom and sit down behind the sign that reads '*Beklagte*': 'Defendant'. I'm ruminating on the strangeness of the word, when I realize it refers to me. Sitting next to me is the publisher, my co-defendant. We have to push our chairs close together so that we can both sit behind the 'Defendant' sign. A tense silence reigns in the courtroom. We are sitting at Formica tables, like students in a seminar room, preparing to take our state exam in Late Medieval French.

The lawyers flick through their files, and I remember what it was like to hold my book in my hands for the first time. I'd impatiently torn off the plastic wrapping, and the spine of the book had cracked slightly when I opened it up. Both reverent and anxious, I had flicked through the virgin pages that smelled of paper and solvent. It's always an intimate moment for me to hold at last a book that previously existed only virtually, as a Word document or an email attachment. Feeling it, smelling it – and knowing that it will now go on to live its own life, independent of me. While I had still been sitting bent over the manuscript, some German friends had asked me apprehensively whether it wasn't dangerous to write a book about the Mafia. After all, anti-Mafia journalists in Italy lived under police protection.

'But my book's being published in Germany,' I'd replied.

———

It is still silent in the courtroom. The two policemen sitting outside the door both have a lot of gel in their hair, one of them has such curly hair that I can't help wondering whether it might be a perm. Aren't perms for men out of fashion?

The judge's bench is slightly raised, and a crucifix hangs on the wall behind. I look to the right, to the gallery, where I recognize a few familiar faces – a friend, a female journalist, a male journalist. The male journalist is thumbing through his notepad. I run my hands over the Formica table, which looks as if it's new. In Italy, courtrooms are always slightly tatty and the microphones never work. That would be unthinkable here, quite apart from the fact that the courtroom is small enough for anyone to be heard even without a microphone.

Seen from distance, my view of Germany had always been that it was the country with litter-free fields and trains that ran on time. Unlike Italy, where everything's a bit haywire, where the Mafia has infested whole stretches of the country, and even penetrated the highest political offices. With every year that I spent in Italy, Germany had become cleaner, more punctual and more incorruptible to me. And my Italian friends reinforced that assessment – perhaps out of conviction, or perhaps only because they were being kind. They exclaimed, '*Ah, la Germania! Tutto funziona!*' when I raved to them about Germany. They praised the Germans' sense of civic responsibility, the functioning legal system and the honest politicians who have to resign when so much as an unauthorized free trip can be proved against them. Never, I thought, could the Mafia really find a foothold in Germany. Because the Germans would take unhesitating and energetic action against it.

———

The door behind the judge's bench is still closed. No one in the courtroom dares even to whisper. Some people clear their throats. Others guiltily turn off their mobile phones, farewell tunes ring out and fall silent until there's nothing to be heard but the rustling of paper. I look at the crucifix and recall a day in the high security courtroom in Caltanissetta, where the trials against the assassins of Giovanni Falcone were held. I was sitting amongst the journalists behind the lawyers, right next to the cages in which the mafiosi sat. The hearing dragged on until late evening. I saw the lawyers of the Mafia bosses Totò Riina and Leoluca Bagarella chatting amicably with their clients. The cages were roped off with only a thin, burgundy-coloured cord, which did nothing to prevent the lively exchange of ideas between the mafiosi and their lawyers. They shook hands through the bars. Late that night I drove back to Palermo, thinking all the way about what I had seen. Should high security imprisonment look like that?, I wondered. They might as well just sentence them to house arrest. Which is, incidentally, pretty much the norm in Italy. As if they weren't Mafia bosses, but badly behaved children. I was convinced that nothing like that could ever happen in Germany.

———

At last the door behind the judges' bench opens, and the court comes in, a female judge and two assessors. I jump up from my chair, like everyone else there I'm determined to show respect to the court. Chairs scrape, and under the bench the wooden platform creaks as the judges take their seats. The journalist in the gallery clicks his biro. My book lies on the table next to him.

Only one day after I first flicked through my book, I set off on a tour of readings in Germany. I read in bookshops, libraries and at literary festivals. Behind the questions of the German readers and journalists, I often sensed the belief that the Mafia was very far away. The Mafia for them was almost folklore, a phenomenon that mostly appeared in backwater villages in Southern Italy, steeped in incomprehensible rituals and archaic blood feuds, with, why not, songs to which the mafiosi danced in their hideouts, songs that Germans liked to listen to as slightly sinister party music. Every bit as if the Mafia were an oppressed little ethnic group that was only trying to keep its customs alive.

I tried to make it clear to the audiences what I had been told by the state prosecutors in Reggio Calabria, Palermo and Naples: that the Mafia had adapted perfectly well to conditions in Germany for decades – because a mafioso can't be bugged either in public places or at home, because membership of the Mafia isn't a crime in German law, unlike in Italian law, and because money laundering is much easier in Germany, because in Germany a mafioso doesn't have to demonstrate that the money he has invested is clean. Unlike in Italy, where the Pio La Torre law meant that even a person who was only under suspicion of Mafia membership could have his or her possessions confiscated. I told them that the German legal clause concerning criminal association was no substitute for the Italian clause concerning Mafia membership; criminal association requires evidence of preparation for a particular crime, which means that in Germany, the Mafia only risks suspicion of criminal activity in exceptional cases – the Duisburg massacre of August 2007 was a very visible 'industrial accident' that they'd love to forget. I explained that a Europe without borders would apply not only to holidaymakers, but above all to the Mafia.

And the audiences looked at me as if I was warning them about a toxic cloud approaching from the distance. A toxic cloud whose effects they didn't need to worry about if they didn't leave the house. Then they asked me: 'Have you ever been threatened by the Mafia?'

That was the question I was asked most often. As if it was entirely natural or at least only to be expected that a journalist who dealt with the Mafia would put their own life at risk.

I gave a hesitant reply to that question, which I found distasteful and almost too intimate. I've actually been threatened twice in the course of my research: once in Corleone. And once in Calabria, in San Luca, the place that the hitmen in the Duisburg massacre came from. I'd been threatened there because I was at the heart of the Mafia's territory, I explained.

———

Now the lawyers are making their case. The courtroom is tense, silent. The journalist hunches over his notepad like a schoolboy, and I think back to the reading I gave in Erfurt. My copy of the book had been around for almost two months, and the pages weren't quite as virginal as before. I'd scribbled on them in pencil, it was bristling with post-it notes, and was slightly battered at the corners. As I walked through the beautiful streets of Erfurt to the bookshop, I thought about how surprised I had been in San Luca that there were so many cars with the German registration EF — for Erfurt — driving through the village.

A few days before the reading, my publishers had received a lawyer's letter threatening action if my book continued to be distributed with the passages about their client. It was already the third interim injunction I had been threatened with — and there was actually a bailiff waiting for me outside the bookshop. She handed me a letter containing the injunction.

It wasn't exactly the best start to the reading, particularly since about a hundred people were waiting for me inside: I tore the letter open and ran my eyes over it. Then I stepped into the bookshop. The bookseller had engaged a presenter for the reading — that's not necessarily common, but neither is it unusual. The presenter was a stout gentleman, and greeted me by saying that my book was full of untruths. And that he was a good friend of the complainant whose interim injunction I was currently holding in my hand.

'Right,' I said.

I'd have liked to tell him that he had every right not to like my book. I would have liked to suggest that he step down as presenter, but it was one minute to eight, and the audience were already shuffling their feet. He had a lot of good friends in Naples, the presenter went on, and I replied: 'Me too'.

Then I read. I read the passage about my trip to San Luca, and I read the passage about money laundering in Germany, what German investigators call *Beweislastumkehr* — a shift in the burden of proof. It is the reason why they envy Italian legislation: in Italy it isn't up to the police to demonstrate that the money is dirty, but the investor to show that his money is clean.

After my reading the stout presenter introduced the discussion by holding forth on how money laundering wasn't possible in Germany, and how it was a mystery to him how I could have got hold of this truly bizarre information.

At this point a gentlemen who spoke in a distinguished and authoritative tone started off on a lecture peppered with legal pseudo-information, which also led to the conclusion that money laundering in Germany was simply unthinkable. Last to speak was the former mayor of Erfurt, Manfred Ruge, who had also found time to come to my reading. He didn't waste much time with an introduction, but launched a frontal assault on me: everyone here in the bookshop knew that I was the guiding spirit behind a recent documentary about the Mafia in Germany, the film in which he himself had been made to say things that he hadn't meant in that way. I tried in vain to point out to him that he was perhaps overestimating my influence, and I'd had nothing at all to do with the documentary, rather the film-makers had done their research independent of me, but had plainly come to the same conclusion: that the Mafia had done a great job of settling itself in Germany for decades. I added that I was, however, flattered by the suggestion, because I thought the documentary was very good.

He now clearly regretted every single word that had slipped from his lips in front of a rolling television camera.

After the former mayor of Erfurt, some of the Italians in the room felt moved to take the floor. A man with a bow-tie

rose to his feet and delivered a long speech in which he defended my accusers, who were, after all, valuable members
of society, by saying that everything that I had written in
my book with reference to documents from the Italian and
German police was a complete invention – that I had therefore stained the honour of the gentlemen I had quoted. Those
same gentlemen clearly enjoyed his speech – which was why
he glanced, looking for approval, at some men sitting next
to him, and then said, 'I admire your courage, I very much
admire your courage, I have a quite extraordinary degree of
admiration for your courage, Frau Reski.'

Thus inspired, the Italians sitting next to him also felt
spurred to speak, but their German was poor, so they attacked
me in Italian, calling me a liar and finally crying, 'You are
the mafiosa here!' I couldn't see their faces clearly, because
I was blinking under a harsh light all the time, and they were
in the shadows.

Until that point the audience had sat there like rabbits frozen in the headlights. But now they started shouting: 'Who
are you? What on earth's going on here?' There was uproar,
and it was a long time before the stout gentleman remembered his role as presenter and called for quiet. At the end of
the event both German and Italian readers came up to me
and asked me anxiously if I was alone in Erfurt, and if they
could accompany me to my hotel.

That evening in my hotel room I thought for a long time
about all that had happened. I knew a turning point had been
reached, and not just for me. My book had been published at
a time when the Mafia, particularly the 'Ndrangheta, were

trying hard to slip back out of sight. Lulling the Germans back into the deep slumber from which the Duisburg murders had startled them.

————

Now, in the courtroom, it's the turn of the plaintiff's lawyer to set out his case. It seems to me that he's trying to hypnotize me. He doesn't take his eyes from mine for a second as he delivers his speech. That nettles the judge, who instructs the lawyer to look not at me but at the court while he's speaking. 'We attach great importance to that,' she says.

The male journalist takes notes and skims back and forth through my book. The first time I held a copy, with the passages blacked out in accordance with the court instructions, it seemed strangely unreal, as if the book had appeared from somewhere underground. As if this was a book that might be dangerous to read. I still expect my fingers to turn black every time I run them over the pages. Shortly after the reading in Erfurt some German newspapers reported on my case – and again I thought of the moment when I first held my book in my hands. I had expected it to lead a life of its own, but not that my book would turn into a 'case'. Italian journalists took a great interest, and wrote with amazement about the strangeness of the fact that a Mafia book could only be published in Germany if it had passages blacked out. Blacked-out content that had already been documented at length by the Italian press, with no judicial consequences.

————

At last the court orders a break for deliberation, and I think about all the little flickering distress flares that were fired off after my reading in Erfurt. Phone calls to my publishers, letters, emails. People who didn't inspire confidence offering their advice. The German police advised me to replace the door to my flat in Germany with an armoured one. And to put up panes of bullet-proof glass over my windows.

Worried friends rang me up leaving unhelpful messages saying 'Hey, you take care,' as if I was notorious for forgetting to look left and right when crossing the road. A friend advised me always to check that the wheel nuts on my car were fastened tightly enough. Luckily I don't own a car. Most of the year I live in Venice.

———

During the break, no one in the courtroom dares to speak in a loud voice. The plaintiff mutters something to the lawyer behind his hand, the journalist leafs through a newspaper, and the two armed policemen crack their fingers. In a whisper, I ask our lawyer if it's normal to have armed policemen at a hearing in the Higher Regional Court. He shakes his head. Clearly the judge has ordered police protection.

I look at my watch and wonder how long the break for deliberation is likely to last. If the court deliberates for more than two or three hours I'll miss my plane. And I'm longing to get back to Italy. At least there I don't have to explain to anyone what a Mafia threat is. And I don't have to explain to anyone what the 'Ndrangheta is. Even my greengrocer would understand. That's the bitter result of Italy's bloody history.

Almost every anti-Mafia law was preceded by the murder of a state prosecutor. Which is why a Bavarian investigator said to me, 'In Germany we have no dead judges and no dead state prosecutors. Otherwise the legislation would be different.'

The atmosphere in the courtroom is slowly getting more and more restless. Clearly the court is showing no signs of coming back any time soon. The lawyers start putting their documents back in their briefcases. We can, they say, find out the ruling by phone later on. At last we leave the courtroom. Through the high windows, bright spring sunlight falls on the Formica tables, on the crucifix, on the empty judges' bench. The policemen remain until the last people have left the court.

In the corridor behind the courtroom the plaintiff rests his hand on our lawyer's arm and says to him coolly, 'Next time make sure she comes with six policemen.'

Marcello Fava

It's always horrible, being present at a murder. Particularly if it's a person you know. And if you don't know why that person is dying or has died. You don't know, and you'll never find out. Because if you're acting as an ordinary soldier, as we call it in Cosa Nostra, they won't give you any explanations.

The man wears his dark-blond hair with a parting. He has sea-blue eyes. A little double chin and womanly lips. He's wearing a midnight-blue, double-breasted suit and clumsily balancing a briefcase on his knees.

He looks at his watch and then at the departures board for our flight from Venice to Palermo. The twenty-minute delay that's been announced is nearly over. When the stewardess opens the gate, he stands up and strokes the material of his suit smooth over his knees. He looks oddly old-fashioned, as Sicilians often look when life has washed them northwards – as if they came from a time long forgotten. Of course, he wears a monogrammed shirt. Sicilians celebrate elegance as something sacredly serious, like the businessman in the pin-stripe suit pacing up and down by the gate, holding a little cigarillo that went out ages ago. Just like in *Prizzi's Honor*. Or the woman with the big earrings and stockings, the tops of which stand out against her tight skirt when she crosses her legs. Just like Sophia Loren in *Yesterday, Today and Tomorrow*. Or the old couple who look like extras in a Dolce & Gabbana advertisement: the wife in a black suit and with her hair in a bun, the husband in a rough checked jacket. A couple who only communicate with each other in whispers and who, you can see, only leave their village once a year, to visit their son who's found himself a job in the Veneto. Which the parents consider a terrible blow. Apart from these visible Sicilians, there are the invisible ones who don't look Sicilian in Venice at all, as if they had grown pale away from Sicily. Who are transformed during the flight. Who, with each minute in the air that brings them closer to Sicily, assume their original colour.

The man in the midnight-blue, double-breasted suit is the first to board the airport bus; he doesn't set his little briefcase down on the floor but carries it under his arm, which makes him look oddly anxious, like a child going on its travels for the first time.

Generally the victim is brought to a house by a friend, his best friend if possible, so that he feels safe. Then they grab him, and if he still has something to say, he says it now. I'd like to see the one who doesn't speak, with a noose around his neck. But regardless of whether he speaks or not, he gets killed anyway.

When we board the plane, I lose sight of him. The Sicilian woman with the garter belt sashays down the rows to her seat. The old Sicilian couple cart plastic bags and tied-up parcels down the aisle, as if they planned to stow all their household goods in the luggage rack. Apart from a few overweight American tourists struggling past the narrow rows of seats, the plane is full of Italians, most of them business travellers. I always take the evening plane from Venice to Palermo. I like to get there at night, just early enough to have dinner. When I'm in my seat, I send another two texts: one to Salvo, my trusted taxi driver; one to Shobha, the photographer I've been working with for so long that our relationship's almost like a marriage. I tell them we're twenty minutes late, and ask Shobha to reserve a table in a restaurant for us.

As always, I plan to do a bit more work on the flight and start flicking through my archive material. Then I take from my pocket the book about the mystery of the lawyer Paolo Borsellino's red diary. When I open it, I immediately have the feeling that someone's reading over my shoulder. Sicilian paranoia is starting even before I've arrived in Sicily. Every time I fly to Palermo I wonder if it's a good idea to read articles about Mafia bosses or investment strategies, or flick through lectures about the Mafia and power. Or even read *Antimafia Duemila*, a newspaper that is always sent to subscribers in a strikingly neutral envelope, as if it were a porn mag. Sometimes I feel a bit rebellious and think: I don't care. We're living in Europe, after all, not in Transnistria! Italy's one of the founder members of the EU! And sometimes I snap my book shut and put it away. As I do now.

When the man in the midnight-blue, double-breasted suit sits down in the same row as me, I'm already flicking unexcitedly through the in-flight magazine, which says that a flat in Venice will lay you golden eggs because you can rent it out all year as a holiday apartment. He gives me a friendly but non-committal nod, the way you greet a stranger with whom you have nothing in common but your flight route. The seat between us is empty and the man sets his briefcase down on it.

Before I had to kill someone, I would cross myself. I would say: 'Dear God, stand by me! Make sure nothing happens!' But I wasn't the only one who crossed himself beforehand and prayed to God. We all did.

I still remember every one of his sentences. To be able to speak to him, I had to apply to the Ministry of the Interior. I had to set out my motives and guarantee that I wouldn't ask him any questions about current trials. Our meeting had to have the agreement not only of the Secretary of State at the Ministry of the Interior, but also of every individual public prosecutor in the Mafia trials in which Marcello Fava appeared, either as defendant or witness. Every week, at first, to check the state of things, I called the *Servizio Centrale*, the department of the Ministry of the Interior in Rome responsible for turncoat mafiosi, whose name sounds like some sort of secret service operation. It was very quickly made clear to me, however, that my inquiries wouldn't speed matters up. 'Don't call us, we'll call you.' For six months I heard nothing at all. And I'd actually given up all hope when I got a call from Rome one afternoon. '*Servizio Centrale*,' said a voice. My application had been approved. I was to make my way to a bar in Rome, which, as fate would have it, bore the name *Lo zio d'America*, The American Uncle.

A few days later, a taxi set me down a short distance from the bar. It looked like one of those labyrinthine Italian motorway service stations which you step into to get an espresso and leave with five CDs, some Sardinian donkey sausage and a lump of parmesan. Behind an endless counter stood barmen with paper hats sitting on their gelled hair. When I was about to order an espresso, my phone rang. I felt in my pocket, from the depths of which it went on ringing, until a man standing next to me said: 'I called you. Please follow me.'

I hadn't caught his name. I walked some distance behind him. For a split second I wondered what would happen if the man I was following wasn't the man I thought he was. I followed him along potholed pavements, past 1960s buildings and box hedges that smelled of cats. The periphery of Rome is so faceless that I had trouble remembering the way. At last, he stopped outside the entrance to a building, where two men stood looking conspicuously inconspicuous, as only policemen can. The hallway smacked of council housing, with greyish-yellow paint flaking off the walls.

Afterwards we would often go out to eat together. Maybe that's sadism. Could be, I don't know. And I don't know what else to call it, either. But that's what happened. We met up in the evening and went out to eat together. You just have to forget the whole business. Nothing happened, nothing at all.

The mafioso Marcello Fava was waiting for me on the third floor. In a flat that had been rented by the Ministry of the Interior under a false name – for 'collaborators with the judiciary', as turncoat mafiosi are known in the politically correct and somewhat euphemistic language of the law. Since Marcello Fava was working with the public prosecutor's office, he, his wife and his two sons had to be protected from the revenge of Cosa Nostra. They had had to leave Sicily and live somewhere in Italy under police protection and false names.

Although the flat was uninhabited, it was still full of traces of other lives. On a wall was a picture of a mountain scene and an almost blind Venetian mirror; in one corner stood a torn, mustard-coloured sofa, and next to it a battered wicker chair, an old gas stove. The stove had seen better days, and on the dining-room table there was a waxed tablecloth scored with knife marks. It was as if the inhabitants had only gone out for a moment; they would shortly open the door and stare in horror at the strangers in their flat – a woman and six men.

The shutters were lowered and the policemen took up their positions. A bodyguard walked up and down on the balcony, watching the street; two officials stood down by the house entrance, another had planted himself in the hallway, another was reading the latest John Grisham. They were all chewing gum and wore ripped jeans, safari waistcoats and earrings. Fava, on the other hand, looked like an employee of the Banco di Sicilia. He wore a midnight-blue suit with a light-blue tie. His face was rosy and scattered with a few freckles, his dark-blond hair carefully parted. His eyebrows had a reddish tinge. He nervously ran his palms over his sleeves, over his trouser legs, as if he lived in fear of something awful happening to his suit. Fava had brought a little briefcase which rested on his knees, and which he initially clung on to. Like a student going to his first lecture.

'*Tranquillo*,' he said, as I switched on my tape recorder. I was completely relaxed. Uttered in a Sicilian accent by a mafioso, the word sounds like an executioner trying to reassure his victim. '*Tranquillo*.' We were sitting by artificial light at the kitchen table and Fava was telling the story of his life. A life that had only really begun when he was 'chosen'.

It was a wonderful thing for me. It was everyone's desire to be accepted into Cosa Nostra. To be close to these people, to be respected by everyone. Wherever you go, no one dares stand in your way. Respect is your due. Even though other people couldn't know, they sensed you were a man of honour. That you were entitled to everything. That's what they're like, the mafiosi of Palermo. And only in Palermo. Not in the whole of Sicily.

He talked about his acceptance into the Mafia as if talking about an awakening. Fava had been twenty years old when he was accepted into the Porta Nuova family in Palermo. Unlike the Calabrian 'Ndrangheta, in which the members of a family are actually related by blood, a family of the Sicilian Cosa Nostra is based on elective affinity. The family is the smallest organizational unit of Cosa Nostra, whose bonds are reinforced by the acceptance ritual. Even today, the Mafia uses an initiation ceremony that seems to have had its origins in the rites of the Freemasons and which makes a deep, almost religious, impression on young and ambitious mafiosi: the presence of the godparents, the drop of blood falling on the holy picture, the invocation of the price to be paid for betrayal, the burning of the picture of the saint — nothing significant has changed for centuries. It was only when mafiosi started turning state evidence in droves that the boss, Bernardo Provenzano, suspended the initiation ritual. The mafiosi must not know the names of the members of their family, so that, if one day they do become turncoats, they cannot betray them.

Because if one person betrays, the others fall too. No other Mafia organization in Italy is as hierarchically structured as Cosa Nostra. After the family comes the *mandamento*, the Mafia district, consisting of several Mafia families. Above this is the provincial commission, which is composed of the district regional heads. And at the very top, for a while, was the *cupola*, the *commissione interprovinciale*, the Mafia council consisting of the heads of the provincial commissions — a council that existed until the boss Totò Riina assumed autocratic power.

The family into which Marcello Fava was accepted wasn't just any Mafia family, it was a clan that had produced some remarkable bosses, some of whom later shook planet Mafia to the core. Tommaso Buscetta was part of the family — the first turncoat boss in the history of the Mafia, of whom the legendary lawyer and prosecuting magistrate Giovanni Falcone once said, he was like a teacher who introduced him to the language of the Mafia. Salvatore Cancemi was a member, the boss who first spoke about the Mafia connections of Silvio Berlusconi and his right-hand man Marcello Dell'Utri – the former manager who became co-founder of the right-wing party Forza Italia, the in-house party of the businessman Berlusconi. By founding the party, he was trying to react to the crisis that had arisen out of corruption investigations that went under the slogan 'Clean Hands'. In 1993, Cosa Nostra had been in direct contact with representatives of Silvio Berlusconi, said the turncoat mafioso Antonino Giuffrè, concerning an alliance between the Mafia and the newly founded Forza Italia party. In 2004, Marcello Dell'Utri was sentenced in the first instance to nine years' imprisonment for supporting a Mafia association. (In Italy, a sentence only comes into effect once it has reached the third 'instance'.) By that time, his connection with the mafioso Vittorio Mangano was already well documented. On the initiative of Dell'Utri, Mangano had lived for two years in Berlusconi's villa as a middleman for Cosa Nostra – officially as a 'stable-keeper'.

Vittorio Mangano also belonged to the Porta Nuova family, as did the boss Pippo Calò, known as the 'Mafia's cashier', who was involved in the murder of 'God's banker', Roberto Calvi, who was in charge of the Banca Ambrosiana and had transacted deals not only with the Vatican Bank but also with the Mafia. Calvi was found hanged under Blackfriars Bridge in London with US$15,000 and heavy stones in his pockets. But Calò didn't become a turncoat, he merely broke with the Mafia, without spilling any beans.

Marcello Fava described his Mafia baptism as rapturously as if he were recalling his meeting with his first great love.

He spoke with high esteem of his godfather, who wasn't just one of the little group leaders who had acted as godfathers to other mafiosi, but a major boss. Fava obsessively described every detail of the ritual of his acceptance into the organization. How his baptism had taken place one morning in a warehouse, in the presence of twelve bosses. Who had all risen to their feet when the godfather came in. And who later withdrew for their deliberations. He had had to wait outside, along with three other boys who were also due for induction.

When I asked him whether his memory wasn't distorting things, Fava became furious. It was something you had to feel, he said defiantly. And he sounded like an unhappy lover, an abandoned lover, a man seduced. He praised the induction ritual as a holy liturgy – the burning of the holy picture, Santa Rosalia, San Giuseppe, the drop of blood dripping on the picture, the prophecy that he would be burned like the saint in his hand if he were ever to betray Cosa Nostra. And now he saw himself burning. A little bit more each day.

Fava would never be able to lead a normal life. A mafioso who breaks his silence becomes an untouchable. Despised equally by the Mafia and by respectable Sicilians: by the Mafia because he has revealed their secrets in order to buy his freedom; by Sicilians because he has only repented in order to save his own skin. In the first few years after the assassinations of Giovanni Falcone and Paolo Borsellino mafiosi had gone over to the law in droves. Now it happens very rarely. Public prosecutors generally fail when they try to persuade imprisoned bosses to leave the organization. One prosecutor told me how, talking to one of them, he had painted his post-Mafia life in the most glowing terms, invoking the future of his children, who would grow up on the right side. The mafioso merely pointed with a smile at the prosecutor's bodyguards and said: 'Mr Public Prosecutor, if you can't rely on your own security, how are you going to protect me?' And the prosecutor hadn't been able to give him an answer.

The first time I was there, it was a trauma for me. Because they hadn't told me anything about it beforehand, and then this boy I knew was brought in; it was terrible, he was crying and pleading, but there was nothing to be done. The decision had been made. No one could help him. He was punished as a warning to the others.

I thought it was odd, hearing a mafioso talking about trauma. Plainly, it was easier for Fava to judge his actions in terms of psychological categories than moral ones. 'Trauma' is an easier word to say than 'murder'.

Throughout the whole of the conversation he clutched a piece of paper on which he had written notes about his life, a life that had consisted of Mafia membership, bank raids, drug deals, murder. Mostly by strangling. It's the Mafia's preferred method of killing: no noise, no blood. Two men hold the victim tightly, a third strangles him – usually with a small wire loop, because strangling by hand is too troublesome. Totò Riina was famous among his men for always setting his own hand to the job. When he murdered the mafioso Rosario Riccobono at the end of a wine-fuelled lunch, the boss called him by his nickname. '*Saruzzo*, your story is over,' he whispered tenderly, as he put his hands around the sleeping man's neck. The two other mafiosi present held the helpless man down. With the strength of a bull, the boss strangled his victim in less than three minutes. That achievement was greatly admired in retrospect, even by the two turncoat mafiosi who later betrayed him.

Fava was used to talking only to public prosecutors and defence lawyers. Perhaps that was why he sought comfort in that piece of paper, that crib sheet for the stages of his life: when he was boss of the Porta Nuova family, when he was on the run, the first time he was arrested, and when he turned *pentito*, defector. When he became an outcast. He wasn't used to talking for once not about dates, facts and names, but about what he had felt.

A mafioso doesn't find it hard to murder. At least, no harder than a soldier does. If Italy were to go to war with another country and an Italian soldier were to shoot fifty or sixty of the enemy, the soldier wouldn't be considered a criminal, he'd be honoured as a war hero. The mafiosi say. Because they define themselves as soldiers, who never murder for personal reasons but only for their state and their people. What the world sees as a criminal organization the mafiosi see as a society, a state, a people. And for that reason a mafioso doesn't have a bad conscience if he kills someone. He's only interested in the judgement of his own people, not that of strangers. Just like a soldier who finds himself in a war and who has no feelings of guilt.

The police gave no clue as to whether they were listening to Fava's descriptions or wondering whether it was time to buy a new mobile phone. They hid in the semi-darkness, behind blank, expressionless faces. They betrayed neither curiosity nor surprise, as if Fava were speaking not about murder and the Mafia but about how to download a software program.

I wondered whether they secretly despised him. Until recently, he had been on the other side. They had been 'flunkeys' as far as he was concerned, not the guardian angels that he called them now. And for each of them, his arrest had meant a promotion and a silver badge nestling on dark-blue velvet.

I was a very clever boy, I'd committed a few robberies — those are things that don't get past Cosa Nostra. So they approached me. I'd spent a few months in prison, and after that I was accepted.

I tried to imagine the twenty-year-old Fava being made a 'man of honour' in a warehouse in Palermo's old town. Rising from a *nessuno mischiato con niente*, a nobody involved with nothing, to a person of respect. Someone who's allowed to jump the queue in shops, is given free coffee and nodded to at the till: 'It's all paid for.' Someone who never needs to raise his voice. Someone below whose window the procession of the Madonna del Carmine, complete with brass band, stops so that he can hand the Madonna a few banknotes from his window. Sicilians are addicted to respect, and the Mafia sells them the dope.

Fava spoke in those Sicilian sentences half of which evaporates, flies away, seeps away. What he couldn't say in words, he said in gestures. He described little circles with his hand, curled his fingers and hooked them together; he pointed to imaginary dirt under his fingernails – he wasn't even worth that! – and stuck out his index finger and little finger to ward off evil.

His voice was amazingly light for a man, and, as Sicilians often do, he used the remote past tense, a tense that sounds very formal and is now used very rarely, even in written Italian. Sicilian has neither a recent past tense nor a future tense; it knows only the present. And the very remote past.

Fava came from the Kalsa. He had grown up in a family of ten – three sisters and six brothers – in a district of Palermo's old town that the city's middle class seldom goes near, and then only with very great caution, as if it were a wild animal that might attack you if you turn your back on it. He had grown up in a world of tufa-stone baroque and alley cats, tinkers and tinsmiths, a world in which the buzz of power saws seared the air and Eros Ramazzotti's voice groaned from the ramshackle speakers of the CD salesmen.

When Fava thought of Palermo, his nostrils were filled with the scent of the fried-food stalls in the Piazza della Kalsa, the smell of seething oil bubbling away in big aluminium pots, the aroma of *panelle*, of chick-pea fritters, of roasted calves' feet. He remembered picking the *panelle* out of their paper and saying hello to the fat man who always sat outside the church of Santa Teresa alla Kalsa in the rectangular shadow of a pollarded tree, cleaning olives and peeling potatoes to make croquettes. He remembered how there were always snails there on a Sunday, snails in garlic, from eleven in the morning till eight at night. And the fact that he would never again walk through the Kalsa with his two sons. Sometimes he consoled himself with the fact that at long last he no longer smelled of fear, fear of the police, of an undercover agent, of traitors in his own ranks, of a mission that he couldn't refuse. Bringing a friend to his executioner.

All his brothers worked in his family's butcher's shops in the Ballarò market, not far from the police headquarters. Fava had worked there as well; no one had asked any questions when he disappeared from time to time, for an hour, for half a day. His younger brother, Giuseppe, was in Cosa Nostra as well. He was arrested ten days after Marcello. And he has kept his mouth shut until now, as befits a man of honour.

When Fava's brothers found out that Marcello had become a turncoat, they closed up the iron shutters of their butcher's shops and laid chrysanthemums outside them. Above them they hung a sign: *Per un crasto*, For a castrated billy-goat. Nothing dishonours a Sicilian more than this jibe. 'We have no turncoat brother,' they said, 'we have only a dead brother.'

I haven't told my children anything about my past. You can imagine what our first meeting in jail was like, after my family had been taken out of Palermo and brought to a strange city where no one knows us. The two boys cried, they wanted to go back to Sicily, to their grandmother, to their cousins. My children have always been spoilt rotten. It was terrible for them, suddenly feeling they were all alone in the world. Then when I talked to them I made them understand that they would never have seen their father again if he hadn't taken this step.

When Fava talked about committing murder, he sounded like a car mechanic explaining the problems that arise when he takes out an old gearbox and puts a new one in. He smiled with a mixture of embarrassment and superiority, the way car mechanics smile when they're talking about torque to weight ratios, knowing that the customer won't have the faintest idea what they're on about. But when he talked about his family he seemed to lose his composure, his voice trembling, as if what he regretted was not the murders but the shame he had brought on his family. There were eighty relatives in his family, counting only the closest blood relations. His children had no relatives now, they would never celebrate weddings with their family, or baptisms, or first communions. All because their father had wanted only the best for them. And had turned into a worm. Into less than nothing.

I remember what it was like when I learned that my god-father had become a turncoat. It was a Sunday when I got the call. Men from my clan rang me up: 'Get on your motorbike right now and come and see us!' They sounded very agitated. I remember arriving at the meeting place outside Palermo half an hour later, where a lot of men of honour had already assembled and were waiting for me, stony-faced. They said, 'Sit down.' At that moment I knew nothing except that my god-father had been arrested two days previously. I thought, maybe they've killed him up at police headquarters. Because he'd tried to escape. Something like that. But then they told me: 'Your godfather has become a turncoat.' And I started laughing like a lunatic. 'That's why you had me almost kill myself driving

*through Palermo on my bike? To tell me some crap like that?'
'What do you mean crap,' the others said, 'it's true.' And then
I really did have to sit down. It was the disappointment of my
life. A myth collapsed for me. My godfather was — something
like that. Someone who had been like a visiting card for me: if
you thought about it, people were always mentioning the fact
that he was my godfather. And now — a nobody. They all went
underground for a while. As for me, I stayed quietly at home
and waited. All around me men were being arrested, I was
the only one who was spared the investigations. And I said to
myself: my godfather's forgotten about me.*

For the blink of an eye, I had the impression that Fava's
face had been set in motion, his eyelids were flickering, his
cheeks trembling and his freckles twitching. But then his
cheeks turned pink and relaxed again, and Fava fell silent.
The woven straw seat of the chair he was sitting on creaked.
It was as if the straw were betraying his insecurity. For a
long time there was no sound to be heard but the squeaking
of the woven straw and the officer sitting by the door making
a rustling sound as he turned the page of his John Grisham
novel. Some noise filtered up from the street, car doors
slamming and the roar of a passing bus.

The fact that his own godfather had become a turncoat
hadn't persuaded him, he said, to switch to the other side.
There was still no need. Plainly, his godfather had covered for
him, in spite of the obligation to tell the truth, the whole truth
and nothing but the truth. He had simply hushed up the fact
that Marcello Fava had belonged to Cosa Nostra since he was

twenty years old. So why should Fava have crossed over to the
other side? There was no need to. No feelings of guilt. He only
experienced those later on, towards his wife. For twenty years
he had cheated on her with the Mafia. His wife had never
known anything, he said, she had never doubted him for a
morning. If I say a horse is flying, my wife will believe it.

But she wasn't as naive as her husband imagined. No Sicilian
woman is naive. She walked to police headquarters when she
heard that her husband had been arrested again. She knew
that he hadn't been a victim of the judiciary, innocently persecuted on suspicion of being a thief and a bank robber, but
someone who had had the end of his prison sentence sweet-
ened by his bosses when they had paid for the baptisms of his
two sons – four hundred guests, very Cosa Nostra. Lobsters
and champagne. She knew that when he went with her to
mass on Sunday he was only waiting for a sign from his boss.
A slight nod of the head and already he was getting up from
his pew to discuss a few matters outside – protection money,
money from public contracts, bribes, new supermarkets and
bingo halls for money laundering, money for mafiosi in jail.
The clan's money was never enough. After communion he
sat back down in his seat. She knew he ignored her when she
said: 'I don't like those people you talk to.' She said nothing
more than that. She knew what it meant when he begged
her to go with him to lunch at the boss's villa. To a christen-
ing in Palermo cathedral. To a wedding feast in Mondello, in
the Palace Hotel, with real swans swimming in the pool. It
would have been a deadly insult to appear without his wife.

His wife's dislike of Cosa Nostra didn't stop her from

following him in his flight from the police. A life that Cosa
Nostra made as pleasant for him as possible. His brother
found him a little villa outside Palermo and a few lads to
act as bodyguards, who checked that the coast was clear, who
went with him on his motorbike, because that's the easiest
way for a wanted mafioso to get around Palermo. The full-
face helmet was his disguise, that and the wigs, the stick-on
beards — which didn't keep the 'flunkeys', as he still called
the police in those days, from storming the villa. Shots rang
out and his wife thought he was injured. While she was looking for him in all the hospitals of Palermo, she didn't know
that they had just been warning shots and he was already
in handcuffs at police headquarters. She was pregnant at the
time. And lost the child. After a week in solitary, he decided
to do the unthinkable. His wife said only: 'Whatever you do,
I'm with you.'

*I have no daughters. That's something I'd rather not talk
about. It's an open wound for me. Because when I was twenty,
I was given a daughter. Who died at birth. I have three dead
children. They all died at birth. That's something my wife
is always reminding me about. Because they're buried in
Palermo. And my wife constantly thinks of them, of those dead
children. I hope I'll bring her back to me one day. So that I can
do my duty at last.*

When he talked about his three dead children, his eyes
welled up with tears. He looked awkwardly in his briefcase
for a handkerchief, he bent down to hide his face, and blew

his nose noisily into it. He saw the miscarriages as a curse from God. As a punishment for his blasphemous life. Perhaps he was thinking about the people who had wept like children before they were strangled. Perhaps he was thinking of the ones who had died standing up, which is what the men of Cosa Nostra call it when a man of honour doesn't plead for his life. Perhaps he was thinking about how he had taken part in the funeral of a victim, about how he had straightened the sash on the wreath, looked the family in the eyes and shaken their hands to express his sympathy. Perhaps. And perhaps not. Had he not acted like a soldier?

I was always very devout. As a child, I was an altar-boy for the Salesians. After that, I drifted away from the church a little, I committed my first burglaries – but I'm still devout even today. As my son is, too. He loves religious processions. When we were still living in Sicily, he wouldn't miss a procession. Sometimes he copied them at home, he wore a veil and a train like the saints in the procession. He has three hundred figures of the saints at home. He's taken them all over the place. And he does that even now that he's eighteen years old and has a girlfriend.

At the end of the interview, Fava got to his feet and cracked his knuckles. The police woke from their slumbers, one of them looked through the peephole and nodded to the other officers. He hoped his observations had been useful to me, Fava said sheepishly. He awkwardly put his crib sheet back in the briefcase. When he opened it I saw that it was empty, apart from a book: *History of the Mafia from 1943 until the Present*. I remembered an old bookseller in Palermo, whose shop wasn't far from the Via della Libertà, telling me that the bosses from the Borgo Vecchio were among her best customers. As soon as she put a new book about the Mafia in her shop window, it sold out straightaway.

'Is there anything about you in that book?' I asked. And Fava replied: 'Yes, on page 568.' He said it like someone who's managed to get an entry in the *Encyclopædia Britannica*.

Then he took his leave of me, very formally, with a small hint of a bow. He seemed relieved. He said: 'There are people who go through life with their eyes open. And those who live with their eyes closed.' At last, four officers flanked him and walked him to the street. I had to wait upstairs in the flat until the car he was in had disappeared.

The two remaining policemen were curious to know whether I'd found the interview interesting. Whether I'd met other mafiosi, and what differences I'd spotted in their personalities. And what Germans know about the Mafia. Then they offered to take me in their car to the nearest taxi rank. Their car looked like a cross between a minibus and an amphibious vehicle, so I asked them if it could drive in water as well.

'We can't tell you that,' the policemen said, 'because then we'd have to kill you.'

———

The man in the midnight-blue, double-breasted suit also cracks his knuckles. We're already preparing to land in

Palermo, the tables are tipped up again, the seatbelt signs are on, and I'm still wondering whether I should speak to him for a moment. But what would I say? 'Remember me? I'm a journalist and interviewed you once, in Rome.' Because I don't think he does remember me. Journalists are never perceived as people. We're nothing but mirrors that people talk into. You speak into them and in the end an article comes out of it. You remember the name of the newspaper or magazine. Or maybe not. In Italy, at any rate, I'm rarely remembered. And he would have good reason not to remember me, because in returning secretly to Palermo he is putting his new life on the line. His freedom, his status as a collaborator with the forces of law and order, his livelihood, the protection of his family, everything. When a turncoat mafioso returns secretly to Sicily, it doesn't augur well. In Sicily everyone remembers the career of Baldassare Di Maggio – mafioso, hit man and driver to the boss Totò Riina. As a key witness in the Andreotti trial, Di Maggio had been responsible, among other things, for describing the kiss on the cheek between Andreotti and Totò Riina – one of the more spectacular statements about the close relationship between the politician and the Mafia boss. Later, Di Maggio had returned to Sicily, where, in his home town of San Giuseppe Jato, he would commit a murder – one that had nothing to do with the Andreotti trial but was a settling of old scores.

When Di Maggio was arrested for that murder, he provided the excuse that was needed to bring about the collapse of the Andreotti trial. The defence wanted above all to prove that the key witnesses whose statements incriminated

Andreotti were not credible. If the witness to the kiss on the cheek was not in fact the turncoat mafioso he claimed to be, but a mafioso who was still committing crimes, even though he was on the witness-protection programme, then it would be a serious error even to listen to his testimony against one of the most important Italian statesmen, let alone take it seriously as incriminating evidence.

Di Maggio was arrested and thrown off the witness-protection programme. But even then he didn't deviate from his account of the kiss on the cheek between Totò Riina and Giulio Andreotti.

Below us, the sea glistens as smooth and viscous as pitch. The plane is already flying at a low altitude and I see the Isola delle Femmine floating in the pitch. The sky is bright with stars, and the mountain, the one I always think we're going to crash into every time I fly into Palermo, stands out in the moonlight. But before fear can really take hold of me, the plane has already landed.

As always in Italy, the passengers are getting up and impatiently clearing out the luggage compartments while the plane is still rolling along the runway. When the engines are turned off, everyone crams into the narrow aisle, the two old Sicilians try to push their way to the front with their plastic bags and parcels, the man in the pinstripe suit sticks his unlit cigarillo in his mouth, the woman with the stockings brushes her skirt straight. When the plane door opens, damp, warm air pours in, smelling of Africa.

We walk across the runway to the airport building; in the pale glow of the floodlights I see the man who was sitting next to me. I watch him furtively as we wait for our bags beside the carousel. He takes his mobile phone out of his briefcase and switches it on. Our bags arrive at the same time. As we plunge into the sea of waiting Sicilians, I almost lose sight of him. But then I see him walking up to a thin man holding up a sign with a name written on it: Mr Berenson. Then he is swallowed up by the night.

And I hear Salvo, my taxi driver, saying to me, 'Ciao, Petra. Still carrying that same old battered suitcase?'

Rosaria Schifani

Salvo makes that remark about the suitcase every time I come to Palermo, it's a solicitous ritual of his. Because Salvo can't understand why I'm devoted to this battered suitcase even though I could easily afford a new one. A neat, smooth Signora suitcase. Not this old aluminium thing covered with stickers which he's now stowing in his taxi with an indulgent expression on his face.

Salvo always drives me when I'm in Palermo, he's done it for years. I've known him for so long that he's got through three fiancées in that time. Now he's got another one, and this time it's serious. Salvo's very thin, with a profile like a mouse. A mouse with alert, black eyes that seem to consist entirely of pupil. Even in jeans and trainers, Salvo always tries to look smart. When he puts his hands on the wheel he sticks out his little finger, the way other people do when drinking tea. It's not as if he's scrambling to drive me around Palermo, it's more that he's doing me a favour — because for some time now he's become the regular driver for a group of old ladies who play *scopa*, the Sicilian game played with cards that look like tarot cards. These old lady card-sharps meet every afternoon, which is why they represent a secure source of income for Salvo: the ladies always have absolute precedence.

I tap in a text to Shobha: 'Where are we eating?' And she answers: 'Everything's shut on Sunday evening. Except Fresco.'

Fresco is Shobha's local, a kind of vegetarian hippy restaurant opposite Ucciardone prison. They serve up a passable couscous, with piano accompaniment on Sundays. The pianist has been wooing Shobha, in vain, for years.

'OK, Fresco,' I reply, and Salvo asks me why I still haven't got a new phone. He proudly shows me his new super-thin Samsung. Of course, he has two *telefonini*, like any self-respecting Italian: one for private conversations, one for business. The private one's reserved exclusively for his fiancées. And his mother.

We drive silently along the motorway. Cinisi. Carini. Capaci. Each sign represents a case file, a police operation, a raid. Against the Alcamo clan, against the Castellammare del Golfo clan, against the Cinisi clan. Some trials have the names of the places the clans come from, others bear names like film titles: they're called 'Storm', or 'Golden Market', or 'Akragas'. And behind the film titles lurk mafiosi who look like janitors. Or bank clerks. Every time I come from the airport and see the sign for Cinisi, I can't help thinking about the boss in hiding, Matteo Messina Denaro — and his submissiveness to Don Tano Badalamenti, an old boss who came from Cinisi and preferred to let his life trickle away in an American jail rather than be disloyal to Cosa Nostra. He spent almost twenty years in a prison in Massachusetts.

Messina Denaro is seen as the new boss of the Sicilian Mafia: young, brilliant and on the run. In Sicily the phrase 'on the run' sounds as normal as a description of someone's marital status. Single, married, on the run. I wonder whether the brilliant Messina Denaro would maintain his loyalty to Cosa Nostra even in an American high-security prison. Perhaps he'd be readier to come clean than people might imagine.

To do me a favour, Salvo puts on Biagio Antonacci's CD and '*Sognami se nevica*', 'Dream of me if it snows'. In Sicily, the metaphor par excellence for unrequited love.

Few men in Sicily are as sought after as mafiosi on the run. Matteo Messina Denaro met up with ladies from the highest echelons of Trapani society at a hotel in Selinunte – and a short time later had its owner murdered because he didn't feel he had treated him with sufficient respect. The boss enjoyed himself at the elegant spa of Forte dei Marmi, adorned himself with Rolex watches, fell in love with an Austrian woman, whom he visited and whose telephone is probably still tapped today, and spent part of his time on the run from the police in Bagheria, not far from Palermo, staying with a woman who wrote him pages of love letters: 'I have loved you, I love you, and I will love you all my life.' She went to jail for acting as his accomplice. When Messina Denaro hid at this woman's home, his pursuers were so hot on his heels that they came close to catching him, except that one of the *carabinieri* had turned off the hidden cameras and given the boss the tip he needed.

Salvo says: 'I don't know what you women see in this song.' And I can't give him an answer.

'What kind of a story are you doing this time?' Salvo asks. He asks more out of politeness than interest; basically, he thinks a preoccupation with the Mafia is a waste of time. On the one hand. On the other, it fills him with a curious sort of pride that I should come here specially from Venice to tell the Germans what's happening in Sicily. As if the island's inhabitants were a people at risk of extinction, of interest to a very few, highly specialized anthropologists. People whom he meets daily in the hall of his building, and whom he otherwise considers overrated. Salvo still lives with his mother, in the district between the Piazza Indipendenza and the Capuchin Crypt, where tourists shudder at the sight of the mummies. It's a normal district of Palermo, which lives equally normally off the drugs trade. Salvo loves describing how the customers meet by the statue of Padre Pio, because the goods are hidden under the saint's feet. A neighbour on Salvo's floor has already been arrested four times for membership of the Mafia, and each time he got out of prison he rose a bit higher in the hierarchy. First he committed break-ins, then he collected protection money — that is, he picked up the envelopes that were laid out ready for him, and if there was nothing ready he squeezed superglue into the locks of the shops that hadn't paid — and now you only ever see him in a suit and tie.

'I'm writing a portrait of Letizia,' I say.

'Letizia?' Salvo asks in amazement, because he knows Letizia, and because he thinks I write about people who are either famous or dangerous, and in his eyes Letizia is neither famous nor dangerous, but just the mother of the photographer Shobha.

'Letizia Battaglia is perhaps your most famous woman photographer,' I say, 'your most famous anti-Mafia photographer.' A Sicilian Cartier-Bresson, I'm about to say, if Letizia wouldn't have taken offence at being compared with someone else. And if Salvo knew who Cartier-Bresson was.

'*Minchia*,' Salvo says. 'I drove her only yesterday, and I didn't know she was so famous.'

'It doesn't matter,' I say. When Sicilians say '*Minchia*' they're really impressed. *Minchia* means 'cock' in Sicilian. In fact, Sicily has tried its damnedest to forget Letizia. There is no exhibition in her honour, no archive of her work, nothing. 'They pretend I don't exist,' Letizia always says. 'As if I were guilty for the things I've seen.'

There are no reminders of her − and she was always more than a photographer: Letizia was a theatre director, city councillor and MP for the anti-Mafia party La Rete. Her surname Battaglia means 'battle' − her life's manifesto.

'And why are the Germans interested in Letizia right now?' asks Salvo.

'Because of Duisburg,' I say.

Because, while there are no corpses, people are inclined to suspect that the Mafia doesn't exist. Before six Calabrians were murdered in Duisburg, a lot of editors saw my interest in the Mafia as a personal eccentricity, a whim − as if I'd become obsessed with some absurd topic like the life of the giant ant-eater – to be treated with a degree of indulgence. Okay, if she's absolutely desperate to write about the Mafia, then for God's sake let her get on with it; on the other hand, next time get her to write us something about Tuscany.

And then the massacre in Duisburg happened and my phone started ringing non-stop. Everyone wanted to send me to Calabria. News websites, weekly papers, monthly magazines. 'Haven't you got a mafioso to hand that you could interview?' one editor asked me. Suddenly everyone wanted to know all about the Mafia, to what extent Cosa Nostra differed from the Camorra and whether it was actually imaginable that something like the Duisburg massacre could happen more often. I heard myself lecturing and doling out definitions – that the word Mafia actually referred only to the Sicilian Cosa Nostra; while the Calabrian Mafia was called 'Ndrangheta and was at the moment the most successful criminal association in Italy; alongside the Neapolitan Camorra, which, unlike Cosa Nostra with its strictly hierarchical vertical organization, was organized horizontally, which also explained the constant gang wars, everyone wanting to be the boss, and you can't have that without corpses; and the Apulian Sacra Corona Unita, the youngest Mafia organization in Italy, which only came into being in the 1980s. And at the end of the phone calls I turned down all the commissions because at the time I happened to be in Poland covering a story – which was a source of relief to me. It was only several months later that I travelled to San Luca and by that time all interest had subsided again.

'The Germans must have been really shocked when that thing happened in Duisburg,' Salvo says with concern. And also some worry. '*Che brutta figura*,' he says — what an ugly image we've given of ourselves. As if he were personally responsible for his Calabrian compatriots. For the 'Ndrangheta massacre. He looks crestfallen and turns the music up slightly.

There's dense traffic on the motorway, the whole of Palermo's coming back from the weekend. As if impelled by a death wish, the cars dash down the tunnel. The sea shimmers like blackish-blue metal, with a strip of pale moonlight. Up by Carini you can't see the sea any more, it's hidden behind a settlement of shacks which stretches all the way to Palermo and looks like a poor district in Calcutta. The rubbish from the weekend is piled up alongside the motorway. The buildings are mostly one-storey houses with rough brick walls, no rendering anywhere; rusty metal rods stick out of the concrete on the roofs. These are Palermo's holiday homes. They're all illegal, and they have been for thirty years. In Sicily they call this 'surveyors' architecture'. It has ravaged the island. In Sicily everyone knows a surveyor who will draw up an illegal building plan for a backhander.

And then we get to Capaci. For a while, there was always a pause when we drove past this place. It didn't matter who I was with, all my friends, taxi drivers, interviewees fell silent. Not any more. Now everyone just goes on talking. Before, the only reminder of what had happened was a bit of red crash barrier. Five hundred kilos of explosives on a skateboard in a sewage pipe. Set off by remote control.

Now, two red marble steles stand here with the names and
the date: 23 May 1992, Giovanni Falcone, Francesca Morvillo,
Rocco Dicillo, Antonio Montinaro, Vito Schifani. One marble
stele in each direction. War memorials for a lost battle, as red
as the Sicilian soil. Sometimes there's a faded wreath with a
sash that's already slightly faded: in Sicily things deteriorate
very quickly.

I'd only seen Giovanni Falcone and Paolo Borsellino once,
from a distance, in the Palace of Justice. Like a lot of other
people in those days, I, too, thought they were immortal.
When they were murdered, it was felt in Palermo that the
killing of the two public prosecutors wasn't a murder like
the previous ones. Not a small death that the city could have
shaken off, denied and forgotten again the following morning, but one that clung to the city in front of everyone's eyes.
'È andata oltre,' people said, things have gone too far. For the
first time, Sicily could no longer dispute the existence of the
Mafia, and the reaction was one of catharsis. Temporarily.

'The mafiosi will pay for it,' Rosaria had said. We were
sitting in a bar not far from the Teatro Politeama, at a white
marble table which had been scrubbed till it had lost its sheen,
when Rosaria suddenly grabbed my wrist and said: 'They'll
pay for it, on the earth and in the hereafter.' What other point
would there be in their going on living after committing
those murders? Were they never to be punished? Then life in
general would have no point, no point at all. 'There must be
something, after all, don't you think?'

And I said: 'Yes, sure.' Because she was looking at me so
piercingly with those black eyes of hers. And because I didn't

have the courage to rob her of her hope. Hope of the divine plan. When I was sitting in the bar with Rosaria, her husband Vito Schifani, Giovanni Falcone's bodyguard, had only been dead for six months.

'They only showed me his hands,' she said. 'His hands. They were the only bits undamaged. He had such lovely hands.'

Rosaria had been widowed at the age of twenty-three and had become an anti-Mafia icon. Her son, Antonio Emanuele, was only four months old. Even today, everyone in Palermo remembers Rosaria haltingly trying to read out a text at Giovanni Falcone's funeral, supported by a priest who kept encouraging her to go on reading – until Rosaria threw aside the pages of her prepared text and cried out her true feelings: 'They're even here in the church, the mafiosi.' And: 'Too much blood, there is no love here, no love of anything or anyone.' And: 'I forgive you. But you must kneel.'

Everyone sensed that this wasn't the usual forgiveness, that empty ritual of absolution that everyone in Italy always has to defer to; before the corpses are even cold, the first television reporter has asked the victims about forgiveness. Only very seldom does anyone have the courage to step aside from this sale of indulgences. Like Rita Costa, the widow of the public prosecutor Gaetano Costa, shot by the Mafia in the centre of Palermo. 'I forgive no one and nobody,' she said. 'I could kill my husband's murderers and then calmly go off and have an espresso in a cafe.'

I had first seen Rosaria when Margarethe von Trotta was in Palermo introducing her film *The Long Silence*, a film that paid tribute to the women widowed by the Mafia. Rosaria wore a sand-coloured blazer, sat next to Rita Costa on the podium, and looked as if she'd rather have been a million miles away. Far from the widows, far from having to set an example, far from Palermo. She almost crept to the microphone as she said: 'When I talked about forgiveness in church, that sentence was my personal affair. Whether a person can forgive is, of course, a matter for each individual.'

Then she said nothing all the way through the panel discussion. She later told me how angry her mother had been when Rosaria had insisted on being seen in public in a sand-coloured blazer and not in black.

We had met at the regional administration, her new place of work. As is generally the case with victims of the Mafia, a job had been hastily found for her to supplement her meagre widow's pension. But she hadn't been given any actual work, just a reason to leave the house in the morning. Her office was empty. The phone was out of order, the desk hadn't been used for ages, the shelves were bare and dusty, and Rosaria talked about the profound shame she felt at never having taken an interest in what Mafia really meant. 'Even two days after my husband's death I didn't know who Totò Riina was!' she exclaimed. After the murder she had approached the public prosecutor Paolo Borsellino. Once she had asked him if he was scared, and Borsellino had replied: 'I'm only scared for my wife and children.' Fifty-seven days after the assassination of Falcone, he too was dead.

After her husband's death Rosaria became a driven woman: one who wanted to know what was happening around her, how it had come to this, how it could have been prevented.

'Tell everyone what happened to you,' one widow advised her. 'Shout it out. Everyone must know, go into the schools and speak to the children. Headlines aren't enough to reach the hearts of the children.'

And Rosaria followed her advice. She took part in demonstrations and panel discussions, she visited schools and juvenile institutions, and she published a book of her talks, dedicating it to her little son. In her open letter to the mafiosi, Rosaria wrote: 'You are murderers. Let's say it out loud, so that your sons can look you in the eyes and see what murderers' eyes look like.'

Perhaps that was the moment when Palermo became strange to her. She was a diva, people said, only interested in getting on television. And she was a lunatic. An attention-seeking lunatic.

Even if her husband had been killed by the Mafia, a Sicilian widow has to deal with her pain in silence. *Fatti gli affari tuoi e campi cent'anni.* Mind your own business and you'll live to a hundred.

Soon Rosaria stopped taking part in panel discussions, in memorial services, demonstrations and candlelight processions. I still heard from her from time to time. I heard she'd left Sicily. That she'd married again. That she'd had another child. She never wrote another open letter. The mafiosi who murdered her husband have been sentenced in the meantime. Some of them have repented. None of them has bent the knee.

Some have even managed to get college degrees, like the boss Pietro Aglieri. And they hope for their sentences to be overturned. Perhaps not entirely without justification. In the years following the assassinations, the anti-Mafia laws were gradually abolished. There is effectively no longer such a thing as high-security detention, no life imprisonment, and anyone who has been sentenced to thirty years' imprisonment for drug dealing can expect to be out of jail again in seven years. The last president of the Sicilian regional assembly, Salvatore 'Totò' Cuffaro, was sentenced in the first instance to five years' imprisonment, which he celebrated with a little communal drink and a tray full of *cannoli*, that traditional sweetmeat that every Sicilian emigrant devours until the day he dies. Cuffaro was celebrating because he knew that he would never have to serve his sentence; by the time it was confirmed by the supreme court, it would have lapsed. But he was wrong: in January 2011, Cuffaro went to prison. You never know what's around the corner.

Today, even the commemoration of the victims is too much. The former president of the Sicilian regional assembly, Gianfranco Miccichè, has demanded that the name of Palermo airport be changed as a matter of urgency: *Aeroporto Falcone e Borsellino* smacks too much of the Mafia.

Perhaps Rosaria was right after all, and all that remains is hope of a divine plan.

San Luca

'*Ma*,' says Salvo, as if he could read my mind. *Ma* means 'but'. In Sicily, though, the word *ma* has many more meanings than that. According to emphasis, *ma* can mean: 'Everyone here has gone mad', or 'If you think so', or 'Do what you like'. And if the *m* is particularly protracted, *mmma* means: 'The longer you think about life, the more you reach the conclusion that everything is in vain.'

We've left the bypass, and we're very close to the Piazza Indipendenza. And we're in a traffic jam. There's always a traffic jam in Palermo, the traffic is in a constant unforeseen state of emergency. A state of emergency that lasts from eight in the morning till midnight. Four-lane bypasses end up in one-way streets. Or nowhere. In the Palermo suburb of Mondello there's a four-lane road that looks as if it could be somewhere in Los Angeles. It comes from nowhere and peters out as a dirt track half a kilometre further on. A boss wanted it.

Salvo opens the window a crack. A hubbub of voices enters

from outside, scraps of music, exploding firecrackers, the wail of a burglar alarm. Faded blue saints glow in the wall of a house, promising two hundred days of absolution to any-one who says the credo before them. Finally we've arrived in Corso Vittorio Emanuele, outside my hotel. The Centrale Palace is my home in Palermo, a home that has survived even extensive renovation unharmed. Where hotels are concerned, I fear nothing more than alterations. That's why I love the familiar faces at the Centrale all the more. The head porter wears a pair of glasses that sit on his nose like a pince-nez, his centre parting looks as if it's been drawn with a ruler. The Tunisian hotel servant has frozen into a statue, and the old maître d' serves the breakfast tea with distracted dignity. Anyone who stays at the Centrale Palace is living not in a hotel but in a nineteenth-century Sicilian novel.

As soon as I enter the lobby, the receptionist bows in greet-ing. He purses his lips as if to kiss my hand and scatters a few compliments: 'Time simply doesn't pass as far as you're concerned, *Dottoressa*!' he says.

Since the day I was picked up by the lawyer defending the Mafia boss Bernardo Provenzano, the receptionist has respectfully addressed me as *Dottoressa*. The lawyer was pleasantly touched not to have had to introduce himself. The receptionist obviously knew his name.

I have my case brought to my room, and rejoin Salvo in the car. To get to the restaurant, we have to turn into the Via Roma. As it is every Sunday, the Via della Libertà is closed to through traffic. The Sunday-evening stroll from the Teatro Politeama to the Teatro Massimo is one of Palermo's sacred rituals. Wives are got up in outfits that look like suits of armour. They hold their handbags pressed under one arm and their husbands under the other. And by the boutique window displays the women sink into a dream-like state – until their husbands drag them away.

Shobha is already sitting on the terrace of the Fresco when I get there. Her blonde hair flashes in the darkness. Piano music drifts from the restaurant, and sitting on the terrace you look down on the yellow volcanic walls of the Ucciardone prison, an old Hohenstaufen fortress with floodlights and sentries behind armoured glass. The mafiosi called the prison Grand Hotel Ucciardone: they had champagne and lobsters delivered until they were released, usually after just a few months. After the assassinations of Falcone and Borsellino, a stay in the Ucciardone temporarily became rather less comfortable. Temporarily. Because lately the prison attracted a certain amount of attention when guards were found to have distributed *telefonini* among the bosses.

'You've got blonder,' Shobha says.

Every time we see each other again, we behave like an old couple who have been apart for a few weeks and are now looking at each other with a critical eye: is your hair shorter or longer? Are your earrings new? Yes, they really suit you, and what wonderful shoes you have, I want some pointed shoes like those. We've been working together for so long that we've decided to stop counting the years, because then anyone would be able to work out how old we are.

The pianist comes to our table, makes sheep's eyes at Shobha and asks if she'll be coming to eat here again tomorrow, then she could go with him to a concert afterwards. Shobha doesn't even turn round, and says: 'I'm busy over the next few weeks. And the next few months, and the next few years as well. I'm sorry. *Scusami.*'

And then we stare at the walls of the Hohenstaufen fortress until the pianist wanders back, shoulders drooping, to his piano and plays something that sounds like Chopin's Funeral March.

'And your mother?' I ask Shobha.

'Tomorrow,' Shobha says. 'We'll get to work tomorrow.' Then she adds: 'At least it's a good story. Not something like San Luca.'

———

At the end of every report we swear we won't do any more Mafia stories. *Basta.* We plan only to cover stories about Sicilian wine and fine hotels. About the wonderful quality of Calabrian olive oil. About Naples without rubbish in the streets.

Somehow we never manage to put our good intentions into action. Even while we were on the ferry from Sicily to Reggio Calabria we remembered our plan to do a report on something positive at long last. But instead we were sitting a short time later in the Grand Hotel Excelsior in Reggio Calabria, looking at a sea that looked as if it was poisonous, shimmering in tones of greyish blue with oil tankers in the glaring light. The 1970s hung in the hotel's heavy curtains; they fell from the neon light of the restaurant and settled on the faces of the hotel guests, who all looked like pharmaceuticals salesmen

passing through. In the lift, one of them asked if we were
hostesses.

'It isn't so bad here,' we reassured each other, like a mantra.

'You don't find such lovely cafes that often. We haven't got
such an elegant seafront in Palermo,' said Shobha.

Like a woman whose eyes are so beautiful that you forget
her short legs, Reggio Calabria is saved by its seafront. The
cafes stood side by side under palms and magnolias and cast-
iron arches. Later, we walked through the warm sirocco night
down Corso Garibaldi and established that you would have to
go the Via Montenapoleone in Milan to find a greater density
of luxury boutiques: Valentino, Alexander McQueen, Versace,
Rolex, Gucci, Prada, Cesare Paciotti. The 'Ndrangheta's shopping mile. Nothing but marble temples with salesgirls who
look like something halfway between nuns and museum at-
tendants. And whose eyes are as icy as the breeze from an
air-conditioning system.

We drove in silence along the coast road to San Luca.
We glided through a diffuse grey light, as if the sky were
filled with sand. We drove past shells of buildings, orphaned
houses, prickly pears and crippled olive trees, past concrete
posts for bridges that had never been finished, street signs
riddled with bullet holes and a tug-boat rusting away on the
beach amidst driftwood and bits of plastic. People-trafficking
is a source of income for the 'Ndrangheta, and the villages
of the Ionian coastal region are its fortresses: Platí, África,
San Luca.

Since the murders in Duisburg, San Luca had become
almost more famous than Corleone. The blood feud had

broken out eighteen years before and since then the clans of the Nirta-Strangio and the Pelle-Vottari seemed to have been persecuting one another with an Old Testament thirst for revenge, as if time were still being measured with hourglasses and honour could only be redeemed with blood. Because the Mafia thrives on symbols, murders tend to be carried out on feast days – Christmas, 1 May, Assumption. Behind this lies the message: 'Until the end of my life I may remember the murder of my wife every Christmas; but for you, Assumption will never again be a feast day because on that day, until the end of your life, you will think about your murdered brother.'

The investigators know, beyond the bloodlust, the Mafia always thinks pragmatically. The blood feud is by no means entirely archaic. The criminal prestige of the family that organized the Duisburg massacre has risen enormously, and that's where economic profit lies. Now they just have to present themselves to a member of the regional government and say: 'We're the people from San Luca.' And the next public bid will be in their favour.

The 'Ndrangheta has divided Calabria up into three territories: the Tyrrhenian coast, the Ionian coast and the city of Reggio Calabria. Even if you didn't know, you would smell it. In the air, which always smells a bit burned. In the 1960s and 1970s the 'Ndrangheta bought up the biggest agricultural enterprises, vineyards and olive groves, and the public prosecutor's office couldn't bring a case against it because the owners hadn't reported the extortionate purchases. The 'Ndrangheta now controls every breath anyone takes, every inch of road, every thought.

When we arrived in San Luca that autumn, after the assassination, the day lay there like a piece of wet grey cotton
wool, between the Aspromonte mountains and the dry bed
of a river called Bonamico, 'good friend'. In San Luca every
hour seemed as long as a day of atonement, as weird as an
endless Day of the Dead when you're forever bumping into
ghosts.

We stopped outside a bar that sparkled like a crystal. One
wall was decorated with the glittering image of the Madonna
of Polsi and the barman ceaselessly polished the marble counter, the glass shelves, the brass-coloured water taps, and served
three young financial policemen their espressos. One of the
cops had flaming red hair. He was constantly checking the
position of his beret in the mirror beside the bar, and Shobha
was so taken with this that she casually took a picture. When
we stepped up to the bar, he told us that on one of their pa-
trols a few days previously they'd noticed a Volkswagen Golf
which, it turned out, had been hired in Duisburg and not
taken back. And they'd found half a kiló of hashish in its boot.
No big deal. But still.

San Luca looked as if its walls had been designed to match
the grey of the sky, unplastered, with rusty iron railings and
electric wires that hung between the houses like washing
lines. There weren't even any street signs: the street names
were just painted on the walls of the houses with black paint.
Shortly after the Duisburg massacre, San Luca had tried to
present itself to the world's press as a village forgotten by the
world, full of unemployed woodsmen, God-fearing women
and one brave priest, a lone voice in the desert, fighting

tirelessly against the Mafia. He was the one we wanted to meet. Don Pino.

Up on the hill, next to the church of Santa Maria Addolorata, a few old grey stone houses clung to one another. When there had been an earthquake a few years ago, these old houses had been destroyed. And not rebuilt, just abandoned. As if it wasn't worth preserving anything. Opposite the church there was another bar, a scruffy little affair with a veranda where a few men sat. When we asked about Don Pino, they shrugged as if they were hearing his name for the first time. A man offered us a coffee. His eyes looked as if he was wearing mascara: his lashes were black and dense, and curved slightly upwards as if he'd used an eyelash curler.

He really lived in Australia, in Adelaide, he said. But then he had started feeling terribly homesick and had come back to his home of San Luca with his wife and two children. Although he regretted that, because there were no jobs here. He smiled politely, and perhaps with some embarrassment.

Because Adelaide is thought of as a stronghold of the 'Ndrangheta, and particularly of two clans from San Luca, the Nirtas and the Romeos, both of which were involved in the Duisburg murders.

Among the Italian Mafia organizations, the 'Ndrangheta has proved to be the most mobile, an unbeatable advantage in business terms; unlike the entrenched Sicilian Mafia, the Calabrian clans are active not only in every region of Italy but all over the world. Even before the First World War, the 'Ndrangheta had invested the money it made from extortion into the cultivation of cannabis in Australia. By the

1950s it controlled the drugs trade in Canada. In America, the Calabrian men of honour joined forces with the Sicilians; according to the FBI, between one and two hundred mafiosi of Calabrian origin are active in New York and Florida. In South and Central America the 'Ndrangheta enjoys privileged trade relations with cocaine producers in Peru, Chile, Brazil, Argentina, Uruguay, Paraguay, Venezuela, Bolivia and Colombia. Calabrian public prosecutors have uncovered links between the Colombian paramilitary *Autodefensas Unidas de Colombia*, the AUC, and the 'Ndrangheta. Thanks to their good connections, the 'Ndrangheta has been able to open up new sources of production and export routes for the cocaine trade, cutting out the middlemen and selling the cocaine more cheaply. That's another unbeatable advantage.

The 'Ndranghetista Roberto Pannunzi had the best connections with the Colombian drugs cartel: he was able to buy his cocaine at a particularly good rate because he took delivery of at least three tonnes a month, and always paid on time and in cash. Pannunzi even sealed his business connections with blood bonds: his son Alessandro married the daughter of a Colombian drugs baron. In 2004, Pannunzi was arrested, along with his son, in Spain − the soft underbelly of Europe, according to the investigators. Spain is the most significant portal for the importation of cocaine from South America. And in January 2008, Pannunzi's henchman in Calabria was arrested: 'Don Micu' Trimboli, who was led away in his tracksuit after he had been tracked down to a bunker under a sheep-pen. When he was arrested, he cursed the politicians who were concerned only with garnering votes. And didn't keep their promises. And behind this there lay an undisguised threat: the politician who was supposed to have been looking out for him had clearly committed a small but significant act of negligence – that was the only explanation the boss could find for the fact that the police had suddenly appeared on his trail. The Mafia had always bought political protection with votes.

The reason Germany is so important for the 'Ndrangheta is because that's where they invest their profits from the drugs and arms trade, which would risk confiscation in Italy. Since 1982 it has been possible in Italy to confiscate the property of individuals who are only suspected of belonging to the Mafia. They have to demonstrate that their property was acquired legally, with clean money. If that proof cannot be supplied, confiscation can go ahead. At least, that's what the law says. So it's easier for the 'Ndrangheta to invest abroad, without bothering about the precautionary measures that are required in Italy. In Germany, a waiter who earns a thousand euros a month can buy a hotel without anyone asking any questions.

According to a report by the BND, the German federal intelligence service, the 'Ndrangheta have bought shares in the Frankfurt Stock Exchange and they've invested millions of euros in hotel chains and restaurants in eastern Germany. The clans from San Luca are particularly active: in North Rhine-Westphalia, in Thuringia, in Baden-Württemberg. In Bochum, and in Duisburg.

And the man from Adelaide said: 'My children were born in Australia, they're homesick for Australia. Here they have nothing to do with their spare time. There isn't a decent sports club, nothing. That's why we'll probably go back soon.'

And I said: 'I can understand that.'

Don Pino

The church of Santa Maria Addolorata in San Luca was painted white and its interior was decorated with the sort of living-room furnishings that you find in department stores: fake marble and figures of saints that looked like shop-window dummies, with a gaudy Christ hovering over the altar and a Saint Sebastian riddled with arrows.

Don Pino would be there at any moment, the curate, Don Stefano Fernando, told me; but, if we didn't mind, he himself would be happy to answer our questions. He wore thick, horn-rimmed glasses and addressed me respectfully in the second person plural, *voi* – that antiquated polite form that has disappeared everywhere except in southern Italy.

Yes, he said, the 'Ndrangheta had become well known in Germany since Duisburg, even though the Germans must clearly have known that the 'Ndrangheta had invested in restaurants and hotels to launder their money. The Germans, he said, had taken the dirty money without hesitation after reunification, they'd turned a blind eye. I'd love to know, he said, what the German government thinks about that now.

Don Stefano Fernando had developed a whole theory about the sad lot of southern Italy: it extended from the economic boom of the 1950s which never arrived, to the secularized society of the present — it's not true to say that people here aren't devout, they're just indifferent! And he would have liked to expound his theory still further, if he hadn't suddenly come over all self-effacing — after all, he was just the curate, and the role of explaining the world fell instead to Don Pino, who was now standing in the door to the sacristy. There were only a few minutes before the start of mass, the bells were already ringing. Don Pino Strangio had ebony-black hair and smiled at us winningly, as if he'd just been waiting for us to turn up. Of course, of course, he would love to speak to us, right after mass.

'Bringing peace to the villages ... not losing faith ... because we must give an account of ourselves before God ... if we could see him with our mortal eyes ...' The words rang out over the church square. Don Pino hovered like a spirit over San Luca; his words rang out from the loudspeakers, echoed against the grey, unplastered walls, and crept into the hairy ears of the men sitting not in church but outside the bar, blinking into the milky morning light.

As in Sicily, churchgoing in San Luca is for the womenfolk. So Don Pino had decided to broadcast his sermons into the church square via loudspeakers. The women who listened to his words were all dressed in black, as if life were a time of endless mourning. Old women, with their thin hair in buns, tightened their wrinkled mouths as the host dissolved on their tongues. Their daughters had faces that could have been carved from olive wood; they wore tight, black skirts, black pullovers and flat, black shoes, and allowed themselves only one piece of jewellery: a wedding ring. Only the granddaughters were allowed to shine. With blonde strands in their hair, Dolce & Gabbana belts and sequined blouses glittering above their naked midriffs. And during prayers the mothers quietly tugged the blouses down over their daughters' waistbands.

At the end of mass, Shobha was surrounded by little girls demanding to have their pictures taken. When Shobha said she didn't like posed photographs, the little girls turned angry. They hissed: we issue the orders here.

The women darted back down the alleys like black birds and I thought of the wife of the boss Bernardo Provenzano who had spent fifteen years living underground with him and their children. At one with the Mafia and the Lord God. After she had returned to Corleone, she was a *signora*. Respected by everyone, a first lady who was allowed to the front of the queue for ricotta. Her husband? Respectable and hardworking, a victim of the Italian judiciary, that was how she described him.

The men in San Luca drank some more beer before they too disappeared and the village looked uninhabited once again. As if everything human had fled — fled the cement-grey colour of everything, the bare light bulbs that dangled above the lintel, by the rubbish bins peppered with machine-gun fire. And fled the words *But the soul never dies* spray-painted on the cemetery wall.

The dead of Duisburg were buried in the new cemetery which, seen from above San Luca, looked like a holiday resort. Their graves were right beside the entrance: rough cement boxes with rusty iron girders protruding from them. On every grave lay a crucifix with a shrink-wrapped rosary. Don Pino had buried three of the Duisburg victims: Marco Marmo, the hit man who had murdered the wife of the head of the enemy clan at Christmas; Sebastiano Strangio, who owned the Da Bruno restaurant in Duisburg; and Francesco Giorgi, at sixteen the youngest victim of the killing spree, and the son of Don Pino's female cousin. 'Mio cuginetto,' Don Pino said, 'my little cousin'. Francesco, the poor boy, had only wanted to visit his uncle in Germany. And then Don Pino praised the piety of his cousin, the boy's mother, who was sitting in the front row of the church. Her daughter, Elisa, was playing organ in church when she learned of her brother's death.

In her pain, the mother gazed into the distance. No doubt she wanted to look her son's murderers in the eyes. But there was no hatred there! She said: 'I forgive you.' And lots of people joined in that forgiveness. Perhaps Duisburg was the end of something and a peaceful rebirth would follow. 'The people are crying out for peace,' Don Pino said sadly.

We were sitting on a wooden bench next to the church — the same wooden bench on which he had received almost the whole of the world's press since the massacre, not just the German daily papers but El País and the Italian broadcaster Rai. Even Japanese television crews had come to listen to Don Pino, who tirelessly stressed that the people of San Luca were

simple and good, and only afraid to say anything to the journalists because you never know how what you say is going to
be used.

'We condemn all kinds of Mafia, with our swords drawn,'
said Don Pino. 'And then they write that we're all like that!
And years ago someone even wrote: "The parish priest
co-habits with the Mafia."'

Don Pino has spent half his life as a parish priest in San
Luca. He was born here, he grew up here, he knew them all,
he baptized and married them, and carried them to the grave.
He was already the parish priest when San Luca grew rich
in the 1980s on the money it raised from kidnappings, when
Jean Paul Getty's grandson had his ear cut off in a neighbouring village, and when the women caught an industrialist who
had managed to escape from his hiding place and held him
until he could be returned to his abductors.

Don Pino was already here when San Luca started invest-
ing its ransom money in the cocaine trade; before, along with
the villages of Platí and Sinópoli, it hosted the elite of the
'Ndrangheta, the wealthiest Mafia organization in Italy –
which today, with an annual turnover of 44 billion euros,
controls the whole of Europe's cocaine trade and has diversi-
fied its activities like a multinational corporation, so that it
now deals just as successfully in arms as it does in people.

Today the 'Ndrangheta is seen as the epitome of a successful criminal organization. It isn't organized hierarchically
like the Sicilian Mafia, but federally: each Calabrian clan
chief makes autonomous decisions. He accepts advice, but not
orders. In Sicily, on the other hand, it's the commission that

makes the decisions: *la reunione dei mandamenti*. And there-in lies the weakness of Cosa Nostra — because, if someone at the top spills the beans, the whole organization collapses. The 'Ndrangheta is a close-knit family, everyone's related — un-like the Sicilian Cosa Nostra, which places more emphasis on the criminal weight of a mafioso than it does on blood ties.

After the assassinations of Falcone and Borsellino, it took Cosa Nostra years to regain its invisibility — the silent acqui-escence of Sicilians, the discreet handouts from politicians and the blind eyes turned by everyone — without which the Mafia cannot flourish. During the years when Cosa Nostra was in the spotlight, the Calabrian 'Ndrangheta rose in its shadow.

With the introduction of a law freezing the property of people who had been kidnapped, abduction ceased to be a viable business. So the 'Ndrangheta left the kidnapping industry and entered the cocaine trade. In Calabria it also controls all public commissions and maintains its power by collecting protection money. It has branches throughout the whole world; in Germany alone it has a network of three hun-dred pizzerias and, like al-Qaeda, connects the middle ages with the globalized future, negotiating by email with cocaine brokers in Colombia, Venezuela, Peru and Uruguay, buying a bank in St Petersburg and whole stretches of road in Brussels, while at the same time its members will only marry a woman from the same village, because the family is sacred. Blood relations don't betray one another. The 'Ndrangheta's only worry lies in being able to launder money before it rots — as it has done in the past, when two bosses buried 25 million

euros in the ground and 8 million became damp and had to
be thrown away.

But what could Don Pino do about that? Does the shepherd
of souls not have to go where evil is? Is he not more responsible
for the sick than for the well?

Evil must be fought with good, says Don Pino, who is
responsible not only for the salvation of San Luca but also
for the pilgrimage site of Santa Maria di Polsi. He is the
spiritual leader there, a role of considerable importance since
the pilgrimage site is effectively the 'Ndrangheta's meeting
place.

In Calabria, San Luca is seen as the mother lode of crime,
and to a great extent the village derives this status from its
proximity to the Madonna of Polsi – a place distinguished
less for its miracle-working capacities than for the fact that
the 'Ndrangheta gather there every year to pay homage to the
clan chiefs. They gather there even today. They no longer do
so at the monastery, however, but in a house nearby. Three
representatives of the Calabrian Mafia stop off at that house:
one representing the city of Reggio Calabria, one from the
Tyrrhenian group, one from the Ionian. These three wise
men receive representatives from all the Calabrian 'Ndrine,
the family clans – from Italy and the whole of Europe, from
Canada, America and Australia. They come to Polsi, they
bring gifts and set out their problems to these three wise men,
who then give them advice. It's a kind of annual 'Ndrangheta
summit meeting, which lasts a month.

'You see, we don't deny that there were certain gatherings
in Polsi in the past,' Don Pino said, and hurried to add: 'but

the people didn't gather there to, okay, let's say, put something or other into action!' It had, as Don Pino put it, been more of a traditional form of devotion, of the negative kind. Which, put like that, sounds decidedly more elegant than ''Ndrangheta'. Don Pino is careful not to use the word. 'Certainly, it's a deadly sin to revere the image of the Madonna and at the same time to commit crimes. But in the face of the Madonna of Polsi even the hardest hearts soften, and people break down in tears.' Don Pino had seen men in Polsi licking the aisle leading up to the altar with their tongues! 'And the only gathering that verifiably took place there was the one in 1967, when everyone was first arrested and then released again because they'd just been looking for mushrooms!' said Don Pino. 'Those are the great dramas of history!'

———

I'm still deep in thought about our meeting with Don Pino when Shobha says: 'I don't want to think about San Luca any more. Let's just do a story about Sicilian aristocrats planting vineyards – suggest that to one of your editors. Or Selinunte, the acropolis – let's do something about Selinunte.'

'Yes,' I say, 'Selinunte. But wasn't the father of the boss Matteo Messina Denaro a famous grave-robber who stole the ephebes from Selinunte? Yes, maybe we really should stop. But maybe it's all a matter of perspective.'

'*Basta*,' says Shobha, orders some more wine, and then turns pale because she thinks she recognizes the youngest son of the mafioso and ex-mayor Vito Ciancimino at the next table.

'I've never seen him here before,' says Shobha.

Palermo reminds me a little of East Germany. *The Lives of Others* is played out here every day. With the arrogance of the powerful. With members of the opposition who end up working with the ruling party, with heroes who aren't. Sometimes a handshake from the wrong person is enough to lose you your credibility forever. Anti-Mafia public prosecutors seldom go out in Palermo.

'Thank God, he's leaving,' says Shobha, looking at Ciancimino's son, who is greeting everyone heartily as he leaves the restaurant.

It's at that moment that the pianist takes a break. He approaches our table in a series of concentric circles and Shobha turns her back to him. 'May I join you for a moment?' he asks, and Shobha says: 'Sorry, but we're just discussing our latest report, it wouldn't be very interesting to you.'

And then she takes out the battered map of Calabria that she still happens to have in her pocket and points to San Luca and Polsi: 'Polsi basically wasn't that far away,' she says, 'but we'd never have made it in our little Fiat Uno.'

———

To persuade us of the holiness of the place, Don Pino had suggested taking us to Polsi in person. You could only get there in a Land Rover, and luckily Don Pino always had a few people at hand to help him with his divine mission: an engineer and a driver, whom Don Pino called his 'jack of all trades', a silent man who drove the Land Rover and nodded when the engineer said sadly: 'God knocks on our door every day, but we don't hear him.'

On a bend in the road the vehicle stopped so that we could enjoy the view of San Luca. Don Pino, the pious engineer and the silent driver looked at the village with as much emotion as if they were seeing it for the first time. We drove for hours through forests of chestnut trees, past goatherds and over gravel, up and down the twisting road. 'We go down so that we can come back up again,' says Don Pino. He saw it as a symbol of the holiness of the place. I thought of the 'Ndrangheta.

In the courtyard of Polsi monastery everyone was already waiting for Don Pino: some women from the village were roasting chestnuts, a group of men were stacking wood. Don Pino dashed off through the monastery, which had been renovated thanks to the largesse of the European Union. We looked at everything, from the eight-hundredweight tufa-stone Madonna, via the coffin of the child who had been brought back to life here, to the recently installed disabled toilet. There were countless plastic bags under the altar. Because Polsi was a spiritual space, Calabrian brides brought their wedding dresses here as votive offerings. Don Pino was drowning in tulle and lace, and sent the dresses on to Africa.

At last Don Pino led us, whispering, to his room and announced a mystery that he wanted to share with us: the sweating crucifix. The cross had been dripping for fourteen days! Jesus was sweating under his armpits! Don Pino took the crucifix from the wall and said: 'Feel it, it's really wet down at the bottom!' Even though the St Anthony right next to it was completely dry. 'I'm going mad,' said Don Pino, and looked up to the sky and added: 'It's a good sign for the people here. For the purity of their hearts.'

Later, he invited us to lunch. We sat down at a long table in the refectory, in front of a mural of the Last Supper, and ate pasta and porcini. There were only men sitting at the table with us, the women stayed in the kitchen. 'You won't find the eyes of the women of San Luca anywhere else in the world,' said Don Pino and smiled, his cheeks slightly flushed from the wine. 'The family protects you against everything,' he said and looked around. 'You know, the true fugitives aren't the mafiosi, they're the politicians. Here every civil right becomes a favour that's granted.'

While Don Pino said grace, I watched the men. They spoke in short, simple sentences because they were used to speaking only in dialect and Italian sounded heavy in their mouths. They spoke of how they had worked in Germany. In Duisburg and in Wolfsburg, for Volkswagen. Their hands were tanned and blistered. And as I watched those men I wondered what it's like when they kill someone.

Shortly after the Duisburg massacre forty inhabitants of the village had been arrested. For membership of the Mafia, arms dealing and drug dealing, for murder, grievous bodily harm, false imprisonment. Almost all of those arrested were related to one another. Almost all claimed their right to silence.

Since I had read all 1,150 pages of the public prosecutor's custody order, page after page of wiretap records, I found it hard to believe the peaceful image of San Luca evoked by Don Pino. There was the hit man Marco Marmo, who had

driven all the way to Duisburg in June 2007 in search of
weapons and an armoured truck for the next assassination.
There were men who talked about buying parabellum ammunition as if they were discussing the artichoke harvest.
There were mothers who moved Kalashnikovs from house to
house, wives who patrolled in camouflage suits, sisters who
ran messages and transported their brothers from A to B in
the boots of their cars – if those brothers weren't actually
living in bunkers, like some members of the Pelle-Vottari
clan, in the midst of an arsenal of Luger pistols, Berettas and
Scorpion machine guns, ammunition and cash, statues of the
saints, an altar bearing the photographs of murdered clan
members, and *The Godfather* on DVD.

He was glad to be able to help people, said Don Pino, add-
ing: 'People come to Polsi with tears in their eyes. And who
is better at drying tears than the mother of God?' At any
rate, he had dedicated an anti-Mafia field at the pilgrimage
site. And at that event the bishop had announced: 'If Polsi
is a Mafia meeting place, then I'm the head mafioso!' Polsi
was, in fact, a holy, miraculous place. 'Lots of women whose
husbands are in jail come here to pray,' he said, and, via the
prison priest, Don Pino was in constant contact with the prisoners: 'Things happen there that you wouldn't imagine!' And
I thought, so much for high security.

On the way back, Don Pino whispered to us: 'If these meetings of the 'Ndrangheta really did take place, in spite of the
presence of the *carabinieri*, then we're not just talking about
people who have this mindset – something's not working.'

In referring so openly to collaboration between *carabinieri* and 'Ndrangheta, he was being very like Padre Frittitta, one of the many Sicilian priests who secretly heard confessions of refugee mafiosi in their hiding places, always justifying themselves by saying that it wasn't earthly justice that would deliver the final judgement, it was the divine kind – and as its humble drudges they were merely performing a service. They were saving souls. That was Don Pino's argument in a nutshell. That was all he was interested in. The soul of the man who drove the Land Rover, for example, and who was a kind of odd-job man in Polsi. The judge had entrusted this young man to him after he had been condemned to two years' imprisonment for attempted murder. He had shot a *carabiniere* in the face.

'But only with buckshot,' Don Pino said, by way of exculpation.

Back in San Luca, he dropped us off at the bar decorated with the glittering image of the Madonna. It was already dark and there was no one to be seen in the streets except for the village idiot, who was standing by the fountain playing the mouth organ. Shobha hadn't said a word on the way back. While Don Pino had been delivering his monologue, she had looked out of the window. When we got to the bar she went straight to the toilet and threw up.

The image of the Madonna of Polsi had also been found in the Da Bruno restaurant in Duisburg. Along with a .223 calibre American assault rifle, a statue of the Archangel Michael, a picture of the same saint with its head burned, a prayer book, some .280 calibre ammunition, various replacement magazines and the receipt for a payment of more than

300 euros for an armoured Peugeot truck, made out to the hit man Marco Marmo, who had driven to Duisburg to get hold of weapons for the next attack on the Nirta-Strangio clan. Marmo had killed the wife of the boss Gianluca Nirta: that was the notorious Christmas assassination that had to be avenged by the bloodbath in Duisburg. Marmo knew that his days were numbered so long as Gianluca Nirta was still alive.

'He has nothing more to lose, and that's what makes him so dangerous,' said Michele Carabetta, Marco Marmo's assistant, who drove with him to Duisburg. There's something unreal about standing in the bar in San Luca and thinking about the wiretap records of the conversations held there. When Michele Carabetta had talked to his sister Sonia, all they spoke about was weapons, 'deer' that had appeared in the village (the term they used for policemen in those parts), house searches by the *carabinieri*, wigs and make-up for hiding scars, messages and ferrying people around in jeeps. About 'them' and 'us'. And as I stood at the bar drinking my espresso, I wondered whether the man standing next to me eating his cream pastry mightn't have been shifting a consignment of bazookas the previous day.

———

A few days later, Shobha and I decided to take a look at the house that stood over the Pelle-Vottari clan's bunker – not the only one in San Luca, incidentally. The important families of San Luca had holed up at the edge of the village in fortresses, five-storey concrete castles. The Pelle-Vottari family had built one such. It was at the end of a cul-de-sac, surrounded by a five-metre-high steel fence. Because the bunker underneath it had been sealed and impounded, we thought the house was empty. A false assumption, as it turned out.

First we just heard a sound. A hoarse cry, then a dull rumble, and at last the automatic gate opened. Like a herd of wildly snorting bulls, ten men came charging down the drive. Quivering, bobbing and cursing, they stood in our way, and in the way of our car. They demanded that Shobha hand over her camera and grabbed for my notebook. The youngest of them was twenty years old at most; they wore white Dolce & Gabbana T-shirts and their hair was gelled into spikes. They hissed: 'Piss off, you miserable whores.' They were boys who pressed their teeth tightly together until their lower jaws trembled. Only one of them was older, perhaps fifty; with his padded waistcoat, he looked like a shepherd coming back from vespers. The men were being urged on by an old woman in a black pleated skirt. 'Break their knees!' she cried. Their faces contorted with fury, the young men rubbed their fists as if they'd already started thumping us. They pressed so close to us that we could smell their breath. 'You stupid bitches, we're going to smash your heads in.'

As they doubtless would have done if a police patrol hadn't arrived and stopped them. A plump policeman got out and pushed the men aside. His voice sounded like a woman's. There was something surreal about standing at the end of this cul-de-sac, between hate-filled mafiosi and a high-pitched policeman trying to calm them down. It was our good fortune that the Duisburg attack had already attracted far too much attention. The Italian secret services had reported on attempts by 'Ndrangheta families to bring about a ceasefire in San Luca. Because if the Duisburg murders were properly avenged, there was a danger that Europe would become aware of the problem that the 'Ndrangheta represented. And the Calabrian Mafia desperately wanted to prevent that. According to the famous Agenda 2000, the European Union's sponsorship programme, huge amounts of European money is flowing into Calabria, and thus into the hands of the Mafia. 'Measures to remove imbalances between the regions', they call it in Brussels. That's why they want peace in San Luca. And that was why we were able to get back into our car and drive away.

———

After that, Shobha and I thought it might be a good idea to give San Luca a wide berth for the rest of our Calabrian story. We decided to drive to Locri, just a few miles away from San Luca. The name of Locri has a strong resonance in Italy: in Locri the regional politician Francesco Fortugno was killed by 'Ndrangheta assassins in 2005, and it was here, shortly afterwards, that the Calabrian anti-Mafia movement *Ammazzateci tutti*, 'Kill the lot of us!', was founded – an organization that emerged from a student group and called for a revolt against the 'Ndrangheta. However, it was Sunday and Locri was nothing but a main street with deserted-looking houses. We walked across an empty, rectangular piazza planted with withered jasmine bushes. Along uneven pavements and potholed tarmac. Locri was the essence of nothingness. No cinema, no theatre, no museum, no traffic.

In the only bar that was open a man told us that a procession in honour of the Madonna of the Clairvoyance would be taking place that afternoon. The high point of Locri life. Outside the church the usual stands stood ready for the visitors attending the procession — selling drills, spanners and steering wheels, gingerbread and popcorn. The brass band from Gerace was waiting there already, in Madonna-blue suits with sky-blue ties. The faithful were sitting in the church saying their Ave Marias. The parish priest played casually with his rosary and strolled along the rows of the faithful, like a beautiful woman who's aware of the eyes of her admirers on her.

Shobha was bored; we were actually used to better processions than this one. The impressive Good Friday processions in Trapani. The spectacular Santa Rosalia procession in Palermo. And here there was nothing to see but popcorn and drills, women dressed in black — and a woman who approached us with undisguised hostility and ordered us to leave the procession straightaway: 'If you want to take a picture, you need a permit!'

We ignored the nun's baleful looks. When the Madonna left the church under her sky-blue baldachin, the priest, who still has a certain standing here, tried to fan the hostility through his loudspeaker by ordering disbelievers to leave the procession. Then he walked ahead, followed by white-clad acolytes, like a pop star leading his fans. Many women in the procession walked barefoot. As the Madonna was carried, swaying on a bouquet of roses, past the houses, the people waiting on their balconies fell to their knees. One man kissed the hem of the Madonna's robe, and an old woman ran in a red dressing gown on to the balcony to greet the Madonna with loud, smacking kisses. The priest was still playing with his rosary.

And we walked along with the others. Driven by bull-headedness and boundless amazement at how it's possible to kiss the hem of the Madonna's robe and at the same time turn a blind eye to the Mafia. Only a few yards away from the church there stood a charred bookshop with the *carabinieri* seal on its door: clearly the owner had refused to pay protection money.

When we left Locri and drove back along the coast road to Reggio Calabria the night had swallowed everything, the ruined buildings and the sea, and even the wreck of the illegal tug-boat rusting away on the beach. Suddenly a car braked sharply in front of us and we saw something flying through the air. It was an Indian migrant worker who had been riding his bicycle and was now lying in a pool of blood. When I bent over him, he asked: 'Are you my mother?' Then he lost consciousness. So he wasn't aware of the car that had just knocked him down suddenly driving away. A man watched after the disappearing car and said by way of exculpation: 'Maybe he was just scared.' Certainly, it could have happened somewhere else. But still.

————

Seven months later I would read in *La Repubblica* that the *carabinieri* had managed another devastating strike against the 'Ndrangheta of San Luca: nine suspects had been arrested, including the head of the Pelle-Vottari clan, Giuseppe Pelle, who had, according to the Ministry of the Interior, been one of the thirty most dangerous Mafia fugitives in Italy. Later, on the news, when I saw him being led away and cursing the journalists as they watched, I recognized him: he was one of the men who had run out of the Pelle-Vottari house and threatened us. Giuseppe Pelle was the oldest one – the one in the padded waistcoat who had looked like a shepherd coming back from vespers. I wondered why the *carabinieri* hadn't come up with the same idea as we had, only earlier: just dropping in at the Pelle-Vottari house. Perhaps if they had done so, they'd have been able to catch Giuseppe Pelle, one of the thirty most dangerous Mafia fugitives in Italy, while he was having his midday snooze.

———

It's night-time and we're still sitting in the Fresco in Palermo. The floodlight from the prison opposite darkens the sky so that we can't see any stars.

'I'm never going back to Calabria,' says Shobha. 'You can do what you like.'

Our couscous has gone cold by now. The waitress brings us the bill and starts impatiently clearing the tables while we're still wondering where to take a picture of Shobha's mother. In Mondello? Too pretty. Outside the Palace of Justice? Too melodramatic. At the Vucciria market? Too folksy. In the end, we put off the decision until morning. The pianist gets his scores in order and shuts the lid of the piano. 'Let's just get out of here,' says Shobha. 'Otherwise he'll want to come with us.'

I bring Shobha to her front door and then walk back to the hotel. Past the jacaranda trees of the Piazza Politeama, past the Piazza Olivella, past rotting walls that are just held together by faded posters advertising singers called things like Mimmo or Pippo, with their shirt collars turned up. The cobbles look as if they're sweating. It smells, as always, of damp warmth. Of petrol. And of the dark soil of Africa.

Letizia

I'm sitting in the breakfast room of the Centrale, trying in vain to order some tea. The old maître d' stands in the corner like a monument that comes to life only intermittently, and all the other waiters are chatting so excitedly that I don't dare to disturb them. Because as they stand in front of the stucco rosettes, with their slicked-back black hair and blood-red brocade waistcoats over white shirts, they look like figures from novels, as if their thoughts, longings and goals were somehow sublime, extraordinary, perhaps even heroic, even if in reality they're only talking about when they can finally get round to dismantling the breakfast buffet.

Two female English tourists run their fingertips across their street map in search of the Capuchin Crypt; an Italian businessman with an imposing knot in his tie flicks through *La Repubblica*. I wonder what sort of business he's going to be doing in Palermo. Selling surgical instruments, maybe? Private clinics are a flourishing branch of Cosa Nostra business, financed by the Italian state. While public hospitals are

crumbling, half of the Sicilian domestic budget is flowing
into the health service, with 1,800 private practices and clinics recognized by the state and financed by the region. By
way of comparison, in Lombardy it's sixty.

Many of these state-recognized and regionally financed
private clinics are run by Mafia bosses. The mafia has learned
that public commissions can bring in risk-free money. Unlike
the drugs trade, the penalties for misuse of public contracts
are extremely low.

Judging by the knot in his tie, the man could also be a
lawyer. Lawyers who come to Sicily for Mafia trials often stay
at the Centrale. In fact, it was a lawyer who recommended
the Centrale Palace to me, a woman who regularly travelled
on Mafia-related business. She travelled from one courthouse
to another defending turncoat mafiosi, ten days in Rome, a
week in Florence, two days in Venice, a week in Palermo.
After she had spent her day in the 'aula bunker', the high-
security courtroom where she passed hours listening to how
her clients had shot, dismembered and burned people, she
spent her evenings in her room in the Centrale, watching
cartoons.

One of her most famous clients was the Mafia hit man
Calogero Ganci: no previous convictions and a hundred
murders. One of his victims was his father-in-law. Business
is business. When Ganci's wife found out, she had a nervous breakdown: 'Tell me it isn't true,' she screamed at her
husband, 'it can't be true that I've slept with my father's
murderer. What am I supposed to tell my children?'

Calogero Ganci had run a butcher's and a drapery shop

in Palermo. He had never come to the attention of the
authorities.

'What scares me most,' the lawyer says, 'is knowing about
the Mafia's perfect disguise. When I walk down the street, I'm
thinking about how the bus driver could be a mass-murderer,
or the man who runs the chemist's next door.'

I look again at the knot of that tie. And at the two English
tourists, who have finally found the way to the Capuchin
Crypt and are carefully marking it on their map. And I think:
Sicilian paranoia. The man might just be a rep for a travel
agent's. Or an olive-oil wholesaler. Or a mathematician. And
in the breakfast room of the Centrale, Palermo is nothing
other than an opulent palace, with red marble columns, capi-
tals and pilasters, chandeliers and mirrored halls, in which
the sultry sirocco air and thoughts of the Mafia are kept at
bay by an extraordinarily efficient air-conditioning system.

At last, one of the waiters takes pity and brings me a green
tea. He looks at me sympathetically. Anyone in Sicily who
drinks tea in the morning must be unwell. Or a foreigner.
I flick through my Moleskine notebook and try to take notes
for my interview with Letizia. It's hard. I've known her for so
long that I almost feel as if we're related. Although it would
be wrong to imagine that you know everything about your
relatives.

Letizia is the first person I met in Palermo, in the spring
of 1989 – which wasn't just any old spring, but *the* Palermo
Spring. It was a moment of hope, the world was finally stir-
ring, the concrete was crumbling in the east and even in
Sicily the foundation on which the Mafia had built its power

for more than a century seemed to be shifting: for the first time Palermo was run by a mayor who sided with the fight against the Mafia. Leoluca Orlando was seen as a shining light, besieged by journalists from all over the world. Letizia was a protagonist of that spring — not a Sicilian Madonna, but a breathless subversive, a photographer at the service of the revolution, her revolution. A flame-haired rebel who had reinvented herself at the age of thirty-six. Who had transformed herself from a bourgeois Sicilian housewife into a legend, a chain-smoking legend: the first anti-Mafia photographer in Sicily.

Leoluca had appointed her as councillor for quality of life and Letizia had thrown herself into politics with the same passion that she had previously shown for photography. She installed benches in the city, introduced pedestrian zones and freed the seafront from the barricades behind which the sea lay hidden as if people were ashamed of it. Today, Letizia's palms are perhaps the only souvenir of that Palermo Spring, which many people, in 1989, thought would go on forever.

We drove along the seafront in Letizia's official car and she lit one of her MS cigarettes, which immediately went out in the airstream. Letizia haughtily tried to ignore the fact, because she was too busy talking to the driver about the shortest way from the harbour to the La Favorita park, telling me about the importance of the freshly planted palm trees along the seafront for the rebirth of Palermo, and crying 'Amore mio' into the car telephone — it being unclear whether she was referring to her partner, one of the city gardeners under her control or a fellow combatant in the battle against the Mafia. And every now and again I tried to ask her questions about her calling as a photographer.

Letizia drew on her unlit cigarette and thought it was too banal to talk about her photographs. Basically it had all been quite easy! When she was thirty-six, she had separated from her husband, moved to Milan and started writing for the communist Sicilian daily newspaper *L'Ora* as cultural correspondent. And she'd only started taking photographs because stories with photographs sold better than stories without. Art can be as simple as that. Shortly afterwards she had moved back to Palermo, where she was appointed photographer-in-chief at *L'Ora*. Letizia was forty at the time and had just fallen in love with a skinny twenty-two-year-old boy, Franco Zecchin, with whom she was to spend almost twenty years, breathing, taking photographs, sleeping, eating, drinking, dreaming, arguing and fighting. And talking on the phone. Every two minutes. *'Amore mio.'*

At last, Letizia and I were invited to lunch by the city gardeners, in the city nursery, near La Favorita park. We ate bread with olive oil and drank red wine, and Letizia moved among the men like a mother, distributing praise and, every now and then, a bit of blame. They chucked around remarks and references that I didn't understand, and I think Letizia felt a bit sorry for me because I knew so little about that Sicilian planet that she had made it her business to revolutionize. She'd already forgotten that I'd actually come here to write an article about her: it was far more important for her to bring my knowledge about the Mafia up from zero to 100 per cent within a week. She bombarded me with names,

murders, Mafia connections; she smiled at me if there was
something I didn't understand; she showed me street corners
where policemen had been shot down, public prosecutors
shredded in a hail of bullets and unfortunate Mafia bosses
executed by their opponents, and explained to me that the
reason the city consisted of such endless stretches of road and
faceless tower blocks was because the *palazzi* of the aristoc-
racy, along with their knot gardens, pergolas and fountains,
had been stamped into the ground overnight by the Mafia. In
the 1970s, when the Mafia boss Vito Ciancimino was mayor of
Palermo, he had issued 4,200 building permits in four years:
3,300 of them to a street trader, a night-watchman and two
bricklayers, all four of them illiterate and straw men for the
Mafia, in an unparalleled building speculation known even
today as *Il sacco di Palermo*, the looting of Palermo – as if
marauding mercenaries had passed through the place. And
what sounded to my ears like a piece of Sicilian puppet theatre
was nothing but the absolute, total, submissive capitulation
of the city.

Letizia dragged me to the headquarters of a legendary
Mafia investigator who had been transferred sideways be-
cause of his success and now sat gloomily at an empty desk.
The investigator was called Saverio Montalbano. He had
Nordic blue eyes and a half-bald crown because at that time
it wasn't yet fashionable to shave your head. In those days
Andrea Camilleri hadn't yet invented his Commissario
Montalbano, and he would certainly have been unsettled to
watch this Montalbano being guarded by two bodyguards
who drove him around in an armoured limousine. I still

remember thinking: What a strange country! The policemen
need bodyguards!

Saverio Montalbano had been active in Palermo's mobile
task force, where he had been responsible for tracking down
Mafia fugitives. He had uncovered the 'pizza connection', the
heroin link between America and Sicily. He had, when he was
running the mobile task force in Trapani, revealed the connections between Freemasons, leading Christian Democrats,
the vice prefect and the local police chief — and by way of
reward the Ministry of the Interior had ordered him to leave
Sicily because they could no longer guarantee his safety. After
that, he was transferred to the commissariat in San Lorenzo.
I found it bizarre that successful policemen in Sicily were rewarded with a disciplinary transfer, but I imagined that soon
this would definitely be a thing of the past — after all, we were
in the spring of 1989 and everyone had this amazing faith in
the future. Everyone except Montalbano. Two of his predeces-
sors had been murdered: Boris Giuliano and Ninni Cassarà.
We were sitting in the courtyard of the commissariat, which
had once been a monastery, with no sound but the lapping of
the fountain and the faint crunch of gravel under the feet of
the odd stray cat. And Montalbano clicking his tongue when
Letizia asked him if he still believed in the future.

Letizia lived in the old town. Her apartment was filled to
the rafters with archive boxes; proclamations were stacked
up on the floor, manifestos spread out on tables. In Letizia's
flat I was reminded of clandestine meetings I had had with
Solidarność activists, and I remember finding that connection rather odd: wasn't Italy part of the free West? And wasn't

the Mafia a criminal organization? Rather than part of the state, for example?

People were constantly going in and out of Letizia's house: trade unionists, communists and women dialect poets, bearded men who had written about the Mafia in their own villages and published their books themselves, singers from ethno-rock groups and mothers of sons killed by the Mafia – activists in a revolution that was plainly just around the corner. Letizia introduced me to everybody; she explained connections, ideas and plans, never losing faith in my capacity for lifelong learning. She introduced me to her daughter, Shobha, who was a photographer in the service of the cause, the inheritor of Letizia's poetic legacy, and was carrying on as a photographer the task that her mother now hoped to accomplish in politics. Together they dragged me to the meeting of the city council in the Palazzo delle Aquile. And as I looked down in amazement at the arguing councillors and wondered how many of them might be mafiosi, Leoluca Orlando sent me a note which was passed to me by a waiter on a silver tray. On it was written: 'The most wasted of all days is one without laughter.'

That small gesture was what won me over to him – that and the trust that Letizia and Shobha placed in him, even though he had once been a Christian Democrat. At the time, the Christian Democrats were irrevocably linked with the Mafia through Andreotti's connections. Then Shobha and I had waited outside the door of his office until three o'clock in the morning, when Orlando finally granted us an interview.

––––

When I look up from my notebook, a waiter is standing by my table. He inquires impatiently whether he can clear my table. 'The breakfast buffet is closing now,' he says. I quickly drink down my cold tea and finally leave the table.

Salvo is waiting in the lobby. He is hopping agitatedly from one foot to the other because his card-sharp ladies have already called three times to ask him where he's got to. Then we make our way painfully slowly through the morning traffic along the Via Roma. Armoured limousines with darkened windows force their way past us, along with swarms of Vespa riders. The city swims in the blue of the sky. It smells of exhaust fumes and the sea. I would recognize Palermo with my eyes shut. By its smell, as unsettling as the scent of a strange man. A smell that both attracts and repels. Palermo is always ambivalent. Always beautiful and terrible at the same time. Like a beautiful woman with an eye missing. Like one of those bearded Madonnas sold by the albino below the church of Sant'Antonio Abate. The bearded Madonna can be seen only if you stand at the right angle in front of her picture. If you stand to the left, a bearded Jesus appears. If you look from the right, you see a Madonna with a flaming heart. But if you stand right in the middle you can see them both merging into a Madonna with a beard.

As we drive past, I see the albino gleaming in the shade of his stall. With his white hair and pale skin he looks very vulnerable, so vulnerable that I have to buy a Madonna from him every time I come to Palermo. And he swindles me every time.

Letizia and Shobha live on the top two floors of a 1970s

tower block which bears a striking resemblance to an air-raid
shelter. The lift cautiously jerks its way up, so slowly that you
expect to come out at the twenty-ninth floor, not the ninth.
I'm still standing in the doorway when I can hear Shobha
on the phone, blowing kisses, *Baci, baci, baci*, dismissing the
caller, *Ciao, ciao, ciao*, 'Yes, yes, see you, no time right now,
see you tomorrow.' Clutching two phones, she gives me a sign
to say that Letizia is waiting on the floor below.

When I go down the stairs I have to have my hand licked
by Letizia's dog, which she picked up somewhere in Palermo,
just like all those foreign journalists she picks up, even now,
like orphan children; there's always someone sitting on
her sofa, sometimes it's a Spanish journalist, sometimes an
American – Letizia helps them all, she makes contacts, spurs
people on, introduces people, all for the cause. Still. A bit.
Sometimes. Often.

For a short time now she's been living in this flat whose
walls look like the walls of a stalactite cave, as if it was made
as a film set for a 1970s domestic drama. If you stand on
the terrace, you can see the Ucciardone prison. She herself
feels like a prisoner in Palermo, Letizia says. It's ridiculous,
in Germany she was awarded the Dr Erich Salomon Prize
for her Mafia photographs, and in Sicily they want to forget
her. She sits in the breeze from the ceiling fan, clutching
an unlit cigarette, and says without much of an introduction: 'I was happier back then. In 1989 we thought we could
change things, in love, in society. We have lost the battle. On
every level.'

And then she falls silent and there is no sound but the

whirr of the ceiling fan, the panting of her dog and the roar of the Palermo traffic. The eighties were also the years of the big Mafia wars: the Corleone family assumed power in Palermo; there were killings almost every day. Not just among the mafiosi but also among public prosecutors, judges, police – and Letizia, Franco and Shobha were always first to the scene. Like all good reporters, they listened to the police radio. And photographed bullet-riddled bodies, pools of blood and widows in the grip of despair.

'We were unfettered. If we travelled off in an old VW van, it was never for longer than a week, because we couldn't bear to leave the city for longer than that. We loved Palermo,' Letizia says. And she sounds as if she's talking about a drug addict that she's hoped in vain to save.

'Today there is no any anti-Mafia awareness,' she says, brushing her dog aside as he tries to kiss her.

Letizia has always been a plain speaker. She has never tried to prettify anything, ever, and doesn't see why she should start now. 'There's nothing left,' she says. All those anti-Mafia meetings, symposia and memorials for the victims were nothing but showcasing, and that's something she's always rejected.

When Letizia talks about showcasing, I immediately see an image of the children by the Falcone tree, that huge magnolia below the house where Giovanni Falcone lived. The death of the murdered public prosecutor is commemorated here every year. A stage had been set up next to the magnolia and children stood on it in green baseball caps. The children danced under their teachers' beady eyes; they read out poems they had written themselves, about a Mafia cockerel that wanted to dictate the law, and sang law-abiding songs.

Standing next to me was a journalist from *Corriere della Sera*, who noticed my astonishment. Glancing at the stage, he said with a shrug: 'An identity ritual. We're Catholics, we need something like this. Like the processions. We have to keep proving our identity.'

As the children were singing under the magnolia, people remembered Falcone and Borsellino in the 'aula bunker', the high-security courtroom in Ucciardone prison, which had been built for the 'maxi-trial', which would go down in history not only because of its sheer size — 474 defendants, of whom 114 were acquitted, the guilty ones being sentenced to a total of 2,665 years' imprisonment — but also because it was the first in the history of the Italian judiciary from which the Mafia had not emerged victorious. A huge scout camp had been set up in the courtyard of the prison: the law-and-order village. The children wore T-shirts bearing the picture of the murdered public prosecutors. The prison fence was draped with sheets scrawled with words like *The Mafia suppresses us* or *Grow up honest!*. One teacher went up to her pupils and hissed: 'Write something! Write something intelligent!'

Inside, the two prosecutors were commemorated with a lot of speeches, a lot of noisy applause, and television films about the Mafia — films in which the mafiosi looked like action heroes with pump-action shotguns and the public prosecutors looked bold and incorruptible. They love films like that in Palermo, where the Mafia is now once more as invisible as it used to be. Aristocratic among aristocrats, bourgeois among the bourgeoisie. The bosses stopped being shepherds a long time ago, shepherds who could barely speak Italian; now they're doctors, businessmen, politicians, the so-called 'white-collar Mafia'. Palermo returned to its normality a long time ago. Only rarely are there diplomatic incidents like the one that year when a student asked the minister of the interior, who was attending the Falcone-Borsellino memorial day, what he planned to do about all the MPs with criminal convictions, two of whom were even on the anti-Mafia commission. The minister didn't say: 'They will have to be thrown out.' Instead, he accused the student of being a little populist. A hint of the Eastern bloc wafted through the 'aula bunker' and lingered in the air even after the minister had disappeared. A speaker addressed the schoolchildren sitting on the floor: 'You are stronger than the Mafia!' And the children cheered, as if they were watching a school play.

'*Niente*,' says Letizia, and draws on her cigarette. 'We're finished.'

She doesn't think for a second of lying to herself with the eternal 'there's-no-work-here-and-that's-why-we've-got-the-Mafia' hypocrisy, with the romantic idea of the healing power of culture, as if the Mafia could be got rid of like a typo. In her hoarse voice, she speaks the truth that no one in Italy wants to hear: 'Barbarism rules on our island! People are stuck in a lawless mindset!'

'And that wasn't even Berlusconi's fault,' she says; the Sicilians had been waiting for him as if he were a seller of dreams, someone who could at last let them forget. Her comrades-in-arms fell silent, crept away. Lots of them jumped on the Forza Italia bandwagon, and, when Berlusconi was deselected and everyone expected the Prodi government to launch a campaign against the Mafia with renewed zeal, Clemente Mastella was appointed minister of justice. This is a man who is seen as an ardent supporter of Giulio Andreotti and who has also demonstrated a certain familiarity with organized crime: in 2000 he was a witness at the wedding of the Sicilian mafioso Francesco Campanella, who had no hesitation in turning state witness immediately after his arrest. Mastella's first action in office was to introduce a mass pardon for convicts, benefitting not only Silvio Berlusconi and the Eritrean human-trafficker Ganat Tewelde Barhe, better known as 'Madame Gennet', but also countless mafiosi who immediately returned to their daily business.

Anti-Mafia public prosecutors uncovering the connection between politicians and the Mafia had long been isolated in the Anti-Mafia Pool. Some were withdrawn from investigations, and Leoluca Orlando, too, failed in his attempt to win back the city for himself. In Letizia's eyes, Orlando was the only one capable of restoring the city's dreams. He stood for mayor and only narrowly lost the election to the Forza Italia candidate. There was the usual talk of election fraud. It was said that people had been told to take pictures of their ballot papers with their *telefonini* to prove to the bosses that they had followed their electoral recommendations. In vain Orlando demanded that the election be declared invalid. A year later, the public prosecutor's office brought an action for proven electoral fraud and arrested two electoral district officers.

For a long time, Palermo has been governed by a triad of mayor, regional president and president of the council. Political best buddies, who won't be shaken by allegations of electoral shenanigans. The innovations of the last mayor, Diego Cammarata, stopped with the introduction of two double-decker buses for sightseeing tours. And the next thing he did was to commission a lawyer to take action against any journalist who criticized the city administration. Regional president Totò Cuffaro was sentenced in the first instance to five years' imprisonment for supporting the Mafia and was forced to step down, but found brief consolation with a seat in the senate until his prison term began. He was replaced as regional president by a soulmate, his former party colleague Raffaele Lombardo. And the former council president Gianfranco Miccichè is a close friend of Marcello Dell'Utri, the senator and companion of Berlusconi who was sentenced in the first instance to nine years' imprisonment for supporting the Mafia.

'So you've met him, Miccichè, when he was still council president,' Letizia says, 'and what do you want me to tell you?'

In fact, Shobha and I did once meet the minister, who isn't really a minister now but is still addressed as such, at the Villa Igiea, the luxury hotel in the Bay of Palermo where the city's upper crust meet, from ministers to Mafia bosses to cardinals. It was a remarkable encounter with a representative of Sicilian politics.

Under Berlusconi, Forza Italia MP Gianfranco Miccichè was appointed deputy economics minister and secretary of state for development, but during his time in office he was better known to the wider public for an inglorious and quickly buried affair involving cocaine: a runner, a Sicilian Forza Italia activist, had delivered the drug straight to the ministry. In Rome, the minister was also responsible for deciding what EU sponsorship money went to Sicily, and was rewarded for this with the highest number of direct votes in the Sicilian election.

At Villa Igiea he introduced his latest gift: a daily soap entitled *Agrodolce*, Bittersweet – two hundred and forty episodes, which were to be produced in Sicily. Supported by EU funding. You can't always talk about the Mafia and nothing else, the minister says, you have to be able to see the positive side as well. In a freezing-cold conference room he presented the trailer to the journalists. He didn't show rubbish in the streets or endless traffic jams; he didn't show the skeletons of burned-out cars in the Borgo Vecchio or the weeds tearing up the motorways; he showed dolphins gliding through a sky-blue sea to the sound of melancholy accordion music, and Kalsa cathedral, which looked as if it had been dipped in honey, and at the end of the trailer the minister wiped tears from his eyes. Next to him sat another party colleague who was equally moved – he was one of the closest political allies of Miccichè and Marcello Dell'Utri: Angelino Alfano, who was appointed justice minister in the third Berlusconi government in 2008 and, since 2011, has been the Secretary of Berlusconi's party, Popolo della Libertà (People of Freedom).

Later, after a generous lunch, Miccichè met up with a journalist from the Berlusconi newspaper *Il Giornale* on the hotel terrace. He didn't want to talk to me because a German television team had once called him a mafioso and he had brought charges against the television channel. But Shobha and I stayed stoically on our wicker chairs and watched a circle of young people crowding around Gianfranco Miccichè and the journalist, Italian neo-cons with turquoise ties, young lawyers and economists, and a young woman with Cleopatra eyeliner.

'We're the Gianfranco boys,' one of them said, and the minister casually rested his feet on the table.

His young admirers were all members of the Marcello Dell'Utri Club: the senator, co-founder of Forza Italia and Berlusconi confidant, found guilty of complicity with the Mafia, is so keen on disseminating his so-called culture that he has established hundreds of clubs all across Italy. When I asked a young man what they talked about in those culture clubs, he told me they often discussed issues such as 'Is Italy a constitutional democracy?' Because in Italy, he argued, people had no protection once they fell into the clutches of the legal system.

I looked at the young man in amazement. Because it didn't seem likely to me that these young people were at risk of falling permanently into the clutches of the Italian legal system. In fact, these ambitious, talented and probably privileged neo-conservatives gave the impression of being intoxicated from their immersion in the sea of Berlusconi's propaganda.

'We want to prove that it's not only the left that does any thinking, we also discuss issues like "Karl Marx and God – what's left?"' said the girl with the Cleopatra eyes.

They all spoke eloquently, word perfect in fact; they talked freely. Only the minister didn't say a word and kept his eyes firmly closed. I wondered if he was bored. Or was it his heavy lunch? In fact, the minister had gone to sleep. He was snoring — it was impossible to ignore. And the Gianfranco boys just went on talking about their cultural activities and about how not everything in Sicily should be all about morality. The minister's head was tilted to one side and his mouth slightly open, noises issuing from his soft palate.

And the next day there was an interview with him in *Il Giornale* in which he promised to bless Sicily with ten golf courses: 'We will bring Sicily back to the fore.'

———

'Hmm, yeah, golf courses,' says Letizia, drawing on her unlit cigarette. For a while she moved from Palermo to Paris because she didn't want her whole life to be eaten up by the Mafia. Because she couldn't bear to stare into the triumphant faces of politicians who were collaborating with the Mafia. The former minister for infrastructure and transportation, the Lega Nord politician Pietro Lunardi, had with disarming honesty told the Italians they must finally get used to living with the Mafia: the Mafia and the Camorra had always existed, he said, and they always would. 'Since then, politicians have lost their shame,' Letizia says.

Up until a few years ago Letizia had also run a publishing company, Edizione della Battaglia, bringing out books about the Mafia and the southern hemisphere. She had sold these books in a little bookshop not far from the Teatro Politeama — until the day a man came in and asked her very politely for a donation for the prisoners. The second time he asked for a donation she closed the bookshop.

'You know, I got the message,' she says, staring with amazement at her cigarette, still unlit.

Padre Frittitta

Letizia's dog wakes up when he hears Shobha's footsteps on the stairs. He runs over and licks her too. 'If I might briefly interrupt your conversation,' Shobha says, pointing at her watch and at the sun, which is already high in the sky. 'Before midday, perhaps we could take a few pictures, in the Kalsa, perhaps, not far from the Piazza Marina.' She had had the idea, she says, of taking a photograph of Letizia in front of the church of Santa Maria della Pietà in Kalsa; Salvo is already waiting downstairs. Letizia nods, somehow resigned. She prefers to stand behind the camera. Particularly since she's just been given a new camera, a digital Leica, which she now throws over her shoulder.

As usual, Salvo has triple-parked, but it's not a problem. Unusually, he isn't in a hurry, the Kalsa isn't far away, and his ladies are still engrossed in their game.

When we arrive in the Piazza Marina, the waiters are already laying the tables for lunch. It's one restaurant after another – and no reminders of the years when the mood was one of permanent curfew and not a single sound. No one in their right mind would ever have thought of setting foot in the Kalsa in those days. No one would ever attend a vigil of their own free will. Forty years of Mafia city administration had led to the abandonment of the old town. Forty years during which the bourgeoisie of Palermo had turned a blind eye to Mafia mayors and kowtowing city councillors, submissive architects and venal city planners. As far as those people were concerned, the decay of the old city couldn't happen quickly enough; ideally, they would have knocked the whole lot down so that they could fill the place with the tower blocks that had already disfigured the rest of the city. It was only since the Mafia had put money into the tourist industry as well that some of the baroque *palazzi* had had their façades restored.

In the middle of Piazza Marina there's a huge magnolia fig tree that has grown into a vast and magical forest. The trunk is reddish brown, like the Sicilian soil, and has transformed itself into some fabulous creature that consists of knotted, frozen snakes, dragons half hidden in the ground and elongated elephants. Every time I turn my back on this tree I half expect it to stretch out its arms and grab me.

Shobha immediately directs her mother to stand under the tree and starts taking pictures and I take notes about Letizia, about her red fringe, which even today makes her look like a Parisian student who's just climbed down from the barricades. She's always been a reporter, commander and spy all at once; she comforted widows, saw her friends die and crept behind enemy lines. She photographed Giulio Andreotti holding out his hand to a Mafia boss — something

that Andreotti still tried to deny decades later, when he was
on trial for supporting the Mafia. But Letizia's photograph
was among the evidence produced.

'And I only remembered that photograph when the police came looking for it in my archive,' Letizia says with
amazement.

When Shobha directs her mother towards the roots of the
magic tree, I hear brass-band music floating across from the
Corso Vittorio Emanuele. Not a day passes in Sicily without a religious procession of one kind or another. Curious,
I walk towards the street to take a look – before coming
back, disappointed: there isn't the usual sea of people, just a
scattered troop of believers following the crucifix. It isn't a
procession as such, just a small penitential pilgrimage. The
Jesus being carried along the Corso has bashed knees and a
slightly crooked crown of thorns; he's followed by a handful
of believers being spurred on by a priest with a loud-hailer.
'Lord, we beg thee,' the believers cry, asking for healing for
the handicapped, for those who have succumbed to alcohol,
for those who have fallen under the spell of evil. Would they
include the mafiosi? Like the turncoat Marcello Fava, for example? Until his arrest he belonged to the congregation of
Santa Teresa alla Kalsa, just a few steps behind us on Piazza
Marina. There he had prayed to Santa Maria del Carmelo,
when he wasn't meeting the other bosses outside the church
to discuss business with them. When I interviewed him in
Rome he repeatedly stressed the importance to him of the
spiritual assistance given to him by a nun after he had decided to turn state witness. But now that I'm standing only

a few yards away from his church, I wonder whether these people here mightn't see betrayal of the Mafia as a greater sin than actually belonging to the Mafia.

Salvo stands next to me. He casts an indifferent, if not contemptuous, glance at the procession moving past us, before staring again at the display of his *telefonino*, because he's in permanent contact with his fiancée. But when the Jesus with the crooked crown of thorns is carried past, even Salvo glances up and crosses himself. Briefly, with his thumb, the way people do in Sicily.

While Shobha and her mother are still trying to find the best perspective in the shadow under the magnolia fig tree, Salvo and I start walking towards Santa Teresa alla Kalsa. As always, a man sits opposite the church in the shade of a tree, frying croquettes in an aluminium pot full of seething oil. Santa Teresa alla Kalsa is a small, sand-coloured church with bashful baroque forms. Stucco saints stand in the niches, sighing for all eternity from their half-open mouths. It's here that we find Padre Frittitta. The priest Don Pino – the priest from San Luca – reminded me of.

'I don't suppose you want to have another chat with Padre Frittitta?' Salvo asks and laughs. I involuntarily stick out my little finger and my forefinger, to ward off evil. Everyone in Palermo knows the name of Padre Mario Frittitta. On one occasion Don Mario had been arrested for supporting the Mafia because he had heard fugitive Mafia boss Pietro Aglieri's confession in his hiding place and had read him private masses. After the arrest of Padre Frittitta, his congregation had organized street demonstrations. Only four

days later Padre Frittitta was released from the Ucciardone
prison: a lenient judge had released him on condition that
he leave Sicily. But even that punishment wouldn't last for
long: we met the Carmelite priest shortly after he returned
to the bosom of his church amidst the triumphant cries of
his congregation.

There was quite a tense atmosphere around the meeting
because Padre Frittitta no longer gave interviews to journalists. He had only agreed to talk to us because we had been
recommended by the lawyer defending the Mafia boss Pietro
Aglieri.

It was a very hot day in October when we met Padre
Frittitta. He was walking busily through his church. Against
the light I could see his Carmelite habit slipping across
the floor and swirling up dust. At first, the only sound was
that of his crêpe soles squeaking across the marble – Padre
Frittitta arranged a bouquet here, straightened an altar cloth
there – until he greeted us very cordially and led us through
his church, past the statues of the saints with their electric
candles, past the church's patron, St Teresa of Avila, past
Sant'Anna, Sant'Antonio and Santa Rita – who actually had
no business in this church, Padre Frittitta observed, but had
been put here for the devotion of the little people, the lower
classes, the *popolino*, Padre Frittitta sighed.

As Shobha prowled around the church taking pictures of
the saints, I sat down on a pew beside Padre Frittitta and became aware that the church air was making me a bit dizzy. It
smelled sweet and sour at the same time: it smelled of faded
lilies, of muttered sins and stale air, of myrrh, of absolution

and of old men. I held the microphone of my tape recorder at arm's length and Padre Frittitta said: 'God is everywhere.'

He told me his favourite saint was Saint Elizabeth of the Trinity, because she had taught him that God dwells within us.

'God is in the mountains, in the sea and in the trees,' Padre Frittitta said. His voice sounded like whispering from hundreds of years ago, a hoarse susurration, a quiet murmur. 'I don't have to seek God in the clouds,' said Padre Frittitta, 'because I carry him within me, and that is what gives me courage and strength. That's what I always preach: "Take God with you wherever you go!"'

So Padre Frittitta had also brought the Lord God to the hiding place of the fugitive mafioso Pietro Aglieri. There, in front of the home altar, he had served the mass to the murderer, had taken his confession and granted him absolution. Since then, the law had investigated the Carmelite priest and Padre Frittitta no longer understood the world. He spoke without waiting for a question, as if he had pressed a button deep within himself. The button of absolution.

Of course, Pietro Aglieri's involvement in the assassinations of the two public prosecutors, Falcone and Borsellino, was a grave matter even in the eyes of Padre Frittitta, not to mention the thirteen other accusations of murder — involvement in the murders of general public prosecutor Antonino Scopelliti, the MP Salvo Lima, the sisters of the turncoat mafioso Marino Mannoia, and murders during the Mafia war in 1983. But still.

'However, it was right for me to go there,' Padre Frittitta

whispered, 'it was right, because Jesus preached: "Go out and bring back the lost sheep!" So I went. Because this individual had to change. The church must help these people: they too have dignity; they too have a soul that shouldn't be kicked and battered with laws. Laws, laws, of course, but to achieve what? What?'

As he spoke, his eye slipped across the pews to the wooden crucifix, the crown of thorns, the wounds, to Jesus, his legs polished smooth by the hands of the faithful who touched him during the Easter processions. 'And Jesus went to the sinners,' Padre Frittitta whispered. 'Yes, he went to them, so I went to them too, and I knew that I was taking a risk.'

Fury sprayed from his mouth in fine droplets of saliva, incessant, dense and sticky. After all, everyone in Palermo knew how devout the Aglieri family was. Her son believed in God, Pietro Aglieri's mother herself had insisted; he wasn't pretending, he respected the Christian commandments, and all the things that had been circulated about him were false. His sister lived in a closed order, his cousin was chaplain at the Palermo polyclinic, an aunt was a nun, and Pietro Aglieri himself had attended the archiepiscopal seminary in Palermo where he had acquired his knowledge of Latin and Greek.

'These people must be saved,' whispered Padre Frittitta, 'and it's not prison that saves them, not solitary confinement, no. Certainly, they must make good their injustice, that's one thing, but the other thing is surely to convert them. And that requires someone who will sow supernatural, moral values in them. And only the church can do that!'

Padre Frittitta groaned, as if he were living through it all again: the policeman arresting him, the dazzling flashlights as he was dragged from his church in handcuffs – all the humiliations, all the insults, all the indignities still lay heavy on his heart.

Then, on the evening news, the whole of Italy had been able to see the pictures of Pietro Aglieri's hiding place with its little chapel, its prayer stools, the statue of Saint Francis, the Bible, the gospels, the books by Edith Stein and the files of the Second Vatican Council, crumpled and scattered on the floor. The newspapers reported how after his arrest Pietro Aglieri had spent hours in solitary confinement immersed in prayer and said at last: 'I have repented before God.' Which, admittedly, he said more to himself than to the policeman who had opened the door and asked with surprise: 'You want to repent?' And Aglieri had replied: 'Before God. Not before you.'

Padre Frittitta wouldn't have expected anything else of him. Who cares about earthly justice?

It's heavenly justice that Cosa Nostra hopes for. Earthly justice it creates itself. Trials can be fixed, judges and politicians bought. The turncoat mafioso Leonardo Messina said: 'Of course my wife and I are religious. I was taught that the Mafia exists in order to administer justice. So there is no contradiction. On the contrary, it's now that I feel like more of a traitor. Before, when I was a murderer, I was relaxed as I walked into the church. Now that I'm a turncoat I can no longer pray with a clear conscience.'

When Nitto Santapaola, the boss of the Catania Mafia

family, was arrested, before the handcuffs were put on him he picked up the Bible and kissed it. And when the boss Michele Greco, known as *il Papa*, the Pope, was called to account for hundreds of murders at the maxi-trial, he merely remarked: 'I have an invaluable gift – inner peace.' On the bedside table in his prison cell there were four books that he read to make his life sentence go by more quickly: the gospels, a prayer book entitled *Pray, Pray* and two liturgical books.

The reference library of Mafia boss Totò Riina is very similar: he never sleeps without pictures of the saints at the head of his prison bed. And Bernardo Provenzano's knowledge of the Bible is legendary. When he was arrested at the end of his forty-two years, eleven months and two days in Corleone, the police found five Bibles with annotations and passages underlined. At his desk the boss surrounded himself with pictures of the saints, the Last Supper framed in dark wood, the Mother of God in various versions, a calendar with a picture of Padre Pio, the boss's favourite saint. There was even a rosary in the toilet. After Provenzano's arrest, the police counted ninety-one sacred statues, seventy-three of them Christ figures with the inscription *Jesus, I put my trust in you*. No one was surprised that Provenzano's messages, the *pizzini*, those little pieces of paper, folded and sealed with adhesive tape, with which he managed to remain invisible in the age of the internet, bugs and satellite surveillance, always ended with the same phrase: *May the Lord bless and protect you*.

The messages to his followers, delivered in the solemn and affectionate tone of a good father, were typed up by

Provenzano on a typewriter. When he was arrested, thirty little pieces of paper were ready to be collected and distributed to their addressees. The Provenzano code didn't just consist of numbers – the boss Salvatore Lo Piccolo was no. 30, his son no. 31; only the boss Matteo Messina Denaro had the honour of being addressed by a codename, 'Alessio' – but also his own personal, individual spelling: Provenzano wrote as he spoke, he confused *t* and *d*, *g* and *c*, in line with Sicilian dialect. But the lines of prayer and Bible quotations were by no means the expression of religious fanaticism, they were the vehicle of a secret code. When the boss Pino Lipari received a prison visit from his son Arturo, it concerned the content of the piece of paper that Arturo had copied down for his arrested father. The content had not been complete, his father complained. When his son justified himself by saying that there had been a lot of Ave Marias in the message, to which he hadn't paid much attention, his father rebuked him: 'Next time, copy out everything, because in the middle of all those Ave Marias there's something that I need to understand, have you got that?'

The commandments of the church are the commandments of the Mafia. But for the Mafia the significance of the commandments is less ethical than practical. God exists in order to be useful to Cosa Nostra.

Thou shalt have no other gods before me: The boss is infallible, a *padre eterno*, God's vicar on earth, master over life and death.

Honour thy father and thy mother: The preservation of the family goes above all else, even one's own life. But only so long as individual family members don't tread the dignity of a man of honour, the clan or Cosa Nostra itself into the mud — a sister who has an extramarital affair that the whole town talks about has forfeited her life.

Thou shalt not bear false witness against thy neighbour: Mafiosi are obliged to be completely honest with one another. A man of honour never lies. Either he says nothing or he tells the truth, because his honesty is of crucial importance to the survival of Cosa Nostra.

Thou shalt not commit adultery: A mafioso may not deceive his wife: the mother of his children could become an unpredictable security risk if the extramarital relationship came to light. And a lover is often less easily tamed than a wife. Besides, a mafioso who is known to have affairs is seen as someone incapable of controlling himself sexually and emotionally, which means that he isn't professionally trustworthy.

There is only one Christian commandment that has not been taken on board by Cosa Nostra: *Thou shalt not kill*. But can a job be a sin? A man of honour kills without passion. For him, to kill is to fulfil one's duty — to his state, his people, Cosa Nostra, which he is sworn to serve, since the all-powerful godfather said: 'Now you no longer belong to this world. Now you are our business. *Cosa Nostra.*'

Do they have guilt feelings? 'Does a judge have guilt feelings when he sentences a defendant to the electric chair or life imprisonment?' the turncoat mafioso Tommaso Buscetta once asked, and told the story of the mafioso who, before every murder, used to light a candle in front of the statue of

Jesus and prayed: 'Jesus Christ, take him! Take him to you!'
But God did not hear his plea. So the mafioso carried out the
murder himself. After that he prayed again: 'Dear God, you
didn't want him. I have sent him to you.' And before every
murder the hit man Leoluca Bagarella went to church to
pray: 'Lord, you alone know that they are the ones who want
to be killed. No guilt attaches to me.'

Since its origins, Cosa Nostra has tried to merge with the
world in which it lives and from which it was born. That
is crucial to its survival. The Mafia wants to be invisible,
it wants to be part of society. It has always relied upon the
Italian dislike of the state, and for centuries it has successfully sold the illusion of fighting for a higher justice — as if it
were fighting for justice for the individual against a powerful
state. This is something it has in common with the Catholic
Church, which struggles to comply with the demands of
earthly justice. In large parts of southern Italy the state is
still seen as an occupying power — as if the Normans, the
Hohenstaufen, the Bourbons, the Aragonese and Austrians
had passed through here only yesterday.

As pragmatic as Cosa Nostra is, it would never dare call the
church into question. Even in the third millennium, Italy is
still a country where, every day, if not the Pope then at least
one of his cardinals appears on television, addresses his subjects and urges them to have more children, fewer divorces, to
play more sport and use less homeopathic medicine.

The church fears for souls, the Mafia for its sinecure. And
for that reason the Carmelite monks defended their fellow
priest Padre Frittitta and instructed the public prosecutor's

office that the church was never against anything, not even Cosa Nostra, but only ever *with*: with the tormented souls, with every individual sinner who needed salvation. And *Novica*, a journal close to the Palermo curia, said this: 'Even the most wanted mafioso in the world must be sure that at any time of day or night he can find a cleric who will hand him over neither to the public prosecutor's office nor to police headquarters.'

———

'And through whose fault was Christ nailed to the cross?' whispered Padre Frittitta. 'Through the fault of people who had sinned! Through the fault of us sinners! Should I have torn the passion story out of the gospels? Jesus is not only the Jesus of blessedness, but also the Jesus of the passion. That's why I went.'

That's what Padre Frittitta says. And I remember that at some point I lost all feeling in my arm. When I turned the tape recorder off I noticed a faint feeling of dizziness. The heat. The lilies. The incense. The smell of old men. Just before I reached the sacristy I fainted. When I woke up again I saw Padre Frittitta bending over me, rubbing a liquid that smelled like Melissa oil over my face, neck and cleavage, and a deathly pale Shobha dashing in and yelling excitely: 'What's going on here? What's happened?' To which Padre Frittitta, bright red in the face, replied: 'Nothing, nothing, nothing!'

Later, as I was washing my face with cold water, he asked Shobha in a whisper what state my faith was in. Shobha assured him that my faith was firmly rooted.

'Is she religious?' he persisted.

'Very religious,' said Shoba. 'She would never miss a procession.'

When we were saying goodbye, Padre Frittitta offered us a peppermint each. I took one. Shobha turned hers down.

'You are a sceptic,' Padre Frittitta said reproachfully.

Corleone

People need values. Even men of honour, who believe in nothing but the power of Cosa Nostra, need a system to provide them with values and bring them into line. Every value system that strives for the absolute, regardless of whether it's communism or the Catholic Church, gives its devotees not just a complete image of the world, a tight-fitting corset of rules and codes for good behaviour, but an ideological foundation as well. The communists justify their thirst for power by leading people to freedom, to equality, to fraternity. To the victory of the proletariat, the eradication of capitalist oppression. The Catholic Church promises its believers salvation and eternal life. The Mafia, on the other hand, can give no metaphysical foundation for its thirst for power. It has no ideological foundation on which to build its system. That's why it needs religion. Using the components of the Catholic faith, it has constructed God in its own image. The God of a tooth for a tooth. The God of the chosen people. The God who levelled Sodom and Gomorrah. A bloodthirsty God.

I was glad that a few days after my meeting with Padre Frittitta I was able to meet a cleric who had always spoken out against the close alliance between church and Mafia. The Sicilian Redemptorist padre Nino Fasullo bears the label of an 'anti-Mafia priest', because even today it isn't obvious that anyone should be opposed to the Mafia. Not priests, not public prosecutors. 'For a phenomenon like the Mafia, which has no intellectual justification at all, religion may represent the only ideological apparatus to which it can refer,' Padre Fasullo said. I met him in his bare office on the periphery of Palermo. He sat at his desk in a plain checked shirt, no habit, no aura of illumination, no incense.

'There isn't a single mafioso who isn't religious,' said Padre Fasullo, and his voice sounded agonized. All the articles he had written on the subject of church and Mafia! All the lectures he had given! Endless. He sighed.

'You know,' he said slowly, 'the church is holy and sinful at the same time. It is clean and dirty, beautiful and ugly. We're all in the church. Even the Mafia. Unfortunately. The church is embroiled in it. But regrettably not everyone in the church is convinced that opposition to the Mafia is necessary.'

What model is the anti-Mafia priest supposed to refer to when even the Archbishop of Monreale, the largest and wealthiest diocese in Sicily, had been up before the court for accepting bribes for the awarding of building contracts? Monreale has the highest Mafia density in Sicily. The diocese includes the little towns of Corleone and San Giuseppe Jato, Prizzi and Carini.

Padre Nino Fasullo despaired over all those pursed lips,

the lowered eyes and closed ears of his colleagues. 'So confession is no longer the sacrament of mercy and forgiveness,
of freedom and courage, but the graveyard of morality?' he
asked. And then he pointed out that hardly anything has
changed since the 1960s – a time famous for a *bon mot* of
the Archbishop of Palermo, Cardinal Ernesto Ruffini, who
said: 'Mafia? Isn't that a brand of soap?' Ruffini played down
the Mafia to Pope Paul VI as a *quantité négligeable*, a band
of petty criminals invented by the left in order to discredit
Sicily, the Christian Democrats and the church. The only one
who had delivered moral sermons, who had condemned the
Mafia as the spawn of the devil and called upon mafiosi to
convert had been John Paul II.

Of course that had been useful, said Padre Fasullo. A useful
indignation. But. But it's a long time ago. And Pope Benedict
XVI hadn't voiced nearly as much indignation against the
Mafia. Even today there isn't a single official church anti-Mafia
document for public reference.

'In fact, the church, paradoxical though it may sound, has
become the Mafia's ethical point of reference,' Padre Fasullo
said bitterly. 'Over time an almost blind relationship of trust
has established itself between them. You might even say,
church and Mafia have, for various and contradictory reasons,
found one another in their common desire for conservatism.'

––––

When, on the pavement in front of the church, I tell Salvo
about my fainting fit in the company of Padre Frittitta, I am
careful to add: 'And even today Shobha believes that Padre

Frittitta put a spell on me.' I can't persuade her otherwise, however convincingly I point out that it had been very sultry a moment before, that I have a tendency towards low blood pressure anyway, and have even fainted in the cinema, in the middle of *The Silence of the Lambs*.

'*Ma*,' Shobha says once more, as soon as she's standing in front of Frittitta's church. A *ma* which, in this case, means 'you can say what you like'. And as if to ward off a curse, she decides to take Letizia's picture not outside the church but a few yards further on, in front of the tufa stone of the Porta Felice.

Luckily, Padre Frittitta is nowhere to be seen. We step inside the church for a moment, but neither inside, amongst the figures of the saints, nor outside, amongst all the Sicilian baroque of the Kalsa, where fish tails spill from the stone, dwarfs ride along on fanciful horses and centaurs stick their tongues out at visitors, is a trace of his brown Carmelite habit to be seen. I wonder what the old men sitting in the shade of a bar not far from the Porta Felice think about him? As we approach them they are staring as steadfastly at the passing traffic as if it were about to bring them eternal salvation. Until Letizia appears and embroils them in a conversation, just as she used to when she was city councillor for quality of life and talked to the people about their town – which many Palermitans found almost impossible to believe. She looks at the holes in the pavement and tells the men that when she lived abroad she always took pictures of things she wanted to see in Palermo: beautiful pavements, public toilets, museums. 'Strange, isn't it?'

The old men giggle as if Letizia had said something sala-
cious. One of them flicks through a copy of *La Repubblica*,
which shows a photograph of Giuseppe Riina, the son of the
Mafia boss Totò Riina, in cashmere sweater and down waistcoat, wearing his shirt tails fashionably outside his trousers,
leaving prison, getting into an S-series Mercedes and, accompanied by his sister and mother, going back to Corleone as if
it were the most natural thing in the world. Even though he
had been sentenced to eight years' imprisonment, he was able
to leave prison because too much time had elapsed between
the judgements of the first and second instances. As soon as
he arrived in Corleone, this son of the Mafia announced that
he would shortly be taking his case to the European Court of
Human Rights and bringing proceedings against the Italian
state for the excessive length of his sentence.

Letizia watches over the men's shoulders, points to the picture of the S-series Mercedes and says: 'So, bearing in mind
that in theory the entire property of the Riina family should
be confiscated ...'

'Only in theory,' says one of the men.

———

In Corleone the children of the bosses now have the final
word: they ensure continuity. A continuity that has continued
for centuries. Every time I go to Corleone I look for changes
and find none. The very first time I came to the city, in 1979,
I was disappointed. I was a student and had driven straight
from the Ruhr to Corleone in a rusty Renault 4 because I'd
been such a fan of *The Godfather.* And then I saw a town

that looked like a meteorite hurled by a giant into a rocky landscape. Grey, bare stone houses, electric wires leading nowhere. Suspicious glances behind fly-curtains. A town without a soul. Not a hint of Mario Puzo. Not a trace of that flaming lion heart promised by the Italian name Corleone.

I had no sense at the time that I was in Corleone at the precise moment when the village was striving for higher things. In the 1980s it was the boss Luciano Liggio who, along with Totò Riina and Bernardo Provenzano, first brought the Corleonesi to the top of Cosa Nostra, which had traditionally been reserved for the Mafia of Palermo. Until then, Corleone had been a little Mafia village like many others – one that, apart from its walk-on role in *The Godfather*, had no remarkable features whatsoever. But this would soon change, in accordance with the will of the bosses. For almost thirty years, the Mafia of Corleone would lead Cosa Nostra, with Totò Riina ruling violently both at home and abroad, becoming responsible for what was probably the most bloodthirsty era of Cosa Nostra, which would reach its climax in the assassinations of the public prosecutors Falcone and Borsellino. Ruling along with his brother-in-law, Leoluca Bagarella, and with Bernardo Provenzano, the diplomat who succeeded in allowing Cosa Nostra to slip back into its cloak of invisibility. Who staunched the haemorrhage of turncoat mafiosi and re-established a social consensus. Because the secret of the Mafia's survival lies in the fact that it hasn't fought against the state and society but has lived in and with them.

Even today, I wonder about Corleone's piety – not least,

perhaps, because I know that Corleone is the town of a hundred churches. The Chiesa Madre right next to the town hall is so big that I lose my way in it. There is said to be room for all of the inhabitants of the town inside it.

As Shobha and I walked through Corleone in search of godliness, we relied on chance, as ever. We simply strolled through the alleyways, stepped inside the churches and hoped to fall into conversation with a priest. In the Chiesa Madre we met Father Vincenzo Pizzitola, the parish priest. Grey-haired, bent and with sagging features, he dragged himself down the passageways and took refuge, so to speak, in an endless evocation of Corleone's saints, the blessed and the anointed: San Leoluca, Corleone's patron saint, keeping guard in a niche; the Capuchin monk Fra Bernardo in the nave aisle, one of the best sword-fighters in Sicily, who entered the monastery because he couldn't get over the death of an opponent; San Martino, the church's titular saint; San Placido, the martyr, also in bits — rotting away in a glass sarcophagus, a piece of his skull, his arm, his heart. Along with dusty pink plastic flowers.

Corleone. City of saints. The priest didn't mention the doctor Michele Navarra. Michele Navarra wasn't just a physician in Corleone, he was also president of the farmers' association, a trustee of the famers' union and supervisor of the region's health insurance body. Even today, one of the front pews bears his nameplate. The godfather of the post-war period. His name was once uttered in Corleone with the same respect as that of San Leoluca. They called him *u patri nostru* and crossed themselves.

One of the adversaries of Michele Navarra was the trade unionist Placido Rizzotto. Navarra commissioned his foster-son Luciano Liggio to remove the trade unionist. Liggio made his victim kneel and shot him three times in the head. The only witness to the murder was little Giuseppe Letizia, who had been watching sheep nearby. Dr Navarra had no qualms about personally killing the child with a fatal injection.

Day in, day out, the priest walked past that pew. 'I don't know which pew you're talking about,' he croaked. 'Navarra, Navarra, I don't even know who that Navarra was, there are countless Navarras here, and anyway I wasn't even here when this pew was made.

'The Mafia! The Mafia! As if there was nothing else in Corleone. I don't want to comment on the subject, but there's one thing you should know: the anti-Mafia can become a form of Mafia too!'

He gasped for air and for his words, which had escaped from his mouth so quickly. He wouldn't hear a word about the Riinas, the Provenzanos, the Bagarellas, all the butchers who had sprung from Corleone's womb and whose wives still say their Ave Marias here.

On Sunday Bernardo Provenzano's wife goes to early mass in this church. *Una signora*. A Sicilian journalist once asked her if she feared the judgement of the courts.

'I acknowledge only divine justice,' she snapped back. 'I no longer believe in justice on earth. I am answerable only to God. He alone will judge us, and he will do it impartially. He alone knows everything, he alone sees everything.'

Shortly after the assassinations of Falcone and Borsellino,

in 1992, she had come back to Corleone, along with the two sons to whom she had secretly given birth, at the same time as Totò Riina's wife, Antonietta, and her four children. Riina had been arrested and Bernardo Provenzano had taken over the business of Cosa Nostra as the new godfather. The women and their children arrived out of nowhere in a taxi and moved back into the house where they had lived before. Corleone welcomed them both without raising an eyebrow.

'I'm not afraid,' said Father Pizzitola, when I asked about Provenzano's wife. His voice was trembling. As if ashamed of his weakness, he corrected himself quickly and said: 'Of course, I mean I'm not afraid of journalists' questions.'

As always, Corleone lay there like an endless Sunday afternoon. Only the old men had been sent into the street. With cautious boredom, they kept an eye out for unfamiliar car number plates. On these cobblestones the bosses accompanied the processions — the Riinas, the Provenzanos, the Liggios — they paid the carriers, those poor devils who earn a few *centesimi* by lugging the crucifix on Good Friday, the statue of Santa Rosalia on the first Sunday in June, and the glass sarcophagus of the martyr San Placido on his name day on the first Sunday in October. The procession usually stopped outside the house of the boss to give him an opportunity to greet the saints with a barely perceptible nod of the head. And that's how it is even today. With only one small difference, that it's the next generation that keeps the ritual going. The women and children of the bosses step out on to the narrow balcony, cross themselves in the presence of the saints and rain rose petals down on them.

'When I married, I swore loyalty to my wife and the Mafia,' the turncoat mafioso Leonardo Messina told the public prosecutors. 'The priest? What was he supposed to say? Do you think he didn't know who paid for the feasts of the saints?' And then the mafioso added that he had always walked beside Sant'Annunziata in the procession: the meaning was there for anyone who wanted to understand.

There's no such thing as chance in Sicily. Not an unthought gesture, not an unconsidered word. The procession is a ritual. From the procession, Sicilians read the distribution of power in their town and their community − who is allowed to carry the saint out of the church, who walks in front of the priest, who behind. Who collected the money for the feast of the Madonna del Carmine, who is granted the right to march in front of the baldachin. Who wears an absent expression as the procession advances down the alleyways, who makes a special effort during the cries of 'Viva la Maria'. They all know about the sacredness of this ritual for the community. And the costs. Processions are expensive, all those garlands, light bulbs, gun salutes, brass bands, fireworks − the priests know that the alms of the poor aren't enough. Neither are they enough for the new stucco frieze, the new organ, the new chandeliers. In the end, one hopes, where possible, for certain concessions. Totò Riina didn't have to give up the idea of a church wedding even when he was living underground. Don Agostino Coppola, the legendary Mafia priest who died under house arrest, married him to his fiancée Antonietta in the spring of 1974, and christened each of their four children.

Those priests who refused to understand the messages

would receive a visit from the men of honour during the religious service, contrary to their custom of attending mass only on solemn feast days. Because a boss doesn't like to make a display of his faith — confession and religious services are women's business. But if it was unavoidable, they would take a seat in the front row and stare at the priest until he understood and got himself transferred to the missionary programme. If he refused to understand, and even fired up the young people against Cosa Nostra, he would be shot in the back of the head, like Padre Puglisi in Palermo.

In 1993 the murder of the anti-Mafia priest Giuseppe Puglisi was arranged by the Graviano brothers. And seven years later his murderer, Salvatore Grigoli, said: 'Padre Puglisi's lips closed. He smiled. Gentle, cheerful, but also resigned. He only whispered a single sentence: "I expected this." I will never forget his smile.'

By that time Grigoli already had ninety murders behind him and asked for a meeting with the Pope. The beatification process for Padre Puglisi has been going on for years. His murderer's statement is seen as an important piece of evidence for the process. Some clerics were surprised by the church's urgent desire to beatify Padre Puglisi, because just a short time before the cardinal had shown his violent opposition to an anti-Mafia document: no one wanted an anti-Mafia pastoral letter. But they did want an anti-Mafia saint.

All this is pure show, however. We'd be better off going to the theatre, Padre Fasullo had bitterly observed.

———

Letizia is still standing in the bar beside the old men, reading on in the article about the release of Totò Riina's son from prison. Shobha takes pictures as her mother reads from the article, standing among the old men. At last, we take our leave and walk a few yards along the seafront. Plastic bags drift among the palm trees planted by Letizia, the flower beds are full of detergent bottles and rotting mattresses.

'I used to feel as responsible for Palermo as a mother feels for a handicapped child,' says Letizia. Used to.

Then we walk on, towards the Foro Italico, to have an espresso. In fact, the bar is an ice-cream parlour, of the kind that is the destination for the Sunday-afternoon family stroll. And perhaps that's what makes Letizia slide uneasily around on her chair. She hates all the places where the well-to-do of Palermo put themselves on display. Not for nothing has she spent her whole life fighting against that. She fought against the pusillanimous bourgeoisie, against clapped-out moral ideas and against arrogant Sicilian menfolk. She fought against her own family.

As the daughter of lower-middle-class Sicilian parents who strove for better things, she grew up until the age of eight in Trieste, where her parents had moved for work. When she returned to Palermo, she attended a convent school and her father locked her in the house in the afternoon because it wasn't seemly for a little girl to play outside. To escape her father, at the age of sixteen she married the first boy who asked her. She married as a virgin. At her wedding she wore a pink lace hat by the French fashion designer Jacques Fath. Her husband was the scion of a Sicilian coffee-roasting dynasty.

She gave him three daughters, one after the other. When she expressed the desire to study, her husband declared that she had gone insane. For fifteen years she led the life of a Sicilian wife, then she suffered a collapse, a psychologically induced heart attack. Her husband sent her to the best doctors in Italy and to Switzerland for a sleeping cure, and, when nothing worked, to a psychotherapist in Palermo. Letizia spent years in psychoanalysis and at the end of it she left her husband, taking her three daughters with her.

'You know,' Letizia says, 'my husband could have forgiven me a lover, but not a job of my own.'

When Shobha and her mother sit side by side today, they might be mistaken for sisters: they look very similar, with the difference that Letizia has smooth, strawberry-blonde hair, while Shobha is a resolutely fake blonde.

'I can remember my daughters when they were little,' Letizia says, with a glance at Shobha, 'but not my life before I was forty. Strange, isn't it?'

Shobha sets her camera down on the table for a moment. I wonder if even your own mother is transformed when you look at her through the lens. Whether she becomes a different person, a stranger whom you approach impartially? During the Palermo Spring, Letizia was a heroine to many women. To Shobha, she was always her mother. Although perhaps Shobha is more maternal than her mother. Shobha is solicitous about everyone, whether it be her neurotic cat or the tortoises that live on her terrace. She even mothers me. She calls me Petruccia. And tells me to eat more pineapple.

When we're working together, Shobha can persuade even

the most intransigent men and the most circumspect women to pose for her, to smile at her, to give meaningful looks, whatever's needed. And as she rules with an iron hand – 'No! Don't look into the camera! Mouth shut! Yes, that's great!' – everyone is so busy trying to please her that I manage to study them all unobserved, to read a raised eyebrow here, notice a false smile there, or perhaps just a trembling of the hands.

That's how it was in Corleone, where we saw five old men sitting in a row, as if for the Benetton photographer. All wearing the *coppola*, the Sicilian hunter's cap, and freshly ironed shirts. At the old men's feet there stood a basket of pomegranates. From the hall behind them came the murmur of appreciative voices and the slap of cards being slammed down on the table. On the wall there was a sign: *A well-mannered person doesn't swear or spit on the floor.* Shobha managed to make them all feel important, shirt buttons were done up and hair combed smooth.

The old men were looking across at the church of Santa Rosalia, jostled by decaying *palazzi* and new grey buildings. Inside, three young girls were waiting for visitors, to teach them about the art-historical significance of the crucifix, the value of the painting by De Vasco, which depicts St John the Baptist and was once stolen but returned immediately, thanks to the Mafia. But no one wandered into the unassuming church. The parish priest had gone to Monreale to see the archbishop, so the girls were whiling away their time. They scampered around the church like elves, climbed giggling into the niche where the crucifix was kept, hid behind the choir screens, behind which the closed-order nuns used to sit, startled the doves in the bell tower, shared a cigarette up there and sounded a shrill and weary little bell until the old men of the Circolo degli Agricoltori pushed back their caps and stretched their wrinkled necks to look at the sky.

Even today, Santa Rosalia is the church of the Riinas and the Bagarellas, those two families responsible for what was probably the most bloodthirsty period of Cosa Nostra's history. Santa Rosalia was also the church of Luciano Liggio – or 'Lucianeddu', the diminutive by which he is affectionately known here – the legendary boss known as the 'red primrose of Corleone', who was once thought to control the weather in these parts, the foster-son of the mighty Don Michele Navarra, Corleone's post-war godfather.

But Don Michele, his former patron, got in the way of Liggio's entry into the modern age because the old man refused to contribute to the modernization of the Mafia and its entry into the drugs trade and the lucrative kidnapping business. Don Michele, an old yard-dog, too old to bark. But maybe not too old to bite. So one August day in 1958 he was shredded in his Fiat with 112 bullets.

Red and yellow bunting stretched across the alley. In the tense nothingness of Corleone, the little flapping pennants seemed to suggest an unexpected outbreak of high spirits. It was the bunting from the parish festival. For a few days Santa Rosalia had had a new parish priest, Domenico Mancuso. A handsome man, the girls said, and sighed. Only twenty-eight. But already putting on a bit of weight. He eats too much!

The handsome parish priest came from Prizzi and, it was said, from a very pious family. His predecessor was Monsignore Liggio, who had overseen the salvation of the people of Corleone from cradle to grave for half a century. Monsignore Liggio lived only a few steps away from his church, with his sister and his niece. An old man in the middle of a still-life of tatted doilies, bunches of dried flowers and polished walnut. He was a pure-blood Corleonese, he said proudly, looking at his white hands and manicured fingers. His eyes were pale blue and alert in his waxy face. He was born and bred in Corleone, and it was in Corleone that he wanted to die. Peacefully, in his sleep.

The boss Luciano Liggio was Monsignore Liggio's cousin. When the boss died in prison, the Monsignore fought tirelessly to arrange a church funeral for his cousin. 'Does not even the lost sheep have the right to be buried by his family?' he had asked at the time.

But for now he was saying nothing. He ran the tip of his tongue over his white, cracked lips. 'Mafia? You are asking impertinent questions,' he said, and a faint irritation played around his mouth. Silence fell around us like a fine dust. And when his old sister gasped, he prodded her with his long thin finger.

'Don't say a word,' he said, 'these matters have nothing to do with us.'

It was at that moment that the sexton of Santa Rosalia pulled on the rope and the bell rang for evening mass. The bell-tower doves flew off in flocks and the sky began to darken. The church filled slowly, mostly with women saying the rosary even before mass began. A muted hubbub of voices, a creaking sound as the women knelt before the Madonna, crossing themselves briefly before loudly kissing their thumbs. Everyone prayed here, butchers and victims, elbow to elbow. Monsignore Liggio wanted to celebrate evening mass along with his young successor. The power of habit. *In nomine Patris et Filii et Spiritus Sancti.* As Monsignore Liggio unsteadily climbed the altar steps, the young parish priest held out his arm. The elves sat in the front row and smiled at the handsome priest.

'Ah, Corleone,' the younger man said later in the sacristy. It smelled of wax and lavender and dusty old tomes.

'Once the soil here was drenched with blood, but that's a long time ago now. Though the Mafia is everywhere today,' he said, and held his arms folded over his belly. His head was young, his body already showing signs of stoutness.

'We don't know who's in the Mafia and who isn't,' he said in his soft, casual-sounding Sicilian. 'And what is said at confession remains secret. It's as if we hadn't heard it.'

He smiled thoughtfully and ran his hand over his hair as casually as he spoke. 'You know, the judiciary can't forbid us to lead even a mafioso to his salvation. We can't refuse the sacraments to anyone.

'It's always been so, and it always will be. The Lord seeks the lost sheep, the lost son, he forgives the sinners. Oh, the Mafia! Couldn't consumerism be said to be the scourge of the modern age? Saving souls! That's a priest's job. If only everyone would do his job, the *carabiniere* the *carabiniere*'s job, the public prosecutor the public prosecutor's — then he'll win respect! *Il rispetto! Il rispetto!* No one in Corleone would dream of disrespecting the parish priest, no one, however young or old.'

As he spoke, Monsignore Liggio nodded to him. And then said, delighted: 'He does it much better than I do.'

When mass was over, the women disappeared as quickly as if the alley had swallowed them up. The old men had already gone home, the Circolo degli Agricoltori opposite the church had closed its tall double doors. The elves had vanished and the doves had withdrawn to their niches in the church tower. The evening light melted the shadows away, silence stretched like a puddle of oil, and Corleone yielded at last to its drowsiness. Monsignore Liggio was walked home by his young successor. He linked arms with the younger man and cautiously matched his pace. Like that they walked sedately along the alley. Both took very small steps.

Palace of Poison

Shobha decides — whether it's melodramatic or not — that the Palace of Justice is at least worth a shot. 'Come on,' she says to Letizia, 'one more photograph.'

Letizia sighs. For years she has avoided the Palace of Justice — still known in Palermo as the Palace of Poison, because deep down it has little to do with justice for all. Time and again public prosecutors have fought not against the Mafia, but for it. Because Giovanni Falcone knew that, he founded the Anti-Mafia Pool, the investigation team to which various anti-Mafia public prosecutors belonged. The chief commandment of the Anti-Mafia Pool was that all investigations should be made accessible to all participating public prosecutors. The investigating public prosecutors of the Anti-Mafia Pool worked on cases together and shared all their information, which first of all removed the threat of a corrupt public servant appropriating a crucial piece of knowledge which might be useful to the Mafia and, secondly, ensured that, in the event of a member of the Pool being murdered, no knowledge should go missing. The Pool was not to be organized vertically, according to hierarchy and years of service: instead, all the public prosecutors in the pool were to have equal access to all inquiries.

And because by no means all politicians in the Italian parliament are involved in the struggle against the Mafia, for years Palermo's Anti-Mafia Pool has been an irritation to many of them, from Andreotti via Berlusconi to former Sicilian regional president Cuffaro – who have all set themselves the goal of destroying the Anti-Mafia Pool. And if they can't destroy it, then they can at least discredit it through political intrigue and journalistic mudslinging, in which the public prosecutors in the Pool are accused, just as they were in Falcone's day, of participating in a personality cult, and are demonized as communist enemies of the state – if not actually as 'mentally disturbed and anthropologically different from the rest of the human race', as Berlusconi felt obliged to remark.

Salvo's chief problem with the Palace of Justice concerns the availability of parking. A large area around it is closed off, less for security reasons than because of the vast building site needed to produce an underground car park – which has already provoked a certain amount of controversy in Palermo. What if the Mafia exploded a car bomb in that underground car park?

Like most of the other Palaces of Justice in Italy, the one in Palermo looks like a fascistic marble block. I always wonder how this discrepancy between a great stone demonstration of power and a plainly powerless judiciary might be explained.

And I can find no answer. The Italian Palaces of Justice look like fortresses of the legal system, but hidden away in their deep interior are outmoded offices without computers, without enough paper, without enough pencils. If you can't force the public prosecutors to their knees politically, then you try to do it by cancelling paper, pencils and the petrol for armoured limousines.

A flight of very tall steps leads to the entrance. The higher you climb, the smaller you feel. A steel fence used to close off the semicircle of the Palace of Justice, and after the assassinations of Giovanni Falcone and Paolo Borsellino soldiers were entrenched there behind sandbags. Today, the Palace of Justice is guarded by just a few *carabinieri*, armed with machine guns, whose readiness for action not even the dogs in the street take seriously. They doze in the shade beside their sentry boxes and don't even blink when you walk past.

From the back, the Palace of Justice looks like a gigantic pink tombstone; the modern extension is extolled by architects and looks no less fascistic than the granite-grey part, except that the colour softens the effect. People passing in front of the Palace of Justice look as small as if they were walking past the Pyramid of Cheops. The square in front of it is called Piazza della Memoria. Here you can read, cast in steel, the names of all the murdered Sicilian public prosecutors.

Shobha gives Letizia instructions that she isn't keen to hear. 'Turn round, head up, yes, that's lovely, no, take your hand away.' Letizia poses ironically, and wastes no time in taking her own pictures with her new Leica, while at the same time delivering a polemic about the stalemate in the struggle against the Mafia. She asks what the Germans thought when the Duisburg massacre took place. Were they surprised? Shocked by the cold-bloodedness of it all? Perhaps dismayed that the Mafia was just as blithely active in Germany as it was in Italy? Letizia's eyes look combative again. Yes, that's it exactly: the arrogance of the Mafia! The presumption of the powerful! What do the Germans think? The Mafia isn't just an Italian problem, after all. If the EU doesn't pay attention, the Mafia will swallow us all up!

Shobha brushes me aside because I've got into the shot again. So I stand to one side and consider the Palace of Justice, some plaster already crumbling away at one corner. In which it resembles the Palace of Justice in Calabria, which, like many public buildings in southern Italy, is in need of serious restoration.

Throughout the whole of southern Italy, the power of the Mafia can be read in the architecture. Like the Mafia in Sicily and Campania, for half a century the 'Ndrangheta in Calabria has had a share of public commissions, 3 or 5 per cent – what the Calabrians, with bitter irony, call a 'security tax'. All businessmen working in Calabria pay this contribution to the Mafia, whether they are building roads, Palaces of Justice or hospitals. And they save that contribution by putting up plasterboard rather than laying bricks, by quoting for steel and using iron, by using cheap rendering that cracks after just a few months, by failing to make windows watertight or walls damp-proof.

The Palace of Justice in Reggio Calabria looks as if Ceauşescu's architect had finally used it to realize his dream

of omnipotence, even though little details, such as properly
functioning lifts, escaped him. Here I met Salvatore Boemi,
the leading senior public prosecutor in the Anti-Mafia Pool,
and Nicola Gratteri, the public prosecutor investigating the
Duisburg massacre. The bearded Boemi has been dealing
with the Mafia for more than forty years; he's the historical
memory of the public prosecutor's office of Reggio Calabria,
a city in which the 'Ndrangheta controls the very air that
people breathe. Boemi looked like a melancholy English aris-
tocrat; there were English leather chairs in his office, which
contrasted curiously with the view from his window out on
to Sahara-coloured Reggio Calabria, which seemed to consist
entirely of flyovers on concrete stilts, ruined buildings and a
leaden sea which merged in the distance with the horizon.

Duisburg was a massacre that was committed in a mega-
lomaniac frenzy, Boemi said. With these murders, the mafiosi
of San Luca had taken the greatest possible risk: that Italy
and Germany would become aware of the threat from the
Mafia and react to it. And there had been no reaction from
the state, either in Germany or in Italy. If nothing happened
now, Germany could soon find itself approaching the Italian
condition, in which the Mafia had elevated itself to a bourgeoisie controlling politics and the economy. 'In Calabrian
society I see no will to get rid of the Mafia − just the will
to get rid of *us*,' said senior public prosecutor Boemi. And he
added: 'The rot in Sicilian and Calabrian politics is boundless.
The criminal system here works closely with politics and the
business class.'

Boemi was excluded from the Anti-Mafia Pool in Reggio

Calabria for five years. Supposedly to keep public prosecutors from turning into 'autonomous power centres', the Berlusconi government passed a law according to which no public prosecutor could work for more than eight years in the Anti-Mafia Pool — like a yoghurt that's past its sell-by date. In this way not only was the work of the Anti-Mafia Pool slowed down, but many Pools were cleaned of those public prosecutors who refused to see the Mafia merely as a problem of public order and who instead investigated politicians who were close to the Mafia. In Palermo, it wasn't just the public prosecutors who had run the Andreotti trial who had been eliminated from the Anti-Mafia Pool — Roberto Scarpinato, Guido Lo Forte and Gioacchino Natoli — but also Antonio Ingroia, who had revealed the Mafia links of the Berlusconi confidant Marcello Dell'Utri and the high-ranking secret service agent Bruno Contrada.

As Boemi spoke, you could hear the wind howling through the ventilation shafts of his office. He acted as if he couldn't hear a thing. He just went on talking, looking out at the lead-coloured sea, as if he mustn't lose sight of it. On the other side lay Sicily.

'We need European laws,' he said. 'It's a task for the politicians, not for the legal profession. We've got to be able to confiscate Mafia property abroad as well, even in Germany, which we thought was immune to Mafia intrigues. People said to us: "The Mafia, that's your problem. Punish them, do what you like — they're Italians, after all." In Europe today you have to take into account the fact that the Mafia is a reality that we're exporting.'

Where Boemi emanated melancholy, his colleague Nicola Gratteri communicated a sense of dynamism — quick, quick, don't waste a minute. When the lift didn't arrive, he ran all the way up the seven floors to the public prosecutor's office, and as he ran he outlined the relationship between the 'Ndrangheta and the Colombian cocaine barons. There has always been a special 'feeling' between them, based on the fact that the 'Ndrangheta had built up more money through its kidnapping industry than any other client — a special relationship that lasts up to the present day: now, the 'Ndrangheta has a monopoly on cocaine importation in Europe.

He drove the armoured Lancia himself, 150 kilometres every day, between Gerace and Reggio Calabria, to the sound of classical music. His three bodyguards followed in the car behind him. He wanted to drive himself, he said, because the journey was the only moment in the day when he was alone.

The wall behind his desk was decorated with the usual investigator's trappings — the shield of US Special Agent, of the Federal Criminal Police Office of Wiesbaden, of the Amsterdam *Politie*. And a framed certificate behind glass, an award that Gratteri had been given for his battle against organized crime — organized crime which, as the Italian text so beautifully puts it, is notoriously able to rely on support from parts of certain institutions.

He worked on a laptop in his office. He had made five copies of the hard drive and hidden them in five different places. In the context of the inquiries into the Duisburg bloodbath he had issued the custody order that had put whole families behind bars. In March 2008, in San Luca alone, he confiscated Mafia properties to the value of 150 million euros. So much for Don Pino's village of poor, God-fearing forestry workers. And pious women. The confiscated property of the two 'Ndrangheta clans involved in the blood feud, the Nirta-Strangio and Pelle-Vottari clans, included furniture, packets of files and certificates from insurance companies in Germany and beyond.

Gratteri spoke just as quickly as he moved. With cool realism he described his battled against the 'Ndrangheta: the word 'Duisburg' had turned long ago from the name of an investigation file into a metaphor for the arrogance of the 'Ndrangheta.

Before Duisburg, Gratteri's commitment to the fight against the Mafia wouldn't have been worth covering – not in Italy, and certainly not abroad: the floodlights of public interest had always been turned on Palermo. Only a few local newspapers in Calabria had reported on the four hundred dead in six years that the 'Ndrangheta had called for. It was only after Duisburg that public prosecutors like Gratteri were invited on to Italian television programmes. Once I saw him in a Rai Due studio sitting next to the then minister of justice, Clemente Mastella. In reply to the question of what needed to be done to fight the Mafia, Gratteri said: 'The opposite of what's been done over the past twelve years.' At which justice minister Mastella corrected the public prosecutor: 'He should just get on with his job.' Politicians would take care of everything else.

'Indeed,' Gratteri said to me. And fired a mocking smile across his desk, piled high with bundles of documents.

Because a short time later the minister had had to step down after being investigated for extortion and abuse of office.

And a similar scenario might also menace Germany if the Germans didn't start understanding what it meant for the Mafia to take root in their country. Meanwhile, neither Germany nor Italy had modified any of their laws in response to the Duisburg killings.

———

While Shobha looks for her shot, Letizia and I sit on a marble bench in the shade and try to imagine some numbers. The annual business turnover of the Italian Mafia, for example. Which is supposed to stand at around 100 billion euros. I fail in my attempt to conjure the image of 100 billion euros in 500 euro notes. What would that fill? A room? An apartment? A Palace of Justice? How many politicians, lawyers, judges could you buy with that?

'A million euros fits in a shoebox,' Salvo says sagely. 'Ladies' shoes.'

'How do you know that?' Letizia asks in amazement.

'From our neighbour,' says Salvo. 'With men's shoes, it's two million.'

'Sorry for asking,' says Letizia, 'but what does your neighbour do with a million euros in a shoebox?'

'He picks it up,' Salvo replies, and purses his lips.

Then we try to imagine the number of *affiliati*, the numbers of members regularly inducted into the Mafia. The newspaper *Antimafia Duemila* reported that in Calabria 25 per cent of the population – a full quarter – belong to the

'Ndrangheta. In Campania 12 per cent belong to the Camorra; in Sicily 10 per cent belong to the Mafia; and in Apulia it's a modest 2 per cent who belong to the Sacra Corona Unita.

And to these regular *affiliati* may be added the sympathizers, relatives and silent helpers. 'And the ones who are too scared to say anything,' Letizia adds. She looks at the passers-by, most of them lawyers with briefcases, tight-skirted secretaries tottering to the entrance of the Palace of Justice.

'That leaves hardly anyone,' says Salvo. 'Or have we miscalculated?'

'Even as a child I couldn't do sums,' I say. And I remember public prosecutor Gratteri giving me a few simple examples that even a mathematical dyslexic like me could understand, explaining the danger that the wealth of the 'Ndrangheta meant for Germany. He sat at his laptop, answering emails and delivering a little lecture on the financial power of the 'Ndrangheta.

The elite of the 'Ndrangheta didn't have the problem of getting rich, just of laundering their money, he said. A small amount was spent on building a lovely house. Then a hotel was built, a holiday village, a supermarket. In northern Italy buildings were bought, and in Germany hotels, restaurants, pizzerias – all with cocaine money. The account of a typical 'Ndrangheta businessman was always in the red. He never had any money in the bank but took out loans and then paid them back very gradually. That was how he laundered his money.

The game goes like this. The businessman buys a product for 100 euros; let's say, coffee. So he pays 100 euros for the coffee, and by selling the coffee he makes a profit of, let's say, 25 per cent. No one can dispute that 25 per cent; the financial police can't, and the public prosecutors can't either. With that 25 per cent profit the Mafia businessman has managed to launder dirty money – not by buying the coffee, but just by presenting a receipt for it. A secretary sits there from dawn till dusk issuing false invoices, because it's in the Mafia businessman's interest to provide evidence of non-existent expenditure – as if they had had huge expenses and made enormous profits – in order to justify the cocaine money. Logically, the Mafia businessman also has an interest in paying as much tax as possible. The more invoices he issues, the more tax he pays, and the more illegal money he can justify.

Of course, this game with fake invoices works particularly well in restaurants, hotels and supermarkets, Gratteri stressed, where goods can go off and many (fake) invoices are issued to suppliers. After a few years the Mafia businessman has bought the restaurant, the hotel, the supermarket with his cocaine money – and they're all quite legal.

The 'Ndrangheta isn't just an Italian problem, he explains, because the fake invoice game isn't just played in Reggio Calabria, it's played throughout the whole of the Western world. But having great mountains of money doesn't just mean being able to influence the market. It also means financing electoral campaigns on behalf of parliamentarians who represent Mafia interests. The whole of democratic life is infected.

While Gratteri was speaking, I thought about how it was that the then CDU representative and now minister-president

of Baden-Württemberg, Günther Oettinger, had emerged
unscathed from the affair surrounding the pizza-chef Mario
Lavorato, even though things hadn't looked nearly so good
at the outset. Oettinger's friendship with the dubious pizzeria owner had got him into difficulties; the Stuttgart public
prosecutor's office investigated the Calabrian Lavorato for
drug dealing and money laundering, on the grounds that he
was supposed to have used his money to support Oettinger's
election. ███████████████████████████████

██

████████████████████████ who had already been mentioned in a Federal Criminal Police (BKA) report in 2000, ███

███████████████████████████ the 400-seat ███████

██████████ restaurant ██████████ — ███████████

████████████████████ who, according to investigators, ███

███████████████ in the Da Bruno pizzeria. Contacts can be
helpful — even if Da Bruno hasn't been top of most people's
lists since the Duisburg massacre. At any rate, Pitanti nur-
tured his connections in Erfurt, by generously supporting the
golf club. ████████████████████████████████

███████████████████████████████████████ they
also bumped into the then Thuringian minister-president
Bernhard Vogel and his minister of the interior, Richard
Dewes. Both men had been staying there by chance, claimed
Pitanti — who also had an excellent relationship with the police: in the course of further searches, the police found an ID
card for an Interpol conference in Rome identifying Pitanti
as a translator for the Uzbek delegation. It had been issued by
the minister of the interior for Saarland.

A quick glance from Gratteri's eyes darted across his laptop to me, as if he wanted to check that I was following him. The arrogance of the young 'Ndranghetisti derived on the one hand from their wealth, and on the other from their knowledge of their de facto immunity from prosecution, he said. Over the last ten years, the Italian state had weakened in its struggle against the Mafia, even gradually relaxing its anti-Mafia legislation, culminating in the large-scale amnesty under the Prodi government. The problem wasn't that 18,000 or 25,000 criminals were allowed to leave. The problem was a different one. Italians were increasingly convinced that there was a solution for everything, but there was no longer such a thing as a bail culture. For twenty-two years he had been investigating the 'Ndrangheta in Calabria: always the same families — he had arrested the same people three or four times for Mafia membership and international drug dealing, and after a short time they had been released again thanks to an amnesty or remission of punishment. It was easy to imagine that the justice system didn't exactly gain in credibility in this way. Besides, these people weren't normal, small-time criminals. Being an 'Ndranghetista or a member of Cosa Nostra was a lifestyle. A philosophy. These were people who had as four-year-olds experienced the police knocking at their doors, in search of an uncle, a brother or their father, a cocaine dealer. For them, the policeman would always be a 'spy', an enemy who had to be fought against.

Every year he arrested between thirty and forty individuals who had been accused of drug dealing and who all came from the same village. Purely theoretically, these people would be sentenced to twenty or thirty years' imprisonment. You could imagine what that meant to a village of three or four thousand inhabitants – if the sentence was actually served. Instead, the punishment was reduced, thanks to various negotiations which were intended to shorten the process, from twenty to seven or eight years. With good behaviour the prisoner could expect a further remission, and in the end an international cocaine dealer could be out of jail in five years maximum. And what was five years' imprisonment compared with the prospect of importing a thousand kilos of cocaine? For one kilo of cocaine the 'Ndrangheta would pay 1,200 euros in Bogotà. The cocaine was cut and one kilo turned into four and a half. And a gram of cocaine would fetch 70 euros in Milan's Piazza del Duomo.

'Work it out for yourself,' said Gratteri. And then he smiled, calmly, as if his calm was the result of long experience.

The Germans believed that the 'Ndrangheta didn't exist in Germany, Gratteri said. It was a careless error to underestimate the situation, as had been the case over the past few years. Unlike in Italy, in Germany the mere suspicion of Mafia membership was not sufficient to justify an arrest, and spying on people in public places was not permitted. In a few years it could be too late for Germany. The German police didn't have any of the tools required to pursue Mafia dealings. Without electronic eavesdropping, investigators in Italy would have been powerless. Germany, he said, had no time to lose. Because if a mafioso buys a hotel, a restaurant or a stretch of road today, in a few years' time no one will be able to prove that he bought the building with cocaine money.

It wasn't just an ethical problem, Gratteri said, it was also
a matter of the law of the marketplace. Unlike normal businessmen, who have to make sacrifices to put up a building,
the Mafia businessman has only the problem of justifying his
money. Or protection money: if there are three supermarkets
in his area who are all paying him protection money, and the
fourth supermarket belongs to the Mafia, he doesn't have to
pay protection money, and for that very reason he can sell
his products 2 or 3 per cent cheaper. That's unfair competition. And when free competition breaks down, the laws of the
marketplace go awry and democracy breaks down as well.
Because democracy means the possibility of choice. The same
possibilities for everyone.

That was what he said. And as we spoke, the electricity
failed once again in the Palace of Justice in Reggio Calabria.

———

Seven months after our meeting it became known that the
public prosecutor Nicola Gratteri was being bugged when he
met with detectives in the Palace of Justice to discuss current
investigations. The bug used hadn't been very technically
sophisticated and had only been able to record conversations
up to a distance of twenty metres. It was said.

Silvio Berlusconi and
Marcello Dell'Utri

'Just one more photograph,' says Shobha, 'over there by the entrance.'

'I'm done,' says Letizia. She's had enough of posing and being stared at by the passers-by. Resigned, she lights another cigarette and walks to the other side of the Palace of Justice, where the armoured limousines stand between the granite columns. Only anti-Mafia public prosecutors enjoy the privilege of being allowed to drive up the ramp of the Palace of Justice, right in front of the entrance.

'Let's go,' says Letizia. 'The Palace of Justice depresses me.'

'Me too,' says Shobha, and presses the shutter release.

When she's packing her camera away again, we talk about how it is that every time we do interviews with public prosecutors here we have a serious-men-in-ties problem. There's nothing more depressing than a photograph of a serious-looking man sitting at his desk. Particularly since all the offices look the same: *carabinieri* calendars on the wall, a picture of Giovanni Falconi and Paolo Borsellino, and paintings loaned from Palermo's picture gallery – rural idylls with ploughing peasants or grim-looking old women. Generally we would persuade the public prosecutors to pose for us on the roof of the Palace of Justice. But even that shot had worn itself out at some point. Photographically, the Palace of Justice doesn't have much to offer, although its inner life is very informative. I've often sat in the corridors and watched the women defence counsels tottering along the marble granite with a metallic squeak. Until early afternoon, the court reporters prowl the corridors as well, sit outside the doors of the public prosecutors' offices, listen to conversations, try to read the click of a public prosecutor's tongue, to interpret a lawyer's nod, spend hours waiting on the red plastic chairs outside the chief prosecutor's office. All in the hope of being in the right place at the right time, finding that missing piece that might finally give a meaning to the puzzle made up of news, suspicions, hints and rumours.

Perhaps one of my most remarkable meetings in the Palace of Justice was the one I had with Marcello Dell'Utri. Berlusconi's right-hand man. The founder of Forza Italia. The senator. The Euro MP. The man accused of supporting the Mafia in Palermo. Which did nothing to dampen his mood that morning.

I had noticed Marcello Dell'Utri by chance in the corridors of the Palace of Justice. I had actually come here to talk to a public prosecutor about a Mafia boss who had gone into hiding. And then there was the senator, just standing there. The morning sun bathed the interior of the Palace of Justice in a mild light, and Marcello Dell'Utri's head was thrown back.

He pouted as he smoked his cigar and watched as the smoke wafted away. The hearing was supposed to have started ages ago, but the judge was still missing. Only a few local journalists were following the trial. Not a single Italian television channel was covering the story and barely any non-regional daily newspapers. The fact that Senator Marcello Dell'Utri, Berlusconi's companion from the very first, Euro MP and Sicilian, was being accused of Mafia association in Palermo, attracted less attention than a television presenter's move from Rai Uno to Canale 5.

The senator stood in the semicircle of his lawyers, bag-carriers and confidants, smoking a cigar. His lawyers were smoking cigars as well. When Dell'Utri laughed, they laughed too. Dell'Utri was surprisingly short, and wore an azure-blue shirt with a blue suit. His lawyers were also wearing azure-blue shirts. His face seemed to sag slightly at the edges, and his heavy eyelids gave his expression a certain veiled quality. The senator gripped people by the arm as he talked to them; he slapped people cordially on the back, shook hands and hugged people. The lawyers coughed with laughter over each of his remarks, and gigglingly spluttered, '*Oh! Senatore!*' The cigar smoke hung quivering and blue above their heads, drifting away into the great expanse of the marble hall.

The public prosecutor who had led the trial in the first instance had told me that on the very first day Marcello Dell'Utri had got to his feet during the prosecution speech and left the courtroom, saying: 'I'm bored stiff.' I didn't seriously imagine that he would answer my questions, but I didn't want to reproach myself for not having tried. So I pushed my way past his bag-carriers, who eyed me suspiciously. When I stood in front of him at last and talked to him about his Mafia indictment, he didn't answer straightaway. He took a drag on his cigar, blew the smoke out and said: '*Bellissima signora*, this trial is so boring, don't waste your time on it. Go and look at the church of San Giovanni degli Eremiti instead.'

And true enough, the trial in the little courtroom lasted only a few minutes. There was hardly time to appreciate the dusty little fan that stood in the corner and to notice that a silver tassel was missing from the public prosecutor's gown. As always, the microphones weren't working. The trial had been adjourned over a formality.

A few months after our meeting, Senator Marcello Dell'Utri was sentenced to nine years' imprisonment for supporting the Mafia and a lifelong exclusion from public office. As usual in Italy, however, the sentence in the first instance had no effect on the defendant's life: until the sentence has been confirmed in the second and third instances, Marcello Dell'Utri remains a free man. On average that takes ten years. And because the period of limitation begins with the start of the trial, like many other defendants in Italy, Marcello Dell'Utri can expect his crime to have lapsed when the final sentence is passed by the supreme court.

I will never be able to get used to this regulation. The three instances rule in Italian law is referred to as *garantista*: a law that respects the rights of the citizen. But it's one that benefits the Mafia and corrupt politicians more than anyone else. I can't get my head round the fact that someone whose guilt has been acknowledged by a court can go on strolling around the place unmolested and carry on being a politician – even in the European Parliament, as Marcello Dell'Utri has done. But equally it comes as no surprise that a judicial reform abolishing this three instances rule would never be passed by the Italian parliament.

At the end of the eight-year trial the judges have taken it as read that Marcello Dell'Utri has worked as a mediator for the Sicilian Cosa Nostra since the 1970s, in the economy and in politics. His contact was Silvio Berlusconi. 'The defendant has represented the interests of the Mafia in one of the biggest companies in the country; from the 1970s until the present day he was at the disposal of the Mafia, and made a more than considerable contribution to the consolidation and reinforcement of Cosa Nostra. He has favoured [it] and received favours,' the judges wrote. The public prosecutors identified Dell'Utri as a kind of insurance agent for the Mafia: he drafted the contract with his client and ensured that it was precisely adhered to.

Immediately after the proclamation of the sentence, the then president of the chamber of deputies, Pier Ferdinando Casini, phoned up the defendant and assured him of his highest esteem and friendship, and also passed this on to the Italian public in an official note. And Berlusconi assured his friend Dell'Utri that he would put both hands in the fire for him. At the same time, Berlusconi warned the public prosecutors of Palermo not to play with fire. Berlusconi has never been terribly skilled in his use of metaphors.

Only a few short steps from the courtroom where I met Dell'Utri, in a corridor that, with its rows of discarded photocopiers and dusty swivel chairs, looked like a furniture storeroom for the next intake of Bosnian refugees, public prosecutor Antonio Ingroia, Dell'Utri's accuser, had his office. A bearded man with an old man's posture, even though he wasn't all that old.

On his desk lay a silver wolf's head as a paperweight; on the wall there were prints and the usual *carabinieri* calendars that every public prosecutor is given as a present. Public prosecutor Ingroia told me how he had come to Rome with over a hundred questions in his luggage to hear Silvio Berlusconi take the witness stand. The prime minister evoked his right to silence. And the public prosecutor regretted this as a missed opportunity to tell the truth.

———

The story of the friendship between the Milanese Silvio Berlusconi and the Sicilian Marcello Dell'Utri is documented in the 2,500 pages of files produced by the Palermo public prosecutor's office. Here one can read that the two men met in 1961, both in their early twenties, at Milan University. Marcello Dell'Utri began his professional life as secretary to Silvio Berlusconi, who was only four years his senior. This first collaboration lasted only a short time, however, and a year later Dell'Utri went to Rome, where he became sports director at a sports centre run by Opus Dei. From Rome he returned to Palermo, where he became sports director of an athletics club, where he became acquainted with the mafiosi Vittorio Mangano and Gaetano Cinà. Mangano was later deployed as Cosa Nostra's middleman at Berlusconi's villa in Arcore. Gaetano Cinà worked as a bagman between the Mafia and Berlusconi, and at Christmas expressed his thanks for his successful collaboration with Berlusconi with ten kilos of cassata cake. But that time had not yet come. In 1970 sports director Dell'Utri became a bank clerk. A particularly skilful one. Soon he was responsible for the allocation of agricultural credits in the Sicilcassa bank.

A few years later, the Mafia threatened rising businessman Silvio Berlusconi with the kidnap of his son Piersilvio, unless Berlusconi paid protection money. Berlusconi didn't report this blackmail, but remembered his Sicilian friend. Marcello Dell'Utri brought his contacts into play and learned that a clan from Catania was threatening Berlusconi. However, the power of Cosa Nostra traditionally lies in the hands of families from Palermo, with which Marcello Dell'Utri had excellent relations – which is why there were several meetings between Silvio Berlusconi, Marcello Dell'Utri and the legendary Mafia boss Stefano Bontade, known as the 'Prince of Villagrazia'.

These meetings ended, to the satisfaction of all participants, with the assurance of the greatest goodwill. The mafioso Vittorio Mangano moved into Berlusconi's villa in Arcore as guarantor of the security of the Berlusconi family, officially as a stable-man. Berlusconi's flexibility was rewarded: from now on 113 billion lire (around 300 million euros in present-day terms) flowed into Fininvest, the holdings in which Berlusconi has bundled his activities as major investor, building contractor and media entrepreneur. Later, in the Mafia trial against Marcello Dell'Utri, even an adviser for the defence had to admit that these payments from Fininvest between 1975 and 1983 had not been transparent. According to the statements of various turncoat mafiosi, during that period the Mafia boss Stefano Bontade invested a considerable amount of Mafia capital in Berlusconi's consortium and thus became an associate in the Fininvest group's private television channels.

In 1976 a daily newspaper in Lombardy reported that a mafioso was working in Berlusconi's villa, whereupon Mangano returned to Palermo. A year later Marcello Dell'Utri left his friend Silvio as well. He had hoped in vain for an executive position in the company, but Berlusconi didn't think he was up to it − only for Berlusconi to change his mind a short time later. The Mafia boss Stefano Bontade had been murdered and the new generation of bosses was no longer satisfied with flexibility and little presents, and instead exerted pressure on Berlusconi. Meanwhile, the former stable-man Vittorio Mangano had been arrested and from prison tried in vain to put in a good word for Berlusconi with the new bosses. Silvio Berlusconi was forced to bring Marcello Dell'Utri back into his enterprise so that he could take care of delicate Sicilian business relationships.

In the meantime, Dell'Utri not only had to assume responsibility for the fraudulent bankruptcy of his building consortium, but also had to establish fresh Mafia connections. Toughened by this experience, he negotiated an annual 'friendship contribution' to the Mafia from his friend Silvio, to the tune of 200 million euros a year. But even that didn't keep the bosses happy. After a bloody Mafia war, the Corleonese

Totò Riina had reached the top of Cosa Nostra and he wanted a reshuffle. As the collaboration between Cosa Nostra and the Christian Democrats no longer prevailed, Riina tried to reach Berlusconi and the head of the Socialist Party, Bettino Craxi, through Dell'Utri. To stress the urgency of this collaboration, in November 1986 he arranged for a bomb to be set off outside Berlusconi's Milan headquarters in the Via Rovani – a bomb that, Berlusconi said, had been placed there with respect, even with a certain affection. When not even a bomb could convince Berlusconi that cooperation with the Mafia was a good idea, a series of attacks was carried out on his La Standa supermarket chain. After this, Marcello Dell'Utri travelled to Catania as an emissary to clarify the conditions of the collaboration.

In 1992 Italy was rocked by the bribery scandal known as Tangentopoli, which dragged the established Italian parties into the abyss. Berlusconi was concerned about how his enterprise might survive without the protection of friendly parties like the Socialists and the Christian Democrats. Marcello Dell'Utri persuaded him to enter politics himself and started to prepare for the foundation of Forza Italia. A short time afterwards came the assassinations of the two anti-Mafia public prosecutors Giovanni Falcone and Paolo Borsellino. The last interview that Paolo Borsellino gave before his death was the one in which he talked about the Mafia boss Mangano's involvement with Dell'Utri and Berlusconi.

A year after the assassinations of the two public prosecutors, Bernardo Provenzano was made the new boss of Cosa Nostra. He negotiated a pact with Dell'Utri. He offered his support for Forza Italia, a renunciation of any further violence – and demanded certain guarantees in return: the end of criminal prosecution and political pressure on the Mafia, an end to the confiscation of Mafia property, and the abolition of the state witness regulations for turncoat mafiosi. Shortly after the meeting with Dell'Utri, Provenzano convened the leading bosses. We're in good hands with Dell'Utri, Provenzano said, let's work for Forza Italia.

———

So there we have the reconstruction of the charges against Marcello Dell'Utri, which would lead to a nine-year sentence. The further course of this friendship has gone down in Italian history. Forza Italia fulfilled its contract with Cosa Nostra to the letter: it declared the reform of the judiciary to be its most important political task – and this meant, among other things, the near abolition of high-security detention for mafiosi, and, thanks to the introduction of various forms of remission, life sentences no longer exist. Both life imprisonment and high-security detention were a thorn in the flesh for the mafiosi. A mafioso accepts a prison sentence without further ado, but not being kept out of the game forever. Or not being able to communicate with the outside world.

There used to be two high-security prisons, Asinara and Pianos, in which mafiosi were actually isolated. These two prisons have now been closed down. High-security detention is practised in normal prisons. There are certain sections there in which prisoners are isolated – always, of course, in accordance with human rights laws, which demand humane conditions even for Mafia bosses. Thus, for example, they have a right to regular association with other prisoners, which often leads to little meetings of Mafia bosses in prison. They can also communicate with the outside world because they are, after all, allowed regular family visits – even without armoured glass if their children are minors. At the present day, high-security detention merely means detention that is slightly less comfortable than the normal kind.

That's why it's hardly worthwhile for a mafioso to leave the Mafia. And it's become harder for public prosecutors to use the statements of turncoat mafiosi in trials. The state witness regulations have been weakened. Today the turncoat must confess to everything that he has experienced in his whole life with the Mafia during the first 180 days after his arrest; statements made later are invalid. This has halved the value of these state witnesses: twenty or thirty years of Mafia life can't be summed up all that simply. And besides, the statement of the turncoat will only be recognized at the trial if it is confirmed by two further turncoat mafiosi. And it sounds like a cruel irony within the history of the Italian judiciary that this state witness law so craved by Berlusconi was passed not by the Berlusconi government but by the left-wing government that came after it – plainly with a view to getting rid of the label of being the party of 'red judges'.

And yet time and again there are moments when the Mafia finds that its demands aren't being satisfied quite quickly enough. The cooperation between the Christian Democrats and the Mafia came to an end in 1992 with the murders of

Salvo Lima and Ignazio Salvo, Andreotti's governors in Sicily. Many people saw a parallel to this when the mafioso Leoluca Bagarella, the brother-in-law of the imprisoned boss Totò Riina, read out a declaration during a trial in 2002. In it, he announced a hunger-strike of seventy-one mafiosi protesting against their conditions of imprisonment and complained that promises made by politicians, such as the definitive revision of all Mafia trials, had not been kept. Results were expected. There was speculation about impending Mafia attacks on Marcello Dell'Utri and Silvio Berlusconi.

For a while there was still a danger for Marcello Dell'Utri and Berlusconi that the two most important witnesses to Mafia deals might hit on the idea of becoming state witnesses, with a view to having their sentences reduced. The problem was solved when the bagman, fellow defendant and Dell'Utri confidant Gaetano Cinà died in Palermo in 2006 — as his death notice put it: at the end of a difficult and honest life. The mafioso and former stable-man Vittorio Mangano had already died in 2000. Vittorio was seen as a Mafia bridgehead in northern Italy; public prosecutor Paolo Borsellino said as much in his last interview, twenty hours before the Mafia blew him up.

Vittorio Mangano came home from prison only once, to die in the arms of his daughters. He had no regrets. It's not only his daughters who are grateful to him for that. His friends Marcello Dell'Utri and Silvio Berlusconi are too. In the 2008 election campaign, Marcello Dell'Utri was even moved to celebrate Mangano as a hero: he died for me, Dell'Utri said, because he was suffering from cancer and would have been released from prison if he had incriminated me and Berlusconi.

And Berlusconi had no hesitation in standing by his friend. Mangano had heroically refused to invent anything about him or Dell'Utri. When he had been living at Berlusconi's villa he had always behaved impeccably, and it was only because of various difficulties that Mangano had fallen into the hands of a criminal organization. But he hadn't been found guilty of anything.

Berlusconi was wrong there. In spite of the slowness of the Italian judicial system, Mangano had been found guilty on two out of the various charges against him, including murder, drug dealing and Mafia membership, and had been sentenced to thirteen years for Mafia membership and drug dealing – of which he had served eleven by the time of his death.

In the eyes of Silvio Berlusconi and Marcello Dell'Utri, Mangano was quite definitely a hero.

After his victorious re-election in 2008, Silvio Berlusconi continued with his tried and tested judicial policy. He announced that he was changing the wiretapping law, which is a source of vexation not just to the mafiosi but also to politicians – which is why the left-wing government's unfortunate justice minister, Romano Prodi, had tried to pass a law that would definitively have weakened the practice of wiretapping. Berlusconi thought he'd be more successful. And both Romano Prodi and Silvio Berlusconi announced that they were going to build a bridge between Sicily and the mainland – a project that has been craved by the clans of Cosa

Nostra and the 'Ndrangheta for years, because, as the boss Provenzano said, when that happens everyone will get a slice of the pie.

As it happened, Berlusconi wasn't successful, neither in the change of the wiretapping law nor the building of the bridge. But it is only postponed. The next new government will doubtless try again. The interests of the Mafia are too big to be ignored.

Anna Palma

'*Basta*,' says Letizia. '*Basta*,' says Shobha, and I say, '*Basta*,' too. We decided to have lunch. When we're working, we stick slavishly to our mealtimes. Regardless of whether we're tracking down Mafia priests, heroic public prosecutors or fugitive bosses, we have lunch and dinner; we have starter, main, dessert and coffee, as if our lives depended on it. For an hour we belong to ourselves again.

'Piccola Napoli,' says Shobha, and I agree. The trattoria Piccola Napoli is an eerily beautiful place with extremely effective air conditioning and fluorescent lighting which takes a bit of getting used to since it colours everything slightly blue and makes you feel like a dead fish on ice. A delicious one, though.

When we come down the steps of the Palace of Justice, we see some public prosecutors driving up and slipping out of their limousines. The public prosecutor Anna Palma greets us briefly as she walks past. I've known her since the trial of the murderers of Paolo Borsellino. Since she's been working on the anti-Mafia commission in Rome and for Renato Schifani, the disputed President of the Italian Senate, she is seen more rarely in the Palace of Justice. Before that, she was in the Palermo Anti-Mafia Pool and responsible for the Mafia in Agrigento, Palma di Montechiaro and Porto Empedocle – the clans that have the closest connections with Germany, where they launder money and hide fugitive mafiosi, who live there as ice-cream salesmen or pizza-chefs, unmolested by the German police.

Anna Palma told me about the arrest of the Sicilian hit man Joseph Focoso, who was arrested in the Saarland village of Spiesen-Elversberg, where he had fled with his wife and children. As a Sicilian son should, he was living there with his parents. The Sicilian police had suspected that Focoso was there since tapping the phones of his relatives in Porto Empedocle and hearing that Focoso's son, who had just travelled from Germany, was given a slap for saying, 'But Dad said ...' That was the confirmation for his pursuers that Focoso was living with his family in Germany. Since bugs have become the essential weapon of the police, every mafioso watches his tongue. Only children blab – and elderly aunts, like Aunt Giugia, who gave away on the phone the fact that she was supposed to be bringing Sicilian fish to Germany. Clearly for her fugitive nephew, because anyone else could simply have gone to Sicily for themselves. In the end it was his craving for Sicilian fish that did for Focoso. Because along with the fish and his aunt came the mobile task force from Agrigento.

Prior to this there had been years of coordination problems

between German and Italian investigators. The Germans demanded proof that Focoso was actually staying with his parents in Spiesen-Elversberg. Regardless of the fish and Aunt Giugia. None of that was sufficient reason to tap the flat, the Germans said. And the Italians said: if we had proof, we would have had Focoso arrested long ago. In the end the Italian officials demanded that the Germans let them search Focoso's parents' flat. And they didn't have to look for long, because Joseph Focoso was in bed, sleeping deeply, and presumably dreamlessly, when he was arrested.

Later, there were further delays before Focoso could be handed over to the Italians because German legislation doesn't allow someone to be sentenced in absentia to life imprisonment — which was the case with the multiple killer Focoso, who had been in hiding for over six years. In order for the mafioso to be handed over to Italy, the Italian investigators had to prove that the lawyers who had defended him had kept their client very well informed about all developments, so that he was able to follow the course of the trial in detail.

If you talk to Italian investigators, Germany is by no means prepared for the battle against the Mafia: membership of the organization isn't a crime in Germany, and eavesdropping isn't legal in public places. In addition, Mafia property can't be confiscated — as it can in Italy, thanks to the Pio La Torre law which states that even if a person is only under suspicion of Mafia membership their possessions can be confiscated. In Germany, on the other hand, property can be seized only if a connection can be demonstrated with a concrete crime. German law does have the crime of criminal association, but, given that the maximum sentence is five years in jail, it amounts to a trivial offence.

When Anna Palma explained the German–Italian imbroglio to me, I couldn't help thinking about Renato Cortese, the head of the mobile task force in Reggio Calabria. Cortese didn't just start working with the German police after the Duisburg massacre, he had already been involved with his German colleagues during the search for the legendary Mafia boss Bernardo Provenzano. Cortese once spent Christmas in Mönchengladbach because the investigators had hoped Provenzano would spend the holiday with his brother who lived in Germany. For two weeks, Cortese lay in wait for the boss in Mönchengladbach, but to no avail. Two years later he would arrest Provenzano, who had been in hiding for forty years, in a Corleone cheese-farmer's hut.

After that, Cortese was promoted to the status of *superpoliziotto*, for which he was awarded a silver medal and transferred to Reggio Calabria. We met in a cafe not far from police headquarters and Cortese looked as if he was one of the two bronze statues of Riace: fished from the sea, put in a pinstripe suit and decorated with a pair of Ferragamo sunglasses.

Cortese set out the contrast between the German and Italian police for us, from his personal point of view. He pointed to the bottle of mineral water on our table and said: 'If I know that this bottle here is the boss, then we go and arrest him. In Germany, they do a "briefing" first. And by the time the briefing is over, the boss has gone into hiding.'

———

A pale noonday haze has settled on Palermo like a pillow
of cotton wool, a pillow that muffles every sound, even the
noise of the tyres of the armoured limousines on the marble
surrounding the Palace of Justice. Salvo looks at his watch
because Piccola Napoli always closes on time. At last we set
off, past the Teatro Massimo, towards Borgo Vecchio, the
heart of Palermo that lives on the drugs trade and looks like a
cross between Baghdad and Bogotá. With fat men in baseball
caps and flip-flops, with piles of rubbish and blocked canals,
with the burned-out carcasses of cars, mangy dogs and a big
statue of Padre Pio behind glass. The Borgo is right behind
the Teatro Politeama with its jacaranda trees; sometimes
tourists stray to this part of town and little boys with iPhones
take pictures of their horrified faces. The Borgo has nothing
of the charming shabbiness of Palermo's old town, which as a
visitor you can imagine as beautiful; the Borgo is nothing but
Mafia arrogance, just a few yards away from the upper-class
elegance of the Via della Libertà.

Written on a wall are the words *Honour the Dishonoured*,
and next to that hangs one of many house altars. Between
narrow curtains a haggard Jesus gazes at a pink Madonna,
surrounded by offerings of plastic flowers and lit by old bedside lights. A short time ago a man was murdered here, in
broad daylight, in front of the fishmonger's stall. No one saw
anything.

A few yards to the rear of the square with the statue of
Padre Pio a goose runs along the road. The goose is called
Candy and she bites anyone who goes near her, because
Candy doesn't think she's a goose, she thinks she's a dog

guarding the front door of a family house. Candy turned out
like this because she grew up with a pit bull terrier, people
say. Originally, in fact, there were two geese, but one of them
died. Everyone remembers the other goose running out in
front of a car, with its chest puffed up.

As we step inside Piccola Napoli the wind from the air
conditioning falls on us like an icy cloth, making us hold our
breath for a second. While outside in the Borgo the rubbish
might be rotting in the gutter, inside Piccola Napoli everything is sterile, with white tiles, starched tablecloths and a
freshly scoured counter on which no drop of water would
stand a chance.

As always, the whole family is at work. Behind the till sits
an old black-clad woman with the eyes of a bird; orders are
taken by her son-in-law, whose red face always looks a bit
unhealthy in the fluorescent light. Behind the fish counter
stands one of those Sicilian women who wouldn't smile even
under threat of torture, her brother works in the kitchen, and
the usual crew are joined by an old man whose degree of
kinship I don't know. He's leaning motionlessly by the old
woman at the till, with his waistband hitched up to his armpits. Depending on the time of day, all kinds of other cousins
and brothers-in-law and aunts and great-nieces and people
I can't tell apart turn up as well.

As soon as we're sitting down, there's white wine on our
table, and green Sicilian olives the size of quail's eggs, and
oriental-scented bread with sesame seeds. The brother-in-
law brings us *panelle*, the chick-pea fritters that I fell in love
with on my first day in Sicily, and sea urchins and a bit of

caponata, the vegetable dish of aubergines, tomatoes, olives and capers which sensitive Italian stomachs find irredeemably *indigeribile*, completely indigestible — which is why it lies for hours, maybe days, even in my belly, formerly inured to such things by my German upbringing but softened by my time in Italy — but which we still find irresistible.

For a second we think guiltily about the heaviness of Sicilian cooking, but it doesn't stop us going on to order tiny fried octopi, swordfish and tuna. And if Letizia hadn't asked about Duisburg, we'd be talking about the food for hours.

What was it like? she asks, suddenly looking like a young girl. More than most people, Letizia has preserved a childish curiosity about life. She soon tires of talking about herself, about things she knows, about repeated situations. But she loves experiencing new contexts, new things, outrageous things. She loves learning. But it all has to happen very quickly.

It's weird talking about Duisburg in Palermo. Thinking about steelworks, blast furnaces and workers' estates when you're surrounded by house altars, baroque churches and palm-lined avenues. And yet the two places do have some things in common. A death toll. When I got into my old Renault 4 that time to drive from the Ruhr to Corleone, because Mario Puzo's *The Godfather* had aroused my curiosity, I never imagined that I would one day make the return journey — that I would travel from Italy to the Ruhr and get out of the train in Duisburg because the Mafia had drenched the place in blood.

Heinz Sprenger

Heinz Sprenger, director of the Duisburg Murder Commission, is waiting for me outside the station. He told me on the phone that he was short, with a moustache. Outside the exit a man was waiting, wrapped in a black leather jacket, the kind of leather jacket I've only ever seen in two places in the world: in the Ukraine and the Ruhr.

If I were casting a police procedural set in the Ruhr, I'd immediately book Heinz Sprenger for the role of a police inspector to whom nothing human is alien and who doesn't waste his words. Sprenger is someone who keeps the ball close to the ground, as they say in the Ruhr. I tried to imagine him in Calabria. Heinz Sprenger in his black leather jacket next to Renato Cortese, the head of the mobile task force of Reggio Calabria, looking in his dark-blue, pinstripe suit as if he had stepped straight out of a Mafia film. Cortese, drawing on his cigarillo and watching after the smoke, and Sprenger, watching his partner with the patient attention of an ornithologist. Working with the Italians had taught him,

Inspector Sprenger says, that it's important to make a *bella figura*.

If he believed the newspapers, he said, the Mafia was being defeated in Italy every day. He was referring to those spectacular mass arrests of thirty or forty people which are always worth a small story even abroad: bosses, policemen disguised in ski-masks, in the background a helicopter in which the mafioso is being taken away − a helicopter that has landed just for the photograph of the arrest. And that flies off again once the picture has been taken, without the mafioso.

Whole clans in Italy are regularly arrested for membership of the Mafia, he said, and no one learns that after a short time many bosses are simply put under house arrest for lack of evidence. Or leave prison as free men once their remand period is over, because the judges aren't able to prosecute them within the designated period.

Heinz Sprenger and I drove to the scene of the crime. The Da Bruno pizzeria is only a few yards behind the station, on the ground floor of the Klöckner building, one of those 1980s buildings that you see everywhere in the Ruhr, buildings that look as if the architect had drawn his inspiration from the *Star Trek* movies. The restaurant looked as if it had been precipitously abandoned, the chairs were dusty and stood randomly around in the restaurant, a yucca palm withered in a corner, and above the counter there was an amateur painting of a pizza Margherita: *Pizza, la specialità di Sebastiano.* Outside was a big terrace with wooden benches; plainly the restaurant had been quite a success, in every respect. The pizza Margherita, and the money laundering too.

I thought about Sebastiano Strangio's grave in the San Luca cemetery. About that crude concrete box with rusty iron girders sticking out of it. And I thought about Don Pino, the parish priest of San Luca, who was a cousin of the murdered Sebastiano Strangio, and who had travelled to Duisburg with the Bishop of Locri shortly after the massacre and held a 'reconciliation mass' outside the pizzeria.

'I don't eat pizza any more myself,' said Inspector Sprenger. He said it casually, without any particular emphasis. Just stating a fact.

The bloodbath had taken place in the drive, just a few feet away from Da Bruno. We were standing in the rain; it smelled of soil and damp leaves, and Sprenger showed me the place where the shots had fallen. It was a driveway paved with those small square pieces of shale that you only get in the Ruhr. The two hit men had hidden behind the bushes planted along the drive. One of the surveillance cameras in the Klöckner building had caught the gunfire, more of a flash behind the leaves of the trees. Sixty shots from two different firearms, followed by shots to the head of each of the victims before the perpetrators fled in separate directions.

Until that night in August 2007, Heinz Sprenger had had nothing to do with the Mafia. He was the director of the Murder Commission in Duisburg, and had, among other things, made his name by developing a system for the monitoring of child abuse. His job was to clear up murder cases. His colleagues were responsible for organized crime. And now, overnight, he was in the eye of the hurricane – a hurricane of journalists, politicians and anti-Mafia parliamentary committees,

lip service, postulations and inferences, of 'Ndrangheta, investigating magistrates and police. A hundred and twenty of
his colleagues, half of all the investigators in Duisburg, were
deployed to clear up the massacre.

At night Sprenger read books about the 'Ndrangheta.
And files about the blood feud of San Luca. About the Nirta-
Strangio and Pelle-Vottari clans, who had been at war since
one side had thrown an egg at the other as a carnival prank.
About a village that essentially consisted of organized crime,
drug dealing, arms dealing and murder. When Sprenger went
to Calabria, he always took his personal interpreter with him.
Not out of suspicion, no. 'Just because,' he said.

His office was in a fascistic-looking red-brick police headquarters, built in the 1930s, like the Italian Palaces of Justice.
There was lino in the corridors; cacti and little ficus trees
were lined up neatly in Sprenger's office and the walls were
hung with organizational charts that Sprenger had drawn
up: family trees of the clans of San Luca, the members of
the warring Nirta-Strangio and Pelle-Vottari clans, assign-
ments of tasks, family relationships and flows of information,
arrows connecting men's heads, women's faces, hit men, victims, witnesses, perpetrators, getaway cars. At once a kind
of wallpaper and a cartography of crime. Hanging next to
it was a photograph of a bin bag with a child's arm sticking
out of it.

Heinz Sprenger had learned a lot about the family relationships of the Calabrian clan, about how almost everyone
in San Luca has the same name and you always have to
know their mother's name to distinguish one 'Ndranghetista

from another. And he had learned that in the summer before the massacre Marco Marmo had driven through Duisburg: Marco Marmo, the instigator of the Duisburg massacre, the 'Ndranghetista who had carried out at Christmas 2006 the murder of Maria Strangio, which had been intended to kill her husband, the clan head Gianluca Nirta.

Since the murder of his wife, the boss Gianluca Nirta had been seen as a time-bomb by the enemy Pelle-Vottari clan, so it was the job of the hit man Marco Marmo to get rid of him as quickly as possible: 'Gianluca must die, otherwise nothing here is going to work. He has nothing to lose now, you see, and that's what makes him so dangerous,' said Michele Carabetta, the hit man's devoted helper, who had travelled halfway across Europe with him, all the way to Duisburg. In a car that wasn't just full of bugs but was also fitted with a satellite transmitter that told Italian investigators its exact location – in Tonhallenstrasse in Duisburg, for example, or Saarstrasse and Mühlheimer Strasse, where the pizzeria Da Bruno stood.

Unlike the Sicilian mafiosi, who are always worried that their flats and cars might be bugged and who therefore talk rarely or in a very coded way about their business, what is astonishing about the 'Ndrangheta is the openness with which they talk about their dealings: the wiretap records of San Luca and the ones from the car in Duisburg suggest a certain recklessness. The killer and his henchman talked quite openly about their plans: plainly they thought they had nothing to fear, from either the Italian or the German police. Who, incidentally, knew nothing about the fact that the two

mafiosi were driving through Duisburg in a bugged car —
and Heinz Sprenger remains angry about that, because of
the not inconsiderable danger that the two men represented.
After they'd been stopped at a roadblock, the hit man told his
henchman that he would have fired if they had been held any
longer. But because Italian wiretap records are illegal under
German law, they are ineligible as evidence.

Behind this lurks what German detectives politely term
'different investigative traditions and legal cultures': the
Italian police try to penetrate the structures of a whole clan,
which it can then finally arrest for the crime of Mafia membership. The German police have to be able to demonstrate a
concrete crime, so they must look for evidence, for DNA traces,
fingerprints, traces of gunpowder. Or, as Inspector Sprenger
puts it: the Italians bug everything, they tap people's phones
for years — and nothing happens.

But where the Italian police have the edge, as far as he's
concerned, is in their ability to seize Mafia property, even
if Mafia membership is only suspected. How many times
have the German police questioned Italians who have come
to Germany without funds, worked making pizzas for six
months, and then bought up half of Duisburg city centre?
And, when they were asked where the money came from,
said, 'From my uncle in Italy.'

All mafiosi cherish this hole in German legislation, and
they exploit it even today. Especially, of course, since the fall
of the Berlin Wall. German investigators noticed this when
mafiosi from Duisburg, Cologne or Dortmund moved to the
east, to Saxony and Thuringia, and particularly to the Baltic

coast where millions of euros were laundered through the purchase of hotels, restaurants and holiday resorts.

There isn't a single Calabrian-run pizzeria in Germany that hasn't got some involvement with the 'Ndrangheta, says Inspector Sprenger. But so long as there is no shift in the burden of proof, so long as the police have to demonstrate that the money comes from criminal offences and the investor does not have to prove that his money was acquired legally, the Mafia's businesses in Germany will go on thriving.

What did he expect?

'I don't think the Germans are going to change their laws because of Duisburg,' he said. 'And if they don't change anything, nothing will change between Italy and Germany.'

For me this accorded with the views of the Calabrian state prosecutors Gratteri and Boemi and the investigator Cortese: all three men were united by the oppressive feeling that Duisburg hadn't really changed anything. That the initial enthusiasm that had inspired Germany and Italy to work very closely together had already dissipated. Cortese saw that his German colleagues were highly motivated, but that they were hampered by the legal situation. German laws were no match for the criminal reality.

———

'So the Mafia has a great future in Germany,' I said to Letizia, who had forgotten all about her swordfish as we talked about Duisburg. The red-faced son-in-law has been lurking for quite a while, and when finally Letizia sets down her cutlery he immediately takes the plates away and tries to persuade us to have a dessert, wild strawberries in orange sauce, or hand-made lemon sorbet, almost compulsory at the end of a fish dinner: 'To lose the fishy taste in your mouth,' he adds. We comply without much resistance and take both. Wild strawberries with lemon sorbet.

By now we're the last guests in Piccola Napoli, the old woman at the till is already starting to cash up for the day. She's a bit like the grim-looking old Sicilian woman that I saw in a pizzeria in Duisburg. A policeman had recommended the restaurant to me: 'I can assure you that the kitchen's clean, we searched the place only recently,' he said.

I had gone to Duisburg with my uncle, an undercover agent in a sailor's cap. My uncle is a pensioner and a former miner, so he's the ideal companion for looking around Duisburg without drawing attention to yourself. We had lunch in the Sicilian pizzeria that had already been searched by the criminal investigation department. No one in the restaurant spoke even halfway decent German; they didn't even speak Italian, they just communicated in a Sicilian dialect which they muttered through unmoving lips, as if they'd been catapulted into the present of Duisburg from the depths of the Sicilian past. My uncle was eagerly wolfing down a plate of salmon with prawn sauce when the old woman came out of the kitchen. She was very short, had eyes like bits of coal and her hair was in a thin bun at the back of her neck. She poured herself a glass of mineral water at the counter. When I saw her, a film played out in my mind's eye, showing all the encounters that I've ever had with Mafia wives. I couldn't help thinking about suspicious glances behind fly-curtains, the severe faces of the black dwarves of Corleone, of Mafia mothers who call their sons vermin when they have left the Mafia. But perhaps the old woman with the coal-black eyes was just a generous Sicilian grandmother helping out in this restaurant for a few hours a day. Perhaps.

But this restaurant was actually only a warm-up. The destination for our outing was the Landhaus Milser. A hotel that was 'the expression of Southern vitality', according to the prospectus. It was on the edge of Duisburg, between meadows and little pieces of woodland.

My uncle stepped into the hotel lobby as if into a church; he crossed his arms behind his back and stepped across the terracotta tiles with great deference. Displayed in a case next to the entrance were medals won by the weightlifter Rolf Milser, who had founded the hotel along with the Calabrian Antonio Pelle. The hotel became famous in 2006 when the Italian national football team stayed there. And when the Duisburg massacre took place. During those August days there was barely an interview in which the Calabrian owner, Antonio Pelle from San Luca, endeavoured to avoid arrest on grounds of kinship: not all Calabrians were mafiosi, he'd rather have been born on the moon than in San Luca.

But I said nothing of that to my uncle. We stepped through the light-drenched hotel lobby, poked our heads into the Da Vinci restaurant and admired the photographs of the Italian national team. My uncle thought everything was very nice, very well cared for.

As we left, my eye was drawn to a gold plaque that hung in the lobby, on which Antonio Pelle was celebrated as a 'successful migrant' who had brought honour on Calabria. The medal of honour had been awarded by the Pro Loco of San Giovanni di Gerace, one of those associations devoted to the fostering of local traditions. The medal was signed by the Pro Loco president, Dr Mario Carabetta. And I'm sure it's a coincidence that the companion of the hit man from San Luca who drove through Duisburg in a bugged car the summer before the assassination bore the same surname: Michele Carabetta.

When Don Pino, the parish priest of San Luca, had travelled to Duisburg to deliver his mass of reconciliation, he spent the night in the Landhaus Milser. As befits a Calabrian. Compatriots always look out for each other.

Mafia Women

When we leave the trattoria at last, the women of the Piccola Napoli look up for the first time. The old woman stares at us and at the money that the waiter brings her on a little silver tray, the daughter-in-law finally stops polishing the counter and wipes her hand on her apron. But not even Shobha can wrest a smile from the daughter-in-law, not even when she takes a picture of her and admires her delicate profile. The daughter-in-law shrugs carelessly, as if she thinks her symmetrical face is entirely uninteresting.

Outside, the light has softened again; we stand irresolutely in the street, Letizia lights a cigarette and looks through the smoke at the clear, endless sky as if expecting a sign.

'We could drive to Mondello,' Shobha suggests. 'We could take a few pictures on Monte Pellegrino first, and then a few on Mondello beach.'

Letizia looks up in astonishment, as if remembering only now that this is all about her. 'Haven't we finished?' she asks. She hesitates for a moment between protest and resignation, and then opts for an aggressive: 'Let's get it over with.'

Shobha calls Salvo, who is clearly in the middle of his siesta, because it takes him ages to answer. He suggests that we go in the direction of Ucciardone prison, where he'll pick us up to take us to Mondello. First he has some things to do for one of his ladies.

'Madonna,' says Shobha, as she puts the *telefonino* away again, 'they've really got him over a barrel.' So that we don't have to wait too long for Salvo, we walk through the Borgo at a leisurely pace, as slowly as tourists, past the piles of rubbish from the market stalls, through air that smells as if it's fermenting. The green of artichokes lies next to burst watermelons and shimmering grey fish scales. Not a single car drives past; nothing stirs around here before five o'clock. A deep silence prevails in the street, on the artichoke-green, on the fly-curtains of the balconies. The silence of paused time. The sacred southern Italian lunch break is even respected by the dogs in the street, which lie snoring in the shade on the pavements. Beside them, fat women sit spread-legged on plastic chairs outside the front doors of their houses. The women sleep open-mouthed, hands folded on their bellies.

The plastic chairs aren't the usual white ones that pollute the world, but chairs stretched with strips of plastic, old chairs that look almost beautiful next to the omnipresent white plastic stacking chairs. It's not just traditions that last longer in Sicily than elsewhere, chairs do too. They remind me of Rita Atria's mother's chair. It was in their living room, made

of white and yellow plastic strips, with an old sofa cushion on
the seat.

———

Rita Atria was a Sicilian girl, about whom I wrote my very
first book. She was eleven years old when her father, a Mafia
boss, was murdered. She was sixteen when her brother was
killed. She took her own life at seventeen. She had grown up
in the Mafia. Rita wanted to avenge her father and brother by
collaborating with the judiciary and telling them what she
knew about the Mafia in her village. Since then her mother
had rejected her.

Rita lived in Rome under a series of assumed names —
with her sister-in-law, her brother's widow, in an apartment
that the Ministry of the Interior had rented for the two young
women. They were filled with hope for a new life beyond
the Mafia, until public prosecutor Paolo Borsellino was murdered. A week after the assassination Rita Atria jumped from
the seventh floor of a block of flats in Rome. She would have
turned eighteen four weeks later.

A state prosecutor gave me a photocopy of Rita Atria's
diary. In it she wrote:

*No one can understand the emptiness that Borsellino's death
has left in my life. Everybody's scared. But the only thing I'm
scared of is that the Mafia state will always win, and the few
poor idiots who tilt against windmills will be murdered too.
Before you start fighting against the Mafia you have to test
your own conscience — it's only when you have defeated the*

Mafia within yourself that you can fight against it in your circle of friends. Because the Mafia is us and our twisted way of behaving. Borsellino. You died for what you believed in. But without you, I'm dead.

Rita's mother didn't come to her daughter's funeral. Eight women from Palermo carried Rita's coffin on their shoulders: they were the women from the committee of 'Women against the Mafia', and one of them was Letizia. Rita Atria's grave was marked with a small headstone with the inscription *The Truth Lives*. Rita's sister-in-law had had this gravestone erected − the sister-in-law who had lived with her until her suicide. It was only months after her daughter's death that the girl's mother visited the grave − and shattered the gravestone with a hammer that she had hidden in her handbag. She went on striking the stone until only a few splinters remained of Rita's photograph and the inscription *The Truth Lives*.

To understand Rita's story, I had driven alone to Partanna, the village in the Belice Valley, south-east of Trapani. A taxi driver from Palermo had brought me to Partanna and promised to pick me up again when I called him. I stood in the road and watched his car disappearing into the distance, and felt as if I had been dropped off on an alien planet. I felt even more abandoned when I moved into my room at the only inn in the village, a narrow room with a metal fly-curtain outside the window which rattled gently when the trucks drove by on the through-road below my window.

The inn was actually a pizzeria that also rented rooms − rooms without phones. You could only make phone calls from the dining room, and you could only do that with coins. The only other person staying in the inn was an old man, a Sicilian who had emigrated from Partanna to America in the 1940s and who, since he had retired, came back to his village every summer. He spent his holidays sitting in the front door of the pizzeria and hoping to fall into conversation with someone. He usually waited in vain. Because he spoke only English – and remnants of the dialect that people in Partanna had spoken in the 1940s and which hardly anyone understood now. Sometimes I translated for him from English into Italian. In the evening the old Sicilian waited for me; he sat in his vest on a plastic chair and told me his house had six bedrooms and wasn't far from Niagara Falls. And I sat next to him and smoked and thought about the day's encounters – with Rita's sister-in-law, who had come back to visit her village under police protection; with Giovanna Atria, Rita's mother.

Everyone in the village knew that I had come because of Rita's story. I could feel their eyes glued to me as I walked along the street to buy cigarettes in the village's single tobacconist's shop, or when I made a call from the only phone box that took phone cards. But when I asked anyone a question, they all acted as if Rita had never existed. Every day I tried to allay the suspicions of Rita's mother, who didn't want to talk to anyone about her daughter. At first, she only opened the door a crack and then slammed it shut again as soon as she saw me. But I refused to be discouraged and stood outside her house every day, hoping to persuade her to give me an interview. Until she finally invited me into the living room.

Even though it was light outside, we sat behind closed shutters in the light of a fluorescent strip, in a room that looked as if it had never been lived in, with a walnut vitrine full of liqueur glasses that no one had drunk from, with a sofa that no one had sat on. I sat on one of the dining-room chairs, which had not had its plastic covering removed in all those years. The only piece of furniture that was actually used was the chair stretched with strips of plastic on which Rita's mother sat. Her favourite place to sit was in a corner behind the living-room window, from where she could see the comings and goings in the street as she sat on her chair, peering out from behind her crooked blinds.

The mother didn't regret rejecting her daughter, nor did she regret shattering the gravestone. The betrayal of the family had to be paid for. Washed away, scrubbed away, chopped into tiny pieces. Giovanna Atria repeated only that her daughter's actions had been wrong, wrong, wrong — and that she had been hexed by her sister-in-law, the hated sister-in-law.

The mother spouted her accusations, her breath rattled, and I had difficulty following her through her thicket of accusations and suspicions. I saw her sitting, legs spread, on the plastic-strip chair in front of me and heard her complaining without once using the word Mafia. I dreamed about her at night. The metal chains of the fly-curtain jangled, and she came flying through the window into my room at the inn, and tried to strangle me.

By day, on the other hand, she reminded me of my East Prussian grandmother. She too had done everything she could to keep her family together. The family here meaning only blood relations. Also like a Sicilian woman, my grand-mother distinguished between flesh by blood and flesh by marriage contract. And my mother was flesh by marriage contract. She had been widowed at the age of twenty-seven, when my father died in a mining accident. When my mother went out dancing for the first time, six years after my father's death, my grandmother cast her out of the family.

'I thought you'd stay on your own,' my grandmother had told my mother. I thought about that as I walked back along the main street with the villagers' eyes on my back, and as I had my dinner in the pizzeria in the evening, eyed sus-piciously by old men who were, as always, the only guests. In one corner of the pizzeria there was a television fixed to the wall, turned on all day. In the evening the old men watched soft-porn films, along with the old emigrant in his vest. And when the taxi driver picked me up at last and drove me back to Palermo, I felt as if I was going back to a city of light.

———

Shobha, Letizia and I sit on a bench by the yellow stone walls of Ucciardone prison, waiting for Salvo. After dinner a wave of fatigue falls upon us, intensified by the heat. Letizia smokes a cigarette and Shobha takes her photograph sitting next to some women. The women are waiting for visiting time at Ucciardone to begin. They sit in the shade, fanning themselves and smelling of perfume. No Mafia wife would neglect to visit her husband in prison. One of them looks like a tragic, crazed Anna Magnani. A face like a figurehead with heavy, blue bags around her eyes. Her hair comes down to her waist and she wears a chain of pearls which falls to her lap. I wonder whether I've ever met her before, perhaps in the high-security court at Caltanissetta?

When the trials of the murderers of Giovanni Falcone and Paolo Borsellino were being held there, with perpetrators, instigators and accomplices all in the dock, the wives didn't miss a single day. Unlike now, when Mafia bosses are usually questioned by video link, the defendants used to be present in person; they sat in barred cages and tried to catch their wives' eyes. They were men with the air of janitors, men in tracksuits. In front of the cages hung a red cord that was supposed to stop lawyers from getting too close to their clients and passing on messages.

The wives were called the 'white widows'. They were the first in the viewing seats in the courtroom in the morning and the last to leave in the evening. It is the duty of every Mafia wife to sit through every day of the trial, from the reading of the names of everyone present to the closing of the last document folder. The crazed Anna Magnani was always first in the gallery in the morning. She always sat down in the same place on the spectators' bench, wrapped a blanket around her shoulders, folded her hands over her belly and didn't rest until the end of the session. Later came the young women – with frothy perms, lilac lipstick and azure, air-hostess eye shadow. Two weeks' honeymoon in the Maldives, a fitted kitchen with a microwave and a video recorder had been enough to buy their silence. The Mafia woos the wives of arrested bosses with a lot of money. They mustn't want for anything. Because if they are unhappy, they could start giving their husbands the wrong idea.

By half past eight in the evening, when the presiding judge declared the trial over for the day, the air conditioning had turned the women's lips blue. That was the moment they had been waiting for since morning. Because before their husbands were led back to the cells, they managed to blow kisses from their barred cages. The women blew kisses back, kneaded their handkerchiefs and swallowed hard. Their eyes welled up. Real Matres Dolorosae — filled with the kind of devotion that women feel only when they're convinced they're on the right side.

———

These women outside the prison walls of Palermo have, in honour of the day, put on their newest outfits, low-cut floral dresses, polka-dot skirts and bustiers. It occurs to me that in San Luca, back in Calabria, I didn't see a single woman who had dressed herself up, unless she was seventeen years old. All the married women wore black, or at best a pair of jeans with a black T-shirt. Did they wear the latest designer dresses at home, away from the public gaze? Like Arab women? The smart boutiques of Reggio must have some customers, after all.

The women of San Luca are also sure that they're on the right side. Wiretap records show that they are by no means the patient, black-clad victims of potentially violent men but that they actively support their husbands, not only in their illegal deals but also in the planning of revenge campaigns. When she visited her husband in jail, Giulia Alvaro, who would later be arrested herself, asked her husband if she should get weapons out of a hiding place for him and bring them to another clan member. Sonia Carabetta made herself useful as an intermediary between her brother and the hit man Marco Marmo. The women disguise themselves, they pass on messages, hide fugitives, prepare murders and maintain the connection between arrested bosses and the clan – which can even win them the honorific title of a *sorella d'omertà*, a sister of silence.

'How many misfortunes, how many tragedies in the south have been caused by women, especially the ones who become mothers,' said the Sicilian author Leonardo Sciascia. As in Cosa Nostra and the Camorra, in Calabria the women pass on the Mafia culture from generation to generation; it's the mothers who call for vendetta, who keep thoughts of the dead alive and prepare their sons for life in the 'Ndrangheta. In Calabria the clan chief arranges for the newborn child to be paid a visit at which a knife and a key are set down by its side. If the child touches the knife first, it has a future as an 'Ndranghetista, but, if it touches the key first, it becomes a 'flunkey', as the police are called here. And to keep this from happening, the key is set down too far away for the child to be able to touch it. The boss also cuts the baby's nails for the first time: that means the child has been accepted into the organization. And the mother understands the symbolism of these gestures.

Father, uncle, brother-in-law, brother, son. The Mafia sits in the living room. It lies in bed, it eats at the table, it comes home with its boots bloodied. And the wives? You can accuse Mafia women of all kinds of things, of concealing things and lying, of turning a blind eye. But you can't accuse them of not knowing anything.

'The only really important woman for a mafioso is, and must be, the mother of his children. All the others are "just tarts". A mafioso who has been married more than once, or who is known to have had affairs, is a wild card – incapable of controlling himself sexually and emotionally. So he isn't "professionally" trustworthy either,' wrote Giovanni Falcone.

The women are the foundation of the Mafia. When he's accepted into the organization, the mafioso must swear not to chase after other people's wives and always to lead a blameless family life. The reason is less moral than pragmatic – a suspect family life, or even a volatile mistress, represents a threat to security. The men of honour play along with the game. They enjoy the respect that is paid to them. They know what they are worth. But they also know that rules are there to be broken. Even in Cosa Nostra. Of course you have mistresses, very discreetly. But the wife is consoled by the certainty that she takes precedence. She must be protected. Because she provides an assurance that the foundations of Mafia society are unshaken.

Formally, a woman can't be accepted into Cosa Nostra, but even without the formalities she's part of it. Giusy Vitale, the first female boss in the history of Cosa Nostra, and, later, a turncoat, didn't just advance the businesses of the clan in the absence of her brothers, passing on messages, taking part in meetings with bosses, she also bribed politicians and gave orders for murders to be committed. Even at the age of six she knew what it meant to belong to the Mafia, Giusy Vitale said. That is the educational goal of a Mafia mother – she rules over the blood family, the core of the Mafia family itself.

It's the mothers who pass on Mafia values: honour and shame, loyalty and betrayal. It isn't the husband who brings up the children in blind obedience to the Mafia, it's the wife. Even if she and the boss don't actually have a marriage certificate. When the boss Bernardo Provenzano was finally arrested after forty-three years of invisibility, he said, when asked if he was married: 'Where my conscience is concerned, yes.' But wiretap records reveal that, even while the godfather Provenzano was living underground, he didn't have to give up the chance of a church wedding. Or the usual customs of a good Sicilian family life. A linguist who was presented with excerpts from wiretap records could tell from the accent of Provenzano's sons, Angelo and Francesco, that they must have gone to school in Trapani. When investigators went to Trapani, some schoolchildren identified the faces of the two Provenzano sons as those of their former schoolmates. Provenzano's wife was recognized by some of Trapani's parish priests when they were shown photographs of her. But unfortunately they couldn't say where the *signora* might have been living with her two sons.

The God-fearing godfather felt bonded, merged, allied with his wife and family – as everyone in Cosa Nostra knew, and as was revealed by the *pizzini*, the little notes with which Provenzano communicated with the world, and in which he always invoked God's blessing. His wife sent him warm socks along with washing instructions – *You can wash them in cold water or in the washing machine* – and she wrote to him in the tone of a wife whose husband has gone to war:

My life, I end my letter with the blessing of the Almighty, that the light of the Lord may shine on you and help you, as it may give us the power and the faith to endure all this. My life, I hug you very, very tightly. My love, if I should have forgotten anything, please let me know.

Unlike the Mafia, the Italian judiciary has always had a less than flattering view of a woman's capabilities. As if she is someone incapable of acting or thinking independently. Even if a wife is in hiding for twenty years with a documented murderer, she doesn't count as an accomplice, she isn't even guilty of being an accessory. A wife can't be forced to give evidence against her husband. That's the law. And that's what makes her so valuable to the Mafia: wives are inviolable. They bring messages to their husbands, whether they are imprisoned or in hiding, and during their husbands' frequent absences they keep the businesses going: drug deals, money laundering, property transfers. The few Mafia wives who have ever ended up in court have been acquitted; many Italian judges have fallen victim to their own unshakeable faith in the patriarchy: women couldn't be held responsible for their actions, they must have been forced to act on their husbands' instructions. Only slowly have they become aware that the image of the innocent wife with no idea of her husband's murderous activities is a myth, and one that the Mafia at least has never believed in.

———

When the gate of Ucciardone prison opens at last and the women push their way through for visiting hours, Salvo drives up, his Fiat sits, indicators blinking, by the side of the road, unmoved by the furious beeping of the other cars behind it. As soon as we've closed the car door behind us, we talk about the women standing next to us outside the prison. Women you wouldn't want to meet on a dark night, as Salvo says.

We drive past the jetty where people stand waving after the departing ferry, then Salvo turns off towards Mondello. As always, he looks as fresh as a daisy, his collar is turned up, his hair combed and gelled; he plainly had time to shower after his siesta, and he smells of aftershave. When we stop at a traffic light, he looks at his watch until Shobha finally asks him if it's new. With a mixture of relief and embarrassment he admits that his brother gave it to him, a first-class imitation Rolex, because it was Salvo's birthday last week, which none of us knew.

'You remember the Rolex in Corleone?' Shobha asks and laughs. The 'Rolex in Corleone' is a phrase I just have to hear to smell again the scent of a rainy morning in Corleone, the scent of the wet paving stones, the smell of my damp leather jacket, the smell of wet cardboard. The water trickled down us in little streams and flowed along the gutters, dragging paper and rubbish with it.

We wanted to talk to the women of the town, to hear

something about the ones who were spoken of in secret as the first ladies of the Mafia. Not the easiest thing in the world. And certainly not when the weather's bad. Because in Corleone, even when it's fine, you only ever see the old men sitting by the side of the road; it's only thought seemly for women to appear in church, at the cemetery and in the supermarket. It was too late for church, too early for the supermarket and too wet for the cemetery. We walked gloomily along the alleyways. In the window of a haberdashery there was a display of *coppole*, the flat caps worn on the island. Because my hair was already drenched through, we stepped inside the shop to buy one. Inside stood two old women dressed in black, asking advice about buying thread. I noticed that one of them held her left arm at so stiff an angle that it looked as if it didn't belong to her. Then I saw a gold, diamond-encrusted Rolex sparkling on her wrist.

A short time later we bumped into the two women again in the Iannuzzi patisserie, which has the best *cannoli* in Corleone – the Sicilian pastries made of cream cheese and candied fruits. The Rolex glittered in the shop's fluorescent light, and pastry-man Iannuzzi hovered around the two black-clad women like a hummingbird: 'One more marzipan cake, *Signore*? Try one of my delicious *cannoli*, tender as peach blossoms!' When Shobha asked the two women if she could take a picture of them, they just clicked their tongues dismissively. Plainly we weren't worth an answer. The two *signore* were used to being treated with exaggerated respect. They condescendingly gave their orders and quickly left the shop.

Who were those two black-clad women? Signore Iannuzzi

shrugged. 'No idea,' he said, and we could see that he was lying. We bought two *cannoli* and decided to go to Totò Riina's house on Via Scorsone so that we could at least take a picture of the place where his wife Antonietta had lived with her children since her husband's arrest. When Antonietta came back to Corleone, she didn't move into the house with the gilded taps, with the walnut doors and the Carrara marble. The police had impounded it. Instead, she moved in with her two old, unmarried sisters, Emanuela and Maria Matilde. A narrow-fronted, two-storey house on a street barely wider than a Fiat Panda.

Antonietta Bagarella had known her husband since childhood. It was a classic Mafia marriage: Ninetta was from an old Corleone family, her brother was rising through the hierarchy. He had the honour of being murdered by his future brother-in-law. Ninetta only found that out when she was already married to Riina. One thing is certain, though: it wouldn't have got in the way of the marriage. Business is business. A woman like Ninetta, who comes from old Mafia nobility, isn't prone to sentimentality.

Unlike her husband, who didn't get beyond primary school, Ninetta studied and gained her teacher's diploma. Among all the mafiosi who haven't even got a proper command of Italian, Ninetta's education is an invaluable advantage; for a long time she was the only one capable of reading a case file and negotiating with the lawyers. The young Mafia wife also attracted the attention of the investigating magistrates. In 1971, at the age of twenty-seven, she was the first Sicilian woman to be accused of Mafia membership. She was suspected of working as a courier for the bosses who were living in hiding. Ninetta played the part of the innocent, persecuted wife to perfection: she wrote pleading letters, collected the signatures of mothers in Corleone, and even appealed to the Human Rights Commission in The Hague. She told the court: 'I am a woman, and I confess that I am guilty of loving a man that I trust. I have loved Totò Riina since I was thirteen and he was twenty-six. Since then I have borne him in my heart; that is my only crime, your Honour.'

The judge passed a lenient sentence and placed her under police supervision – which she soon escaped by going into hiding.

The Riinas' family life was flawless, even during the years when the family was in hiding. The Mafia saw to it that they had every possible comfort: a priest to marry the couple, a honeymoon in Venice, a place in the obstetric ward, well-guarded villas in the middle of Palermo, holiday homes by the sea. Antonietta taught the children their times tables, while at the same time hit men were recruited and assassinations planned. Hear everything, see everything, just don't say a word.

When journalists dared to ask her a question at the end of a day's trial, she said only: 'My husband isn't what you think he is. He's an elegant man. I wish everyone was like him, an exemplary father. He is too good, and he fell victim to circumstances.'

I was thinking about that as I stood in front of her narrow house and noticed that there were white lace curtains over the windows and a rubber tree on the tiled balcony. Suddenly

I heard cries. At first I didn't even notice that the cries were aimed at us. 'Whores, wretches, damned souls,' came the shouts from the window, 'you've been running after us all morning. Clear off, or you'll be sorry.'

Plainly the two black-clad women were the sisters of Ninetta Bagarella. Shobha blanched, lowered her camera and said: 'Let's get out of here.'

We ran back to our car, which was parked only a street away. I drove off as quickly as I could, towards the slip road for Palermo. Shortly before I got there I noticed that we were being followed by a white Fiat Uno. As I turned off towards Palermo, I saw a heavily guarded security van driving in the distance in front of us. I tried to follow it. I stayed glued to its back bumper all the way to Palermo. At some point the white Fiat Uno turned off.

Shortly after our visit to Corleone, Giovanni, the eighteen-year-old son of Totò Riina, was arrested, for fighting, perjury, blackmail and Mafia membership. And murder. His mother saw him as a victim. Again she sat down and, in her even, schoolteachery handwriting, wrote an appeal which she sent to *La Repubblica* – a masterpiece of Sicilian maternal love. 'As a mother, I have decided to open my heart, overflowing with grief over the arrest of my son,' she wrote, and accused the judiciary and the public of condemning him simply because of his family. 'My children are being found guilty of being born the children of father Riina and mother Bagarella, an original sin that cannot be erased. Why can my children not simply be seen as young people like any others?'

Later, Giovanni Riina was sentenced to life imprisonment

for the murders of four people. His younger brother, Giuseppe, who had also been arrested, was charged with Mafia membership and extortion – and got out of jail on a technicality in 2008. After six years' imprisonment he returned to the narrow house in Via Scorsone, keenly awaited by his mother, his sisters and his aunts. That's what I can't help thinking of when I see a Rolex.

———

Salvo drives slowly along the twists and turns of Monte Pellegrino. Palermo stretches out below us in a veil of heat haze, endless rows of houses, satellite dishes and a sea that blurs with the horizon. Every time Shobha and I work in Palermo, we make a pilgrimage to Santa Rosalia, as if we were obeying an inner voice. And this time is no different, in spite of the mild protests of Letizia, who accuses us of heresy. For a moment we immerse ourselves in the view of the Bay of Palermo, transformed into the *Conca d'Oro*, the golden seashell, then we pass through a tunnel and we've arrived at the top of Monte Pellegrino, up by Santa Rosalia, the patron saint of the city, buried here under mountains of gold and precious stones.

As usual, I get the urge to splurge at the stall set up by the bearded dwarf-woman beside the steps below the pilgrimage church, and buy a bag full of devotional objects: Santa Rosalias supine and haloed, light-up Madonnas, oversized, glow-in-the-dark rosaries and, of course, Santa Rosalia candles as thick as your arm. Thus equipped, we climb the steps to the chapel, and notice a woman, who has plainly climbed Monte Pellegrino barefoot, now throwing herself to the ground and sliding up the steps to Santa Rosalia on her knees. She's young, perhaps less than thirty. Somehow her fanaticism strikes us as weird, so Shobha and I run past her, giving her a wide berth, clutching our candles as if they were amulets to ward off the evil eye.

What does the barefoot woman of Santa Rosalia wish for? Her husband's release from prison? A child? An illness healed? The chapel is full of votive gifts: silver calves and eyes, wax hearts and legs, dangle from the walls. Every time we come here there are different gifts hanging in the chapel. This time we spot a steel-boned corset with a note that says: *For the mercy you showed, Mimma.* Hanging beside it is a plastic bag containing a ponytail, and beneath it children's shirts and bibs, and a rubber ring decorated with blue baby ribbons.

The chapel is in a cave in Monte Pellegrino, so cool that it makes you shiver even on the hottest days. Here two Rosalias wait for the faithful: one dressed in black, holding a death's-head in her hand, her right arm reaching combatively into the air; and a lasciviously draped Santa Rosalia lying in a glass coffin, a Santa Rosalia who lies in her shrine full of precious objects, on a bed of rings, pearl necklaces, armbands — a sleeping beauty who has just fallen into a deep slumber.

Apart from us and the barefoot woman, there is no one in the chapel, no faithful sitting on the pews, no sexton collecting the burned-out candles — no one. Not a sound but drops of water falling from the ceiling on to metal runnels, from which they are guided to the floor. The moisture creeps not just into the silver calves but also into the countless notes bearing wishes and expressions of gratitude; the paper is curled and mottled, and I wonder who actually reads the notes.

As we stand by the saint's glass coffin, the young woman comes sliding along on her knees. She kneels next to us, prays with her head lowered and starts crying. She sobs till her back shudders.

Carla Madonia

Letizia is still captivated by the sight of the weeping woman beside the glass coffin as we drive down from Monte Pellegrino towards Mondello. She looks out of the window and doesn't notice the ash falling from her cigarette. Perhaps Letizia is thinking about the photograph that she herself once took here, showing the bare feet of a woman sliding up to Saint Rosalia on her knees. Maybe she's also thinking of the photograph of the widows whose faces were reflected in the windscreen of a hearse; maybe she's thinking of the picture of the men peeing against a wall. Or maybe not. Although even her photographs of shredded corpses, mouths gaping in death, and hysterical widows always look as meticulously composed as if a neo-realist film director had organized the horror, her first concern was always the struggle; art came second. She fought for women and for the insane. Against men and against the powerful. She opened a theatre for women, edited and continues to edit a magazine for women, published books for women. She was the leader of a revolution, because when Letizia took charge of her own life divorce wasn't even possible in Italy. In its place, there was the crime of honour killing: a man who killed his unfaithful wife to restore his honour could, until 1981, expect mitigating circumstances. From that point of view, in the 1960s it took a lot of courage to leave your husband and lead your own life.

As if she can read my thoughts, Letizia now says: 'I have a very pronounced sense of family, but I don't let it cramp me. And I don't cramp the ones I love. I believe in coexistence, in love, in freedom. I've always been very free, even in the upbringing of my daughters, and even if that wasn't always what they wanted. It's complicated.'

Shobha is sitting in front of her, and I see her looking out of the window and then awkwardly cleaning the lens of her camera with a little chamois cloth. And then Salvo turns the CD back on. Antonacci: 'Dream of me if it snows'.

———

'A woman's thoughts revolve around flesh,' they say in Sicily. Flesh by contract and flesh of the flesh. *Carne di contratto, carne di carne.* And husbands often learn the hard way that their wives, when they have to make a choice, will naturally feel closer to the flesh of the flesh. It's something learned by those mafiosi who have decided, against the will of their wives, to leave the Mafia. Giuseppina Manganaro burned her husband's clothes when she discovered that he was collaborating with the judiciary. She could no longer stand his smell in the house, she said, and dressed in black. The sister and mother of Emanuele and Pasquale Di Filippo went so far as to call a press conference where they told the news agency Ansa of their contempt for the two traitors. The sister was so ashamed that she attempted suicide shortly afterwards, the mother cursed the day she gave birth to her sons, the wives cast out their unholy husbands and cried: 'Our sons no longer have fathers.' The mother and mother-in-law of the turncoat Vincenzo Scarantino chained themselves to the railings of the Palace of Justice to declare that he had been forced into becoming a traitor.

Agata Barresi said nothing when the Mafia murdered the first of her five sons. She also said nothing when the Mafia murdered the last of her five sons. She didn't even open her mouth when the policeman asked her for her personal details. She remained silent until her death.

The mother of the mafioso Enrico Incognito wept when her son was killed. But what good did it do? The shame had to be eradicated, honour re-established. Enrico's brother Marcello had shot him to stop him from going over to the other side, the side of justice. The murder was accidentally captured on video, because at the very moment that his mother and his murderer entered the room, Enrico was recording his statement on tape. 'No! Marcello, no!' Enrico cried, begging for his life. In vain. Then the mother left the room so that she didn't have to watch what was about to happen.

And Vincenzina Marchese, sister-in-law of the boss Totò Riina and wife of the boss Leoluca Bagarella, disappeared when her husband was arrested. He wore her wedding ring on a chain around his neck, as one would with someone who had died, and put fresh flowers by her photograph. A note was found in her handwriting: 'Forgive me, everyone, my husband is worth his weight in gold, it's all my fault,' read the message on squared paper. Later, the police learned from two turncoat mafiosi that Vincenzina had supposedly hanged herself. Not only was she the wife of a powerful mafioso, she was also the sister of one of the most important state witnesses against the Mafia. Vincenzina had wanted to erase the shame, people said. Her body was never found.

Those bloodletting times, when the mafiosi had turned state evidence in droves, had been the times of the Mafia women. Of the cold-blooded mothers, the wives who were as self-sacrificing as they were vengeful. During those hard times, the Mafia women had become more valuable than ever. After all, no wave of arrests, no law, had done so much damage to the Mafia as the statements of its own men. There were men who talked about how they had strangled a little boy and dissolved his corpse in hydrochloric acid, about a man having his arm chopped off before being killed, about a pregnant woman being throttled. Now the wives were called upon to play their part, to praise the sacredness of the family, to extol the infallibility of the husband, to level accusations against the judiciary – wives who were willing to do anything to make the image of Cosa Nostra shine again. In the end, it was all about their children's future.

———

We drive along the seafront of Mondello, past the pier where the Charleston restaurant stands, looking, with its turrets and curlicues, like a Russian railway station from the days of the Tsars. It smells of oysters and burned almonds. The fish restaurants are on their afternoon break, and people jostle each other at the stalls selling sunglasses and fake Vuitton bags as if there were something to be had for free. The turquoise sea looks like a tourist poster, and lovers lie embracing on the beach.

We plan to have a coffee in the piazza in Mondello, and I desperately crave some *cannoli*, regardless of their proven indigestibility, to which Shobha refers me once again.

'I haven't been to Mondello for ages,' Letizia announces with amazement. She stares at the passing couples, who all look as if they've allowed themselves a lunch in Mondello today, with their parents, their sisters and in-laws, their children. As if they've had swordfish at Al Gabbiano, preceded by a few oysters and sea urchins and spaghetti with clams. The son-in-law will have chosen the wine, perhaps a light Tasca d'Almerita, for which his father-in-law will have despised him because he himself drinks red wine with fish. Now they've taken a stroll along the shore, along the quay to the little white statue of Mary at the end, past the fishing boats and back to the stalls of the Vietnamese street traders selling cigarette lighters in the shape of hand grenades. Exhausted by this effort, they slump on to a chair in the piazza, for an ice cream, or perhaps just one tiny *cannolo*. In a moment the mother-in-law will say that the *cannoli* aren't bad, but not nearly as good as the ones she makes herself, which are as light as a breeze. Then they will all argue about whether the *cannoli* from Pasticceria Alba on Piazza Don Bosco are really the best ones in the whole city, and the father-in-law will dare to announce that the best *cannoli* come from Piana degli Albanesi, which will put his wife in such a huff that she won't talk to him until dinner time. 'That's what it'll be like,' says Shobha.

And we sit next to the couples, at one of the wobbly little tables; columns of cars drive noisily past and suddenly, at one of the neighbouring tables, I think I recognize a woman that Shobha and I met in this cafe a few years ago: Carla Cottone, daughter-in-law of one of the most powerful godfathers in Palermo, Francesco Madonia, who ruled the Resuttana clan with his four sons.

I point at her, but Shobha shakes her head. 'No, that's not her. Although it does look very like her.'

Carla Cottone, Madonia by marriage, was wearing a dark-blue suit and a pearl necklace when she collected us that time from the cafe on the piazza in Mondello. Everyone turned to stare as she crossed the piazza, because since her appearance on the Maurizio Costanzo talk show she had acquired a certain degree of celebrity. It was the first time that a woman from one of the most powerful Mafia families in Sicily had spoken publicly. But not to condemn the Mafia, as the presenter had hoped. Since her husband, Aldo, had been behind bars, Carla had embarked on a goodwill tour through the media to convince the public that her husband had fallen victim to a miscarriage of justice.

Carla Cottone had married Aldo, the youngest son of the Madonia clan, one of the most bloodthirsty Mafia families in Sicily, a clan that could boast of being involved in almost every 'excellent' murder in the 1980s and 1990s: the assassinations of the regional president Piersanti Mattarella, the prefect Carlo Alberto Dalla Chiesa, the police chief Ninni Cassarà, the public prosecutors Falcone and Borsellino. And the Palermo businessman Libero Grassi, who had publicly refused to go on paying protection money to the Mafia. Aldo Madonia was the last of the four Madonia sons to be still out of prison. He was also known as *dottoricchio*, little doctor, because he was the only one in the family to have graduated from college. His subject had been chemistry. He was arrested after a turncoat mafioso had stated that Aldo had been involved in a drugs deal in which 600 kilos of cocaine from Colombia was delivered to the beach of Castellammare del Golfo. Aldo was said to have been present at a business meeting between Sicilian and Colombian drug dealers. One of the Madonia brothers who had already been sentenced tried to convince the turncoat that it was a case of mistaken identity. It was he, not his brother, who had taken part in the meeting.

In reply, the state witness said to him: 'Why do you address me with the familiar *tu*? I don't know you, I only know your brother Aldo.'

Carla Cottone had thought that we, too, were propagandists, who were going to deluge her with a flood of imprecations, accusations and entreaties as soon as she'd asked us into her villa in the centre of Mondello, with all its security alarms and high steel walls. She raged, as if she could prove her husband's innocence simply by shouting. She cursed Palermo's judges and all the turncoats who had denounced her husband. Her irreproachable husband Aldo a mafioso? All lies told by rats in return for promised privileges. Aldo was innocent, she cried. She turned into an animal when she heard those accusations; the problem was just that he bore the name of Madonia.

Until his arrest, it was in this house in Mondello that Aldo Madonia had led the blameless life as a pharmacist that his wife evoked. Shobha and I sat in the midst of an idyll of period furniture, family photographs in silver frames and little porcelain figurines, and wondered why a respectable pharmaceutical adviser would need to protect himself with high steel walls. And as we sat there and wondered, Carla Cottone compared the Italian judiciary with the medieval Inquisition and the fascist era, and painted a romantic picture of the Mafia which many people in Sicily joined only because they were in financial difficulties. 'They're unemployed, and life is expensive. So they choose to fit in with something,' she said.

Not a bad word about her husband's family crossed her lips: it was all just dust that was being raised about all his supposed crimes. There was nothing behind any of it. Aldo had always said that his father was a very loving man.

On the day of our meeting with Carla Cottone, I learned that a car-bomb attack had been launched against Maurizio Costanzo, the host of the talk show on which Carla had so volubly defended her husband. Costanzo had survived only by the skin of his teeth. The bomb had gone off just before his car drove past.

Costanzo had long been a thorn in the flesh of the Mafia because of his critical attitude towards them. In his programme, not only had he challenged Carla Cottone to condemn the

Mafia but he had also wished a tumour upon a mafioso, after
the man in question had managed to get himself transferred
from jail to hospital with a faked illness. When the hard core
of the Corleonesi decided, after the assassinations of Falcone
and Borsellino, to continue with their murderous strategy, the
suggestion that Costanzo become a target had been carried
unanimously.

———

'Let's walk along the beach for a bit,' Shobha says to Letizia
and me. I feel like doing that as well. To feel the wind in my
face and the water on my feet. Finally to feel a bit of movement. Because when I think about our meeting with Carla
Cottone, about the attempt on Maurizio Costanzo's life, I feel
the torpor of Sicily settling on us.

'Chemistry,' Shobha says. Just that one word, and we laugh.
No subject could have suited Aldo Madonia better. In the late
1980s Sicily was the centre of the heroin trade and heroin
refinement. At the time there were lots of rumours about the
heroin refineries around Monreale, and Shobha hadn't given
them enough credence. One day when she came home to the
little house not far from Monreale that she had rented shortly
before, her eye fell first on the light bulb that hung from the
ceiling, which was still swinging back and forth, as if it had
taken a knock — a furious, raging knock that had shattered
all the furniture in her flat, bed, cupboard, table and chairs,
books, clothes, plates and cups, all smashed and shattered.
Only her saints had been left unharmed, the statues of Santa
Rosalia, Santa Rita and the Madonna of Trapani.

The next time they were a bit more polite. When Shobha came home, two men were waiting for her in a Mercedes. Men who moved as if they were being filmed. Economical movements, sparse sentences. She had half an hour to pack her things and get out, they said. No one was allowed to live in this area. Her furniture would be taken away in a truck, she could pick it up from a garage on the edge of Palermo.

Shobha packed her most necessary belongings and fled. Later she drove to the garage they had described. It was empty.

Even today Shobha is angry with herself for believing the two mafiosi. Believing in honesty, in a sense of honour.

'I left Sicily after that,' says Shobha.

———

You never hear from any Cosa Nostra women any more. After the numbers of turncoats dwindled almost to nothing, the women became invisible again. They disappeared into nowhere, like rabbits that a magician had pulled out of his hat before conjuring them back again. Once again they became as invisible as Cosa Nostra itself.

The Calabrian Mafia women learned from the deployment of the Sicilian Mafia women: each time the clans are temporarily weakened by waves of arrests, the Calabrian women appear in public. A well-aimed stab to the maternal heart always works in Italy. A year after the Duisburg massacre, the wives of various arrested 'Ndranghetisti in San Luca even joined an anti-'Ndrangheta march, in which they had no hesitation in holding banners demanding *True*

Justice – for their husbands, brothers and sons: wanted murderers, arrested clan chiefs.

Carla Cottone and her blameless husband went on living their respectable life. Once his period in custody was over, Aldo Madonia was able to leave prison and wait comfortably at home for the further judgements of the higher court authorities. In 2003 he was acquitted by the supreme court. He was defended by the Mafia lawyer Nino Mormino, who finally became a Forza Italia MP and worked under the Berlusconi government as vice president of the parliamentary judiciary committee. There he campaigned for an amnesty, which would apply not least to legally sentenced mafiosi. It was only when the Palermo state prosecutor's office investigated Mormino that he stepped down from the judiciary committee. Even now Avvocato Mormino is one of the most sought-after Mafia defenders in Palermo. He defended Berlusconi's friend Marcello Dell'Utri in the second instance against the charge of assisting the Mafia, and also the former Sicilian regional president Totò Cuffaro against the charge of helping the Mafia, both with great success. Cuffaro celebrated his lenient sentence from the court of the first instance: five years, for favouring the Mafia. Originally he was to have been sentenced for supporting the Mafia – not just a difference in the choice of words, but in the length of sentence as well. And Marcello Dell'Utri can consider himself lucky that public prosecutor Ingroia, whose indictment brought him a nine-year sentence for supporting the Mafia in the first instance, was not in charge of the trial in the second instance.

The blow of Cuffaro's resignation as Sicilian regional

president was briefly softened for him by a seat in the senate, where he could feel that he was among friends. Giulio Andreotti, sentenced for supporting the Mafia − whose support for the Mafia until 1980 was proven, and is now deemed to have lapsed − sits in the senate, as do Marcello Dell'Utri and the president of the senate, Renato Schifani. Schifani wasn't sentenced for supporting the Mafia, but founded the company Sicula Brokers in 1979 together with a number of Mafia bosses − which, for a man appointed senate president by prime minister Berlusconi, and who therefore holds nothing less than the second-highest political office in Italy, is at least slightly awkward. Particularly since one of those Mafia bosses, Nino Mandalà, boasted years later of his friendship with Renato Schifani − something recorded in the files of various Mafia trials. Unlike politicians, the Mafia doesn't forget. Not even decades on. Favours must be returned.

———

When she thinks about it she feels ill, Letizia says. She draws on her cigarette and runs her fingers through her fringe. Clouds roll across the sky, turn pink at the edges and pull apart. The last bathers stand in little groups like members of a congregation after church; a boy shuts the parasols and collapses the deckchairs. We go on walking along the water, it slowly grows cooler, and the shadow of Monte Pellegrino falls on the shore. The sea swallows our footprints. Shobha takes casual snaps.

Rosalba Di Gregorio

Salvo is waiting outside the Charleston restaurant to bring us back to Palermo. The sky has assumed a faint purple tinge, which seldom happens in Sicily. Usually night falls from the sky like a black cloth, as it does in Africa. By the time we drive through La Favorita park, it's already so dark under the canopy of the magnolia fig tree that the eyes of stray dogs gleam like little dots in the headlights.

I'm thinking about the dog. Its fur was dirty grey, with a beard under its jaw. I only saw the beard later, because the dog appeared from nowhere like a white plastic bag being blown out of the bushes. I braked abruptly, but it was too late. I still remember the feeling. It was as if I was driving over a bump in the road. Even though the cars behind me honked their horns, I drove to the side and pulled the dead dog out of the road. And saw its beard. And its eyes.

When I told a friend about the dog later on, he said: 'Funny. Human beings are killed here every day, and you're crying over a dog.'

I think about that as we're driving along the avenue, and about the fact that I can't tell Shobha about the dead dog because she'd never forgive me.

And I think about the young, fair-haired cameraman whom we met when we were waiting for an interview with the then Sicilian regional president Totò Cuffaro, who was charged with favouring the Mafia. Collesano lies in the Madonia Mountains, in the hinterland of Cefalù. It was very hot. We sat in the shade of the church and waited for Cuffaro to talk to us after mass, having followed him all the way round Sicily. Next to us waited a few of Cuffaro's bodyguards, who whispered into their jacket sleeves from time to time. Photographers were hanging around, and so was this young cameraman who was supposed to be delivering new pictures of the president. We fell into conversation: at first the usual shop-talk among colleagues, just to kill time, then a cautious approach, the sort of discreet questions that people ask in Sicily when they're trying to work out which side the other person is on. And then, with no need and no real cause, the cameraman told me how once, at night, after a day's shoot in western Sicily, as they drove past he had noticed a parked car with its doors open. Someone was sitting inside and there was plainly something wrong with them. Even though his journalist colleague urged him to drive on, the cameraman stopped. And walked over to the car. In it was a man, bound hand and foot. His hands were tied to his feet, his legs bent back and tied to his arms, and his feet tied to a noose around his neck — a noose that tightened around his neck the more his legs stretched.

Incaprettato, tied up like a goat — that's what they call it when the Mafia condemns its victim to a slow death by suffocation. The man was already black in the face, his veins swollen as thick as fingers, the cameraman said. He cut his bonds and the man groaned like someone who had been underwater for a long time. Then the journalist demanded that they clear off. On the way they called the *carabinieri*.

Later he learned that the man had survived, the cameraman said.

———

Letizia's face is slightly sunburned, like a child's face after a day on the beach. She looks at the display of her Leica and checks her last shots. Shobha holds her camera at the ready on her lap. When we are on Via Ruggero Settimo, we notice that the traffic is being diverted for a procession, and we can't turn round. We are stuck in Palermo's 'street of wealth' — wealth that comes from the drugs trade, embezzled EU funds and extorted protection money — and see smartly dressed women walking past our car, the usual crowd for Palermo's early-evening shopping expeditions. The women walk past the shop windows of the jewellers and the luxury boutiques: Versace, Chanel, Dolce & Gabbana. Girlfriends walk arm-in-arm, mothers are dragged from window to window. Some women linger a bit longer by the shop windows, others walk past them with the apparent indifference that can be mustered only by people who could easily buy up the whole lot if they felt like it. The self-confidence of the elect. A class pride like that emanating from the Mangano women: the three daughters and wife of Vittorio Mangano, the mafioso whose discretion Berlusconi and Marcello Dell'Utri never tired of praising.

It was thanks to the Mafia lawyer Rosalba Di Gregorio that Shobha and I met the Mangano women. Up until her death, Rosalba Di Gregorio defended the mafioso Vittorio Mangano, whom the papers called 'Berlusconi's stable-keeper' and who had worked for two years in the entrepreneur's villa — and who said nothing of what he knew about Silvio Berlusconi, Marcello Dell'Utri and many other businessmen, politicians and lawyers. Right up to his death. It's thanks to Rosalba that Vittorio Mangano was able to die in the arms of his daughters. At least she managed to do that. Even though she'd hoped to get him placed under house arrest.

It wasn't a chance acquaintance as far as we were concerned: the Mangano women hoped to use a media charm offensive to soften hearts, to ensure that the father's high-security imprisonment was turned into house arrest. Rosalba Di Gregorio always defends, first and foremost, the interests of her clients. The Mafia has known for ages that the struggle can no longer be waged with bombs, but only with leading articles, interviews and television reports.

That's why the three daughters and the wife had declared themselves willing to meet us for an interview in her chambers. It was Rosalba Di Gregorio who thought her client's wife and daughters should be given the opportunity to set out their view of things.

They remembered their time in Berlusconi's villa as if it

had been paradise. She had always played with Berlusconi's eldest son, said Cinzia, Vittorio Mangano's middle daughter.

For her and her sisters, Loredana and Marina, it was unimaginable that their father could ever have turned state witness. To fall from enlightenment to disgrace? To become someone for the judiciary to wipe their boots on? They would have had to kick him out.

He would never have destroyed the image she had of a father she had always admired, Cinzia said. He had always said: 'I will leave you no wealth, but I will leave you dignity.'

They were beautiful young women, the ones sitting at Rosalba's desk. Not black-clad women, but cultivated young women who played the piano and were interested in art. Mafia princesses. Loredana, the eldest, was a restaurateur, Cinzia a painter and Marina, the youngest, was still at school. They weren't women whose lives were all *casa* and *chiesa*, as you would normally expect of Mafia women: they didn't say the rosary, they watched films by Nanni Moretti. Women like you and me.

The mother was an elegant, blonde lady with a pearl necklace. Loredana had long, curly hair and wore a floral dress; her sister Cinzia was in trousers. She was the leader of the three daughters, black-haired, modest and confident. She casually appraised us. The youngest daughter, Marina, was so thin that her knees pointed through the material of her jeans.

Marina sat on the edge of the chair, constantly ready to get up and run away; her mother watched her apprehensively from the corner of her eye. Loredana sat bolt upright in her armchair, straining for a lady-like effect, while her sister Cinzia sat in front of us in that comfortable and confident posture that is usually reserved for men. Like a well-travelled woman with nothing to fear.

Their name made them proud, it reassured them: 'We know who our father is,' said the Mafia princesses.

'Our father is someone with high moral principles,' said Cinzia, 'and of course we miss him in the family, as a support and as a human being who has a solution for everything.' A father who's a friend — even if he was indicted for Mafia membership, two murders, extortion and drug dealing. And even so, their name had never been a burden to them, said the Mangano daughters.

The arrest was really terrible. Papa had a meeting with his lawyers here; my mother and I were waiting in the car because we hadn't found a parking space. Then he came down, and as we drove down the Via della Libertà, Papa could already see something coming. Cars driving towards us, more and more of them, and he said: 'Don't worry, don't be alarmed; they might detain us.' And I said: 'But, Papa, what are you saying?' And all he said was: 'Stay calm, don't worry.' Then we turned into a side street off Via della Libertà and they jumped out of the car, with their guns cocked, and stood in front of us. It was really very horrible. They cut us off. It was really loutish the way they behaved: all the people were looking at us; it was a perform-ance as much as anything, it was theatrical. Papa said: 'Put your guns down, these are my wife and my daughter, one of them will go off and there'll be an accident.' They were nervous and smoking. They searched Papa. We weren't allowed to call home; my sisters got really worried because they didn't know where we were. They took us to a barracks and we didn't see Papa again. While we were in the barracks they searched our house. My sisters didn't know anything; they came with cars and guns, it was terrible. They could have done it differently too, they didn't have to be so rough. After all, Papa hadn't gone into hiding or anything. And then it said in the papers that we'd gone for a walk on Via della Libertà, but Papa had been coming from his lawyers and none of it was true.

When Loredana, Vittorio Mangano's eldest daughter, described her father's last arrest, her eyes filled with tears. She kneaded a perfumed handkerchief in her manicured hands. Loredana Mangano was the spitting image of her father: she had the same narrow face, his long, narrow nose. That father that his three daughters never tired of praising. A good father, who unfortunately only very rarely had the chance to prove his love to them. Of the last twenty years of his life, he had spent only five in freedom. The girls' mother constantly lamented their bitter lot. And what did the Mafia have to do with it?

I don't see the Mafia. For me it's history; it could also be another way of life, I don't know. At any rate, I don't see them, and that's my opinion. In my mind it doesn't exist. What should I say? I can't make a judgement about it. So, if I had to see it, I'd see it everywhere, in the civil service, in the most unlikely places, at school, but I don't see it amongst ordinary people.

'The Mafia is everywhere,' said Mama, because she knew that every Italian agrees with this assertion. We're all guilty, so we're innocent.

The public relations work of the Mangano ladies was exemplary. They complained about the victimization that they were exposed to on their prison visits. They complained about charges based on the statements of turncoats, they complained about the judiciary. They were victims.

But what happened to the values of life, to justice? It's a regime. I often watch that film Schindler's List. *It makes me cry. But every time I turn on the video recorder I get new strength from it. Because there are lots of things that are very like our situation, and the situation in other families too. The same feelings, the same torments, as if there is no way out because they have superior numbers. But the judiciary can't be like that. It can't be like that. If someone isn't well, at least he has the right to have his health taken into consideration. That's normal. Even for a dog. The prisoners in high security are the Jews of the Second World War. There's no difference. The Jews were killed, and a slow death awaits the prisoners.*

Cinzia Mangano was the most voluble. And the most confident. The ideal ambassador for planet Mafia. Cinzia was convinced of what she was saying. She wasn't hypocritical, she didn't lie, she was fundamentally honest. She had grown up in the Mafia: she divided the world into inside and outside, like a mafioso who feels no guilt when he commits a murder against the outside world. Cinzia was a soldier in the war. Her father could be proud of his womenfolk. They weren't shy with an answer. Not even when we talked about the murders of Falcone and Borsellino.

When the assassinations happened in 1992, when Falcone died, someone I knew very well told me: 'It's the beginning of the end.' Because to do something like that you must have fallen so low that you can't see a chance any more. Because there had been men who had embodied the Mafia as an ideal of progress; the Mafia had once been a dream of the future, the epitome of doing something — and all that was left behind was scorched earth. They've destroyed everything, everything.

Cinzia's remark about the meaning of the Falcone assassination was perhaps the most thought-provoking observation made by this Mafia princess: she regretted Falcone's death less than its consequences for the Mafia. Like many other mafiosi, she wasn't convinced by the strategy of terror that the boss Totò Riina was responsible for. Cinzia had understood very clearly after the murder of the two public prosecutors that the Mafia faced difficult years ahead if they were to become invisible again, to be a part of society, to be influential again.

The only one of the three Mafia princesses who hadn't yet managed to lay her conscience on the line was the youngest Mangano daughter, Marina, who had been four years old when her father was arrested for the first time. She had grown up with a father whom she only knew from prison visits.

When he got out I was fourteen. It was a real drama. I spurned him. I was convinced that it was his fault that he wasn't with us. I didn't want to know why he had been in jail. I was convinced that he was the one who had left us in the lurch. 'You abandoned us,' I said, 'so now you have no right to hug me either. Or to say to me: "Come here, give me a kiss." Because it was your fault that you weren't there. And that's it.' When I last saw him in jail, he said: 'I'd so love to hug you. With any luck I'll soon be released from high security and back in normal jail.' And I — yes, I thought: No, with any luck this pane of glass will stay between us.

That was the moment when Rosalba, the mother and the sisters lost their composure. They struck the desk with their palms and shouted: 'No, no, Marina, you didn't really think that. You didn't think that.'

But Marina assured them: 'Yes, I did think that. I really did think that.'

Then she wept. Her sisters, her mother and Rosalba stroked her cheeks, her head, her shoulders, and Marina sobbed into the Kleenex tissues that Rosalba took from the box on the desk. And I turned off the tape recorder.

———

Finally things get going again on Via Ruggero Settimo, the traffic is rerouted, and Salvo curses because he has to take a detour. Suddenly we find ourselves back by the Piazza Pretoria, next to the city hall. On the steps in front of the fountain lies a bride, draped there like Santa Rosalia in her sarcophagus. The train of her wedding dress flows down the steps. The bride has, apparently just by chance, pulled the dress up to her knees. A wedding photographer is giving instructions, and Shobha calls out to Salvo: 'Stop!' Because she loves throwing wedding parties into chaos. I once saw her, apparently uninterested, approach a bridal couple who were standing on Trapani beach, posing very stiffly for a wedding photographer, along with other guests. After a minute, Shobha had sent everyone climbing on to shipwrecks in their evening wear, between carcasses of boats and rusty anchor chains, and persuaded the bride to push her cleavage out for the camera, like a figurehead.

It was pretty much the same when we were guests at the wedding of the Mafia lawyer Rosalba Di Gregorio, but that time Shobha didn't need to use her powers of persuasion all that much. Rosalba automatically assumed the right pose in front of the camera: she sat down on the aerial roots of the magnolia fig tree in the garden of the Villa Trabia and smoked. She blew smoke rings into the air, which floated quiveringly above her head until they became invisible, and sometimes Rosalba exhaled the smoke through her nose. It's not for nothing that she's called the devil's lawyer.

Before the wedding, Rosalba had had a scorpion tattooed on her wrist. When she smoked – and she smoked a lot – the eye was inevitably drawn to the bluish animal on her skin. Her wedding dress was made of apricot-coloured silk taffeta. It rustled with every step she took. Her copper-coloured hair was piled up in one of those masterpieces of the Palermo hairdresser's art, notable for looking studiedly casual: solidly sprayed to look like flowing drips of liquid, her curls played around the back of her neck, both artful and casual. The make-up artist had sprayed her face so that the lipstick didn't creep into the little wrinkles around her mouth, her mascara didn't run, her aubergine-coloured eyeshadow didn't smudge the line of her eyelids.

Under her apricot-coloured taffeta Rosalba wore the 'ribbon of bliss', a thin blue satin band tied around her right thigh. When she momentarily lifted her dress for the photograph, her alabaster skin gleamed. And her tanga. After all, she had a reputation to lose. It's no coincidence that she's the best-known Mafia defender in Sicily. The only woman who defends Mafia bosses. And her groom, too, the Mafia lawyer Franco Marasà: thanks to Rosalba's dedication, Dr Marasà had been acquitted of favouring the Mafia. Various turncoat mafiosi had accused him of passing on messages to imprisoned bosses. Rosalba had prepared his defence; two colleagues conducted it. For a year the bar association had withdrawn his certification. Rosalba took over his clients for that period. They included Angelo Provenzano, eldest son of the boss Bernardo Provenzano, who was in hiding. Dedication that was to pay off – because when the boss was finally arrested, after forty-three years, his son Angelo turned to Dr Marasà and asked him to undertake the defence of his father. So in the end everything stayed in the family.

The official wedding of the illustrious lawyer couple took place in Palermo, in the Villa Trabia, one of the Sicilian nobility's feudal villas: faded glory in the midst of palm trees, box hedges and a forest of gigantic magnolia fig trees, whose branches look like enchanted dragons and centaurs. The marriage vows were to be taken under one such monster.

Rosalba smoked, jabbed the air with her freshly manicured fingernails and talked about high-security detention for mafiosi, about the possibilities of appeal in all Mafia trials, about turncoats – until it finally occurred to her that the wedding wasn't a day in court. Again she flared her nostrils and expelled the smoke. She didn't stub out her cigarette until her daughter laid the bridal bouquet of apricot-coloured calla lilies in her arm and urged her to go. It was Rosalba's second wedding at the Villa Trabia. The first had been to a bank clerk. When her son was four and she was in the fourth month of her next pregnancy, she sat her law exam. And shortly afterwards dumped her husband. She still loves her former mother-in-law, even today. Rosalba invited her to the second wedding.

The groom was in pinstripes; he was slimmer than usual, and waited for Rosalba along with the registrar. Dr Marasà knew what he had found in Rosalba. As a sign of that, he took her name: Franco Marasà-Di Gregorio.

Avvocato Marasà enjoys the greatest respect in Palermo. I once went with him to a bar in a side street off the Via della Libertà where we waited for Rosalba. When he ordered a prosecco for me, the barman emptied the open bottle down the sink in front of our eyes and opened a new one. A small but significant gesture.

Bride and groom had appointed their children from their first marriages as witnesses. Apart from the family, their colleagues from their chambers were all there: from the

curvaceous, mini-skirted secretary to the legal intern who
spoke and smoked like a cloned Rosalba; from the fellow
lawyer who defends the Graviano brothers and always ostentatiously goes to sleep when the judge hears renegade mafiosi,
to childhood friends and two journalists from the Ansa news
agency. The ladies in the wedding party proved that anything is wearable – everything was represented, from tiny
pink dresses with glitter straps to the silver-grey lampshade
look with tassels. The two Ansa journalists couldn't take their
eyes off a blonde in a tiny pink dress whose bosom seemed to
have sprung from the pages of an anatomy textbook.

The registrar chewed gum. As he started his speech, the
women's heels slowly sank into the red Sicilian earth. He
had been very pleased to learn that he was going to wed this
famous couple, he said. They were, after all, well known in
the city. He ran his hand along his official sash and gave a
sphinx-like smile. Certainly, some kind of synergy could be
expected from this marriage. The couple had already accom-
plished many wonderful things, he said. And he hoped that
things would continue in that vein, so that they could still
accomplish a great deal more!

He smiled cryptically, and the guests applauded when
the bride and groom finally said yes. After the registrar had
declared them man and wife, Franco and Rosalba kissed pas-
sionately in front of the frozen centaurs of the magnolia fig
tree. Dust shimmered in the sunlight. For one brief moment
Rosalba was silent. And, touched, her children smiled.

After that she stood on the first-floor balcony and threw the
bouquet down among the unmarried women, to choose the

next bride. But the bouquet was caught by an eight-year-old girl. Everything was different at this wedding, in fact. Unlike the usual Sicilian weddings — with at least seven hundred invited guests, Little Tony or some other Sicilian singing star, two video teams who don't miss a single glance between the couple, and at least one member of parliament to give them a silver tray, which may one day feature in a public prosecutor's bill of indictment as proof of Mafia involvement.

I gave Rosalba an antique table runner as a wedding present. Would it, too, one day be used as evidence? At any rate, Rosalba said that the antique table runner went very well with the antique French book, *La princesse Rosalba*, given to her by Marcello Dell'Utri, that éminence grise who is somehow impossible to avoid in certain circles in Sicily.

And so it is that the darkness of the Italian republic lurks within the heart of this apricot-coloured bride. In Rosalba Di Gregorio's chambers the destinies of the most important Cosa Nostra bosses cross paths with those of Italian politicians: Bernardo Provenzano and his family, Vittorio Mangano and his family, Pietro Aglieri, Marcello Dell'Utri and Silvio Berlusconi.

A niece of the new godfather, the fugitive boss Matteo Messina Denaro, the supposed successor to Bernardo Provenzano, had recently had an internship in her chambers, Rosalba said. And I thought: Why not?

Rosalba had travelled to her wedding at Villa Trabia in her dented Renault Twingo. Her last car had been a Twingo as well. She crashed it into a wall when an accidental contact caused a short circuit. Her garage discovered that a bug, acting as a tracking device, must have been removed from her car a short time before. Her client Pietro Aglieri had just been arrested at the time. After that, her journeys clearly hadn't been interesting enough to keep spying on her, said Rosalba. 'They turned me inside out like a pillowcase, I was X-rayed, I was vivisected. But they didn't find a thing.'

When Rosalba invited me to her wedding, we had already known each other for a few years. I had first met her in the high-security courtroom at Caltanissetta, where she was defending her client, the boss Pietro Aglieri, on one of his fifteen counts of murder. I had been struck that Rosalba was the only Mafia lawyer who had been listening during the trial. All the others ostentatiously fell asleep when a turncoat mafioso began to speak. That kind of effect was too cheap for Rosalba. She listened attentively, if reluctantly, so that she could object at the right moment.

It might indeed be the case, Rosalba said, that her client was a mafioso, but there was still no proof about the indictments of murder. And without proof there was no guilt.

And then she smiled with pursed lips. There was a principle at stake, she said. The principle of the freedom of the individual. And just by chance this individual was a mafioso. Are we not living in a constitutional, democratic state? Does a mafioso not have a right to be defended like everyone else? Well then.

Regardless of whether she is waiting for a trial in the Palace of Justice or visiting her clients in jail, Rosalba is always dressed in a way that makes respectable Sicilian women blanch. She wears jeans with holes. Or a pinstripe jacket with

a studded belt. Or army boots. Or a deep cleavage. Or everything at the same time. And her lawyer's gown is thrown
casually over her arm.

Rosalba Di Gregorio doesn't defend just any old Mafia
bosses. But she does defend the ones accused of blowing up the
public prosecutor Paolo Borsellino along with his bodyguards
outside his mother's front door. Some of them are in jail, others in hiding. Rosalba communicates with them via their
relations. Sometimes I met them in the corridor of Rosalba's
chambers. The brothers and sisters of fugitive Mafia bosses
were courteous people who greeted me cordially.

'My clients tell me they're innocent,' Rosalba says firmly.
'You can believe that or not. It doesn't matter at all. At any
rate, according to our legislation the client is deemed to be
innocent until the judge delivers his judgement. The prosecution must present evidence, the defence must present
counter-evidence. That's how you get close to the truth. Or
whatever the truth might be.'

When the Mafia boss Pietro Aglieri was arrested in
Palermo in 1998, after eight years in hiding, he said just one
sentence: 'My lawyer's name is Rosalba Di Gregorio.' In those
days the papers couldn't get enough of the fairy-tale of the
Beauty and the Beast. The Beast had the air of a seminarian
and was considered the leading brains behind the current
Mafia generation. The mafiosi call him *u signorinu*, the little gentleman. A Mafia boss of the kind that Sicily craved:
an ascetic, constantly described by journalists as having read
Kierkegaard in his hiding place and prayed with the priest
Padre Frittitta before a house altar. Someone who could make

himself understood in grammatically impeccable Italian —
unlike the bosses arrested up until that point, who only had
a command of Sicilian dialect and looked like the janitor next
door. And a woman was defending him. That was the loveliest
thing about him. Today, Pietro Aglieri is studying theology
in jail, by correspondence course with Rome University. His
professors are full of praise for him. He only ever gets the
best marks.

Rosalba has a pragmatic view of her job: she isn't supporting monsters, just defendants. A moral problem would arise
only if someone who had already been sentenced brought
guns into jail. But until a sentence is passed, she assumes
that she is standing by saints in their martyrdom trials. She
looks at me ironically and draws on her cigarette.

Every time I leave Rosalba's chambers I have the feeling
of being under anaesthetic. This has to do on the one hand
with her extreme cigarette consumption, and on the other
with 'mafiology', that self-referential area of study that has
blossomed into an art form in Palermo, and in which Rosalba
is an expert. Sicily is a world of interpretation, in which you
read things into silences, into the pauses in the wiretap notes,
into raised eyebrows, into the way someone lifts his coffee
cup. Where you puzzle over what is hidden, could be hidden, should be hidden, behind each tiny gesture. As if reality
were only a question of interpretation. As if the truth could
constantly change like the sky in springtime.

Regardless of the apricot-coloured wedding dress and the
ribbon of bliss, Rosalba didn't allow the merest hint of solem-
nity to appear at her wedding. She talked as she always talks.

As if she were sitting behind her glass desk in her chambers, amidst yard after yard of files tagged with the names 'Vittorio Mangano' or 'Borsellino', in the middle of a menagerie consisting of a cloth swallow that sits on the desk lamp, a cloth snake that serves as a back rest, a horned computer with a leather cover and a fire-red rubber stiletto in which she usually rests her *telefonino*. Since she's used to talking to her secretary in the outer office, Franco in the side room, the wife of a jailed mafioso on the phone and the legal intern in the armchair opposite her, all at the same time, Rosalba talked away nineteen to the dozen to the whole wedding party, witnesses and bridesmaids included. She whooped, cooed, growled and cursed. As if what was at stake was not the cupid's bow of her lips, the curve of which everyone praised, but paragraph 41b, the one that prescribes high-security detention for mafiosi — which Rosalba fought against tenaciously and successfully and anti-constitutionally, on the grounds that it contravened human rights.

Defending mafiosi as a lawyer is no longer the exception in Sicily but the rule, although it is an unusual career for a woman. So far Rosalba is the only one. She originally wanted to study medicine, but then it was law — for her mother's sake. Her father died when she was sixteen and, as the only daughter of a single mother, Rosalba wanted to do everything particularly well.

Her timetable has always been dictated by the destinies of the Mafia. At the time of the maxi-trial she met her present husband, Franco. When the first turncoats appeared as witnesses in the trials, they started going out together. After the assassination of Falcone and Borsellino, they became a couple. Two years after the murders, Franco was indicted for favouring the Mafia. Ten years after the murders, they married. Rosalba doesn't take holidays, she doesn't participate in Palermo's *mondanità*; she is so much a lawyer, to the exclusion of everything else, that all question of a life outside her job is forbidden. What a child's first tooth might be for other people was, for Rosalba, an appeal or a reform of the code of criminal procedure. The maxi-trial of 1985 was a milestone in her life: on the one hand, because she and Franco, her former colleague in chambers and future fiancé, were defending a dozen mafiosi in the trial; on the other, because it was the first spectacular trial led by the anti-Mafia chief investigator Giovanni Falcone, who had whole clans arrested. For the first time, the Mafia was forced to experience what it was like not to have a trial 'adjusted', *aggiustato*, as they say in Palermo: sentences weren't quashed in the subsequent instances, as they traditionally had been, but were confirmed in all instances – and for public prosecutor Giovanni Falcone that meant a death sentence. Of the mafiosi defended by Franco and Rosalba, however, only one received a life sentence.

Rosalba's actual life is played out in chambers. When she comes back from her days in the courtroom, she often sits in her office until after midnight, preparing defence papers – below the oil painting in which horses loom in pink and turquoise, and also below a small icon. She knows what's right and proper. After all, her clients are devoutly religious. Then, if she can chat to the court reporters, with blond Lirio from the Ansa agency, or little, round Enrico from *La Repubblica* who always breathes '*Sei bellissima*' and kisses her hand, or the reporter from Radio Capital, and can make a few mocking remarks about some public prosecutor or other, then Rosalba is in her element. Where, between the rows of files and the red rubber stiletto, she draws up strategies that might be useful to her clients.

After the arrest of Bernardo Provenzano in April 2006, and his successor Salvatore Lo Piccolo in November 2007, aftershocks were expected on planet Mafia. The power had to be redistributed. Backgrounds had to be clarified. Because in Sicily people don't believe in chance, they believe in prophecy. They believe in the divine plan and the urgency of fate. And fate decreed that Bernardo Provenzano's game of hide-and-seek would end, thirty-four years on, where it had begun, in Corleone. And on the day after the parliamentary elections. Not one day before. What would have happened if the godfather, the *capo di tutti capi*, the one everyone called 'Professor', had been arrested the day before the elections? Would Cosa Nostra have filled in their voting slips for Forza Italia even then? As it has done since the day Berlusconi's party put itself up for election for the first time. And no one thinks it's a coincidence that it should have been a bag of laundry – tracked by the police from his family to his hideout – that sealed his fate.

Since the statements of the turncoat Antonino Giuffrè, every child in Sicily knows that in 1993, after the murders of Falcone and Borellino, and after the arrest of his predecessor Totò Riina, Bernardo Provenzano negotiated a pact with Forza Italia. The Mafia boss offered his support and a renunciation of further violence, and demanded guarantees in return: an end to criminal prosecution of and political pressure on the Mafia, an end to the confiscation of Mafia property, and the abolition of the state witness regulations for turncoat mafiosi. This has been on record since the Mafia trial against Berlusconi's right-hand man Marcello Dell'Utri in November 2004, when he was sentenced to nine years' imprisonment in the first instance for supporting a Mafia association.

That Provenzano should have been arrested regardless of his connections meant only that he was no longer of use – either to the Mafia or to his political friends. Now the way was open for a power struggle in the Mafia: the young, ambitious Mafia is waiting outside, while in jail the old Mafia is sitting around Totò Riina, spending years hoping their trials will be subject to appeal. The next generation is greedy for power: Matteo Messina Denaro, for example, the boss of an old Mafia family from Trapani, once a devoted ally of Totò Riina and Bernardo Provenzano, later their competitor. Messina Denaro has been wanted since 1993, and is deemed to be the boss with the political intelligence required to lead Cosa Nostra into the modern age: when money no longer comes just from the drugs trade and protection money, but from public funds – tenders on behalf of the Mafia.

Since the arrest of Salvatore Lo Piccolo and his son, Messina Denaro has been the undisputed number one in Cosa Nostra. Until then, Cosa Nostra had been led by both in a kind of co-sovereignty – a leadership that came to an abrupt end during the hours of the morning in November 2007 when investigators arrested Lo Piccolo and his son. They had met up with other mafiosi for a business discussion, when forty officers surrounded the house and fired warning shots. Lo Piccolo tried to flush down the toilet the *pizzini* he was carrying, the little notes by which mafiosi communicate in these times of eavesdropping. But he didn't get the chance to push the handle.

And yet Lo Piccolo must have been relieved to realize that it was only the police who had lain in wait for him, and not the hit man who had been waiting for months to get rid of the Mafia boss at the behest of his enemies. In times of changing allegiances, Lo Piccolo had made himself unpopular. He had facilitated the return to Palermo of the Inzerillo family, who had fled to America in the 1980s. This had brought upon him the wrath of Totò Riina, who had tried to eradicate that same family in a bloody Mafia war. Lo Piccolo hadn't wanted to leave the drugs trade in the hands of the Calabrian 'Ndrangheta and the Neapolitan Camorra any longer and hoped to use his American connections to bring back the glory days of the mid-eighties when Sicily had, through its alliance with its American cousins, risen to become the hub of the international heroin and cocaine trade.

And then Berlusconi had triumphed in the parliamentary elections and moved into parliament and the senate with fat majorities. Those are the themes that stir Rosalba; those are the scenarios that she likes to think about in peace – much more than taking part in the social life of the city. Much more than drinking a turquoise aperitif in the middle of a wedding party – even her own.

After the wedding, Rosalba had changed and was now

wearing a turquoise dress that matched the aperitif. The wedding guests had driven in convoy to the Villa Giuditta, a restaurant where we sat at long tables under bitter orange trees in a garden – a garden where nature had been tamed to the extent that it looked like a living room. The bitter orange trees were drilled never to lose a leaf, and seemed to grow not from the earth but from a parquet floor, a gleamingly beautiful parquet, with which the whole garden was laid. Between sea salad on couscous and chicken risotto with green apples, the couple were celebrated. After the three-tiered wedding cake was cut, Rosalba put one leg on the table, her heel among the plates of remnants of cream cake, and hoisted up her turquoise dress. Then she pulled the blue ribbon of bliss from her thigh and threw it among her admirers. A young agency journalist caught it, held it appreciatively under his nose and closed his eyes. Satisfied, Rosalba got down from the table and straightened her dress. As she did so, the moonlight caught the tattoo on her wrist. The scorpion's claws were open.

———

The same black-blue sky that stretched above Rosalba's wedding party spreads over us, too – over Shobha, Letizia, Salvo and me, and over the Piazza Pretoria. The gods and nymphs that stand on the rim of the fountain look heedlessly down on us. Shobha has managed to turn the whole wedding party into a tableau vivant. The parents of the bride, witnesses and flower-girls are in position, the bride has already decided to jump into the fountain – and then Shobha lowers the camera, thanks them politely for their cooperation and gets back into the car. Letizia is urging us to leave, saying that her dog must feel abandoned by now.

The smell of fried meat wafts over, along with the smell of the crowd coming from the avenue and now pressing into the bars. Scraps of music fly through the air, Vasco Rossi shrills out of the speaker of an illegal CD seller, *'Voglio una vita spericolata,'* Salvo joins in at the top of his voice, that hymn to the fearless life: 'to the unruly life, a life where nothing matters, a life in which it's never too late and you never have to sleep, a life like a life in a film. A life, you'll see, what a life.'

Carmine Sarno

When Salvo drops us off on Via Carini, not far from Letizia and Shobha's house, both his *telefonini* ring at the same time. One of the calls is his fiancée, the other one of his ladies — and both want to know when he will finally have time for them. While Salvo tries to placate both the lady and his fiancée, we gesticulate to arrange a meeting for the following morning. Then I follow Shobha and Letizia. We've decided to have dinner on Shobha's terrace. The lift creaks its way up to the ninth floor.

Exhausted by the heat we slump into the armchairs. Shobha turns on the television, and on Rai Uno we see a report on the death of a Camorrista. In Campania, the father of a turncoat has been shot, the Casalesi clan has wreaked revenge on the renegade. A country lane is shown, a bare stone farmhouse, a barn with bullet holes in the wall, a pool of blood on the ground. Mafia corpses in Italy are as inconspicuous as car-crash corpses. Then life goes on with reports of traffic jams, with people coming back from holiday, with pictures of the beach at Rimini.

'*Ma*,' says Letizia, stretching out the *m* for so long that her *ma* sounds like 'all striving and straining is in vain'. Then she slowly walks down the steps to her flat. When Shobha calls after her to ask if she doesn't want to stay to dinner, she declines. She doesn't want another bite, with all due respect to Shobha's *caponata*, but the very thought of aubergines with tomatoes and pumpkin makes her feel bloated.

Shobha showers, and I turn off the sound when the news returns to the rubbish in Naples. 'Now there's rubbish on the elegant Via Chiaia, too!' I see a sea of blue, black and white rubbish bags, bursting, fermenting, rotting rubbish bags — fruit crates, cardboard pasta boxes, detergent bottles, nappies. I don't want to hear for the thousandth time the commentators describing the rubbish as some sort of mysterious force of nature which sweeps across the city like a hurricane every few months, leaving behind it a trail of devastation. Each time, politicians wholeheartedly announce an irrevocable victory over the rubbish, waste incineration units will be put into operation straightaway, the army moves in, special commissioners are appointed and dismissed again, special trains are loaded with rubbish and sent to Germany — and no one says the evil word: 'Camorra'. It makes money out of the waste disposal and landfill, both legal and illegal, with which it has contaminated the whole of the Neapolitan hinterland, with industrial waste that it imports to Naples from all over Europe, and with toxic waste that is illegally burned and which has poisoned the groundwater and the air with dioxins.

'At least here in Sicily we have no problems with rubbish,' Shobha says, coming out of the shower with freshly washed hair and pointing to the pictures on television. She adds ironically: 'Having the water supply in the hands of the Mafia is quite enough.'

When Shobha moves, her bracelets jangle. She brings them back by the kilo from India, where she spends the winter. In this way, she escapes not only the damp climate but also Sicilian reality − where people try to change things in such a way that everything stays exactly as it was. Today I sometimes wonder what it would have been like for me if I'd grown up not in the Ruhr but in Sicily. If my first flat of my own had been not in the university district of Münster, but in Monreale, near Palermo, where mafiosi would have destroyed all my furniture. In that case I'd probably have yearned for India too.

When Shobha was back in India, I was in Naples. As befits an old married couple, we sent each other text messages and said: 'Wish you were here!' Instead of Shobha, I had a bald photographer by my side, which didn't exactly make my research easier. Men always arouse suspicion in southern Italy. Women, on the other hand, are generally underestimated, particularly if they're blonde. And being underestimated is the best thing that can happen to a journalist on an assignment.

That's why Carmine Sarno wasn't even slightly suspicious when I stepped into his music agency, La Bella Napoli, and asked him about the lyrics of the songs he had composed. Sometimes you can strike up an acquaintanceship as easily as that.

'You know who I am. You know my name,' Carmine Sarno said softly.

He didn't need to say anything more than that. He sat with his legs crossed on a little gilded rococo chair, a dainty man on a dainty chair. Carmine Sarno has very small feet for a man; he's unusually delicate overall, his waist as slender as a woman's. His shirt was open to the navel and revealed an almost hairless chest and a heavy white-gold chain from which hung a heart-shaped medallion and a portrait engraved in gold. In his trouser pocket he carried a roll of 20 euro notes, held together with a thin rubber band. With this he was paying a man who had printed up some posters for him for a concert by the singer Antony. 'Is that spelled right?' the man asked, pointing at the name 'Antonj'.

'I think that should be a y,' I said.

And Carmine Sarno said: 'That's how we spell it here.'

———

Carmine Sarno belongs to one of the city's most powerful Camorra clans. The Sarnos rule in Ponticelli, that peripheral quarter of Naples into which neither tourists nor Neapolitans stray: a landscape of containers, forgotten by the world, a district that consists largely of oil refineries, arterial roads on stilts, warehouses and potholes. And which is only ever mentioned if another Camorrista is murdered. Or if a gypsy camp is set on fire, as happened that spring, after a gypsy had tried to abduct a child in Ponticelli. For respectable Neapolitans, Ponticelli is a far-off galaxy, its existence known only from the newspapers.

The Sarnos have ruled in Ponticelli since the early 1980s. Seven brothers and five sisters. Three of the brothers were in jail; altogether, sixteen members of the Sarno family were in jail. The oldest brother is called Ciro; even at the age of thirty he was one of the most dangerous Camorristi in Naples and had been in jail for almost eighteen years, with interruptions – which is why Carmine Sarno had dedicated the song '*Ciro, Ciro*' to him, lamenting his brother's lot. Because Carmine Sarno wasn't just a member of one of the most powerful Camorra clans in Naples, he was also a poet.

We had only known each other for a few minutes when Carmine awkwardly told me how his first wife had put him in prison. He had stuck the barrel of his gun in her mouth, his wife had told the *carabinieri*. Shortly after that, they arrested Carmine Sarno. He was behind bars for nine months for attempted murder. When he was released from prison, his wife really wanted to kill him.

'I'm telling you all this because I see you as a sister,' said Carmine Sarno.

How had we got on to the story of his wife? Oh, yes, it was all about love. Lots of his songs are about that. In '*Ci soffro ancora*', 'I'm still suffering', an abandoned man confides in a friend. '*Mi telefoni*', 'Call me', is about a secret adulterous affair. Then there are titles like '*Notte d'amore*', 'Night of Love'; '*Brivido*', 'Shiver'; or '*Estate d'amore*', 'Summer of Love'. Sometimes love is not requited, sometimes it lasts only a heartbeat, sometimes it is a dead end. But it is always heartbreaking. Carmine had composed two dozen songs, at night when he couldn't sleep because he was nervous or filled with longing, or because inspiration had suddenly come upon him.

Carmine represented the best singers in Naples. In his agency, one wall was papered with his stars' posters. They were men whose tattoos crept from their shirt collars, men with pin-sharp sideburns who called themselves Alessio or Nello Amato or Maurizio, men at the sight of whom girls in Naples started weeping as hysterically as if the blood of San Gennaro had just liquefied in front of their eyes.

'*E carcerate*' was the name of one of the hits from Sarno's workshop: 'The Prisoners', a martyrs' hymn about men who aren't allowed to see their children growing up. Carmine Sarno is a man with a soft heart. And armoured glass in his window panes. The armoured glass was necessary because sinister characters made the area unsafe from time to time, he said. Which was an elegant circumlocution for the Camorra war between the Sarno and Panico clans – manifest now in a car bomb, now in a bullet to the head. The war between the clans had also killed Sarno's nephew, whose face, engraved in gold, rested on his chest. The boy had been blown sky-high by a car bomb meant for his father: only his hands were left, Carmine Sarno said.

Later, he invited me to lunch. We ate with one of his friends, an impresario who looked as if he'd been dressed by a costume designer: with a lot of hair gel and an awful lot of artificial tan, a light-grey suit, a white shirt open to the chest and the usual medallion with the picture of a dead person around his neck. The impresario was telling Carmine Sarno that he had been checked by the DIA, the *Direzione Investigativa*

AntiMafia, the national anti-Mafia office. Turning to me, he added apologetically that it must have been a case of mistaken identity: 'We're always talking about various artists on the phone,' he said. The police, he explained, had confused that with some sort of secret code.

Carmine Sarno saw my interest in him as a piece of jewellery that you pin on yourself. After all, there had been bosses in Naples who had dictated legends from their lives straight into the notebooks of selected journalists. Unlike the Sicilian or Calabrian bosses, the bosses of the Camorra are not embarrassed about putting their wealth on display. Camorristi are known for building themselves Hollywood-style villas and speeding down the alleyways of the Spanish Quarter in their Ferrari Testarossas. When I accompanied a Neapolitan wedding photographer to the baptism of a Camorrista's child in the Spanish Quarter, I witnessed the mother giving the godfather a diamond-encrusted platinum bracelet. And the godfather responding with a diamond-encrusted platinum cross for the child. The clan of the Giulianos, the legendary Camorra family that ruled Naples until the 1990s, loved making a show for the cameras: the photograph of Diego Armando Maradona, lying in the Giulianos' scallop-shaped pool drinking champagne, became a Camorra icon.

The smart restaurant where I ate with Carmine Sarno and the impresario rose like a chimera from the wasteland of Ponticelli, with a marble terrace and brightly coloured awnings; the waiters served frittered *fruits de mer* and we drank wine adorned with slices of fresh peach and delicate mint leaves.

'Without parsley for you, as always, Carmine,' said the waiter as he served the pasta, and Carmine Sarno's eye drifted carelessly over the businessmen who greeted him. 'Carmine, you're the greatest!' a man called from the next table, but Sarno didn't respond.

Unusually, he drank wine, in my honour, although he had just had a serious stomach operation. 'To your health, Petra,' he said, and straightened the red ruby ring on his right hand – a present from someone thanking him for a favour he had performed. Then Carmine spoke quietly about the benefit concerts that he organizes every year: one for children at Epiphany, and one for the physically handicapped in September.

Why did he do that?

'Because I have been lame since childhood,' he said.

Carmine Sarno lived in one of those industrialized blocks on stilts of which the whole eastern edge of Naples seemed to consist, all the way inland. Ponticelli was the Sarnos' fortress. With solariums called *fuego*, fire, and the Coppola bar, in which young, nervous men drank tumblers full of whisky sour even in the morning. Before going on to sing a verse from a love song. When they saw Carmine Sarno, they smiled so broadly that I could see their cocaine-eroded gums.

Nothing stirred here without the consent of the Sarnos. Bodyguards reported every suspicious movement – a hidden investigator, a turncoat clan member, a motorbike driver in a helmet. In Naples only hit men wear helmets. Unlike the old town of Naples, Ponticelli couldn't hide behind the enchantment of Renaissance marble cornucopias, baroque churches

decorated with death's-heads, and rococo *palazzi*. There were
no frescoes here, no marble columns scattering poetry like
jewels over everyday life among the Camorra; there was
nothing here but rubbish bags which flourished like carbun-
cles along the roadside ditches, and which at night, once they
had been lit, blazed like beacons of perdition.

Unlike the Sicilian Mafia, the Camorra is organized horizontally: there is no hierarchy and there are hardly any rules,
everyone wants to be the boss, and that doesn't happen without
a murder. Every third day someone is killed in Naples. A few
months before I met Carmine Sarno, the police in Ponticelli
had arrested seventy-one clan members: for nine murders,
two attempted murders, three instances of grievous bodily
harm and one thwarted assassination attempt; for robbery,
profiteering, drug and arms dealing. Kalashnikovs, rapid-fire
rifles, pistols and explosives had been smuggled into Naples
in the buses bringing Polish home helps into town. Thanks
to the arrests, an attack by the Panico family on the Sarno
clan had been thwarted; the prepared explosives had been
impounded, along with twenty businesses, properties worth
millions, cars and yachts. And in Ponticelli you saw nothing
but burned-out car wrecks, home-made house altars and the
graffito *My breath belongs to you.*

Carmine's brother Ciro was called *o' sindaco*, the mayor,
because he had appointed himself master of the *Terremotati*,
the people displaced by the 1980 earthquake, who occupied
Ponticelli's ruined buildings, shells left behind by Neapolitan
speculators after they had cashed in their grants. Ciro *o' sindaco* had allocated the flats. And taken care of electricity, water

and gas connections. And thus won himself the unconditional devotion of people who had nothing more to lose. When Ciro Sarno was arrested in 1990 for illegal arms possession, there was a revolt: frying pans, flowerpots and crockery rained down on the police. One clan member relieved Ciro Sarno by assuming responsibility for the illegal arms possession. Ciro was released again. Temporarily.

Carmine Sarno didn't like to talk about such sad things. He preferred to talk about his songs, which were, he said, always inspired by true stories from Ponticelli. The song 'Frate mio', 'My Brother', is about a pair of lovers who discover they are brother and sister. Social workers make the couple part. 'Mi telefoni', 'Call me', is about a secret adulterous affair and 'Sora mia', 'My Sister', is about the death of a woman who dies of an incurable illness at the age of only thirty, leaving behind a little daughter.

Later, when we were sitting in his agency again, Carmino Sarno tried to make it clear to me he didn't use the sources of his inspiration without their permission: of course, he always asked the families beforehand whether they minded him writing a song about them, he said. Like the parents of little Francesco Paolillo, for whom he had written the song 'Insieme con Gesù', 'Together with Jesus'. Francesco died while playing in an unsafe derelict building. In memory of him, Sarno had produced a video clip and had a little altar built near the spot where he had fallen to his death.

At that thought Carmine felt silent, leaving nothing but a feeling of piety and a gentle summer wind that passed through the agency. The breeze drifted over a withered yucca tree, a Padre Pio watching over a keyboard, and a cabaret artist sitting mutely in a corner. He humbly unrolled a poster and tried to excite Carmine about his programme which was guaranteed family fare, simple lyrics, no swearing. He performed with his daughter, who was nine and a half and a natural talent; the act was capable of further development and equally suited to first communions and weddings, to baptisms and confirmations. Then he told a joke from his act. And laughed. Carmine Sarno didn't laugh. He just looked out of the window into the street. And casually returned the greeting of a passing youth. And the cabaret artist rolled his poster back up again.

A Sarno doesn't fritter himself away, either in words or in gestures.

Carmine Sarno didn't lose his composure even when he received an unexpected visit in my presence: two men in sunglasses. One of them had white hair and looked like Richard Gere, the other had black hair and looked like Al Pacino. Richard Gere wore a pinstripe suit and a thin D'Artagnan beard, Al Pacino was dressed entirely in black.

'Financial police,' said Richard Gere, taking out his ID.

Because I wanted to be polite, I made as if to leave the agency, so that I wouldn't be witness to what might turn out to be an unpleasant conversation for Sarno. 'No,' he said. 'Sit right where you are, Petra, it's not a problem.'

'It's about the income from Alessio's concerts,' said Al Pacino. 'We want to know how many tickets were sold, things like that.'

Sarno fell silent.

'Can't you help us in any way?' asked Richard Gere.

'No,' said Sarno. 'I don't deal with that kind of thing.'

Then he went to a shelf and took out a folder. He opened it awkwardly. There were documents in it, yellowed licences, which Carmine Sarno looked at as if seeing them for the first time.

'Perhaps your tax adviser might be able to help us. What's his name?' asked Al Pacino.

'My what?' asked Carmine Sarno.

'Your tax adviser. You must have a tax adviser,' said Richard Gere.

'I don't know the name of my tax adviser. My wife deals with things like that.' And then he called to the joiner across the street: 'Do you know the name of my tax adviser?'

The joiner yelled back: 'No idea.'

'Perhaps we could have a word with your wife,' said Al Pacino. 'She might be able to drop by later,' said Richard Gere.

And Carmine Sarno answered: 'No, that's not possible. My wife is in Lourdes right now. On a pilgrimage.'

———

'Things like that only happen in Naples,' says Shobha. And please note that the only real question in Italy is what kind of Mafia you can live with most easily – the Sicilian, the Calabrian or the Neapolitan?

I tap the remote control again, turn over and see the domes of Noto cathedral. On a local channel there's a programme about Sicily's baroque town. The presenter is currently raving about how the Sicilian baroque celebrates the moment, movement, the *effimero*; and Shobha and I are only thinking that there's resignation in the air today. And not only in Sicily. In Calabria and Campania too.

While Shobha makes *caponata* in the kitchen, bracelets jangling, I lay the table on the terrace. Here, above the rooftops of Palermo, you can sometimes forget reality. Only recently we spent an evening on the terrace of Marzia Sabella, the Sicilian public prosecutor who led the investigating unit that arrested Bernardo Provenzano. You could have aimed at the terrace from various windows and balconies, but the prosecutor didn't care. From here you can see the sea: that was more important to her. Marzia Sabella had decided not to be frightened.

But when Shobha and I told her about Calabria and Duisburg she shuddered. Calabria makes even Mafia-tested Sicilian prosecutors uneasy. Just as Sicilians sneer at the Neapolitan Camorra. Even the public prosecutors have a certain local patriotism; I often had the feeling that they felt a certain ironic bond with the criminal organization that they fought against every day. The Sicilian public prosecutor thought the Sicilian Cosa Nostra was criminally superior to all other Mafia organizations, at least where its political influence was concerned. The Calabrian public prosecutor thought the Calabrian 'Ndrangheta was nimbler and therefore better equipped for the future in the long term. And the Neapolitan public prosecutor was amused that the Neapolitan Camorristi had always managed to swindle Cosa Nostra whenever they smuggled cigarettes together, regularly failing to share a cargo with them.

In Naples, everyone knows that the Camorra isn't a foreign body but has been part of the city for two hundred years. Today the reality is that a hundred Camorra clans rule the city, and that in 2006 alone one tonne of cocaine and six tonnes of hashish were impounded in Naples – no more than 10 per cent of the drugs traded in Italy, however – while politicians justify the existence of the Camorra as a kind of social shock absorber which keeps public order because it guarantees the survival of whole social classes.

The morality of lawlessness denounced by the judiciary has produced a network of Camorra, contractors and politicians from which all three participants derive great benefits. In economic theory this is known as a win-win situation. The politicians support the Camorra to guarantee themselves votes. And they ally themselves with the contractors in order to enjoy bribes in return for public contracts. The Camorra in turn receives bribes from the businessmen for public contracts, as well as contracts for subcontractors, which enables the Camorra to create jobs and thus assure itself of social legitimacy. And the politicians guarantee the Camorra protection from prosecution by the police and the judiciary.

The benefit to the contractors in this business lies in the fact that by eliminating their competitors they always obtain public contracts, that the safety of building sites is guaranteed, no kind of pressure can be exerted by the trade unions, and the conditions for tax avoidance, slush funds and investments in tax idylls are all in place.

And thanks to its inexhaustible sources of money, the Camorra no longer needs to resort to violence. It operates quite

legally by buying up the market: every espresso drunk in a
cafe is controlled by the Camorra. It dominates the markets
of everyday consumption – meat, mineral water, coffee, dairy
products, cattle feed – without any kind of hygiene control.
Not to mention the waste business.

———

As I'm straightening the chairs on Shobha's terrace, my foot
bumps against something that looks like a stone in the darkness, but reveals itself to be a tortoise: the terrace is home to
two tortoises which have belonged to the family for over forty
years. Shobha likes to talk with them as if she still hasn't
given up hope, even after forty years, that they might one
day reply.

The two tortoises stick out their little pink tongues and
creep towards the food bowl. Mafia wars, murders, blood-
baths and trials drifted across Palermo. The Corleonesi
slaughtered their enemies, they murdered everyone who got
in their way – 'illustrious corpses', as they say in Palermo
when a politician or a civil servant is killed. The Palermo
Spring came and faded; bed sheets bearing the words *Down
with the Mafia!* were hung out and brought back in again.
Giulio Andreotti – 'Uncle Giulio', as the mafiosi called him –
was accused, acquitted and finally sentenced for supporting
the Mafia, a crime that had already lapsed when the sentence
was passed. Cosa Nostra sealed a pact with Berlusconi's Forza
Italia, Onwards Italy! Minister-presidents, senators and mayors were accused of supporting the Mafia and acquitted. And
the two tortoises did nothing but eat bits of chopped apricot,

banana and tomatoes. Organically grown tomatoes – Shobha sets great store by that.

In the distance you can see the harbour, with the ferries that are lit up at night and lie there like whales with their mouths wide open. When I was in Naples, I took a drive through the mountains of containers at the harbour, with two 'falcons', the name given to the plain-clothes policemen who patrol on motorbikes. Since Roberto Saviano's book *Gomorra*, the world knows that the Neapolitan port has no competitors when it comes to the smuggling of forged goods, which are sold in Germany and elsewhere – by Camorristi like the ones in the Licciardi clan, who not only dealt in forged trademarked products, from clothes to drills to cameras, but also in drugs and who, after the fall of the Berlin Wall, extended their area of activity from Germany to Hungary and Poland. When I talked about that with the Neapolitan public prosecutor Franco Roberti, Duisburg came up once again. Duisburg hadn't been a coincidence, the prosecutor said, Germany was just as solid a basis for the Camorra's businesses as it was for those of the 'Ndrangheta, with restaurants and clothes shops used for money laundering.

'In Germany, if you see a Neapolitan or a Calabrian opening a shop, you should take a closer look at where the money comes from,' public prosecutor Roberti said.

———

The traffic snarls up from below, police sirens wail, and even up here on Shobha's balcony Palermo's breath smells of sulphur, dark soil and corruption. And basil, oregano and thyme, all the herbs of the Mediterranean. Shobha has transformed her terrace into a thicket, a thicket of jasmine and bougain-villea, of palms and olive trees, geraniums and little lemon trees. She loves picking off dry leaves, watering and fertiliz-ing. In another life, I'm sure she would have been a gardener.

'And have you seen this Carmine again since?' asks Shobha. The episode with the two financial policemen cheers her up. Is life in Naples tragi-comic? Or is it more that it's tragic and you can only endure it by looking for comedy?

The founder of the Institute for Philosophical Studies in Naples once said to me: 'The low-lifes are still in power, even today. The Camorra are the bourgeoisie of Naples! They're the people that power talks to. The state has no monopoly on force here! The evils of Naples are the evils of Italy! Europe has to get moving! It can't afford to lose Italy!'

Just as the Bourbon King Ferdinand IV of Naples always tried to stay close to the notorious *lazzaroni*, the low-lifes whom he showered with gifts as a way of securing his power, even now Italian politicians are wheeling and dealing with the Camorra in just the same way.

After the financial police had left Carmine's agency with unfinished business, Carmine Sarno had suggested showing me the video that he had had made for the boy who died in the accident. For Francesco Paolillo. Sarno closed up the agency and walked to his car, a silver S-series Mercedes. As we drove past he showed me the chapel of the Madonna dell'Arco, which he had had built between the rows of houses and which looked like a little mosque. A bit further along, at the edge of the road hung the house altar that Carmine Sarno had had built for the dead boy: *For that little blossom that was stolen from the earth to flower in the hands of the Lord.* That was what the inscription said. Signed by the Sarno family.

Sarno quickly climbed the stairs to the Paolillo family's flat. He didn't knock, but stepped inside the flat just as naturally as a king coming to greet his subjects.

The mother had her late son's name tattooed on her lower arm. For months she had slept in a tent at the spot where her son had died, to demonstrate that children have to play in derelict buildings here. At the weekend a sports ground was due to be opened in Ponticelli. It was that mother's victory. Against defeatism, against resignation. Regional president Antonio Bassolino and mayoress Rosa Russo Iervolino had announced their arrival, the dead boy's brother, Alessandro, proudly informed us – a tall, fair, unemployed kid. Neither the regional president nor the mayoress had ever set foot in Ponticelli; it was all down to his mother that the politicians were interested in their fate, he said, and his mother mutely put on the DVD of Sarno's video.

The clip was shot in black and white. Carmine Sarno had seen it thousands of times and still had tears in his eyes at the end. 'Everyone has his feelings,' he said later.

Shobha has turned up the music: David Bowie, 'We can be heroes, just for one day'. The music has startled the tortoises, which are now pretending to be dead. Often when we're travelling in Sicily or Calabria, Shobha and I feel the need to listen to music at deafening volume and sing along. Driving through Brancaccio, Castellamare, Cinisi, through all those Mafia villages with their Padre Pio statues behind glass, with the fat men sitting on plastic chairs lined up at the edge of the street, waiting for their *telefonini* to ring, while we screech 'Is there life on Mars?' Displacement activity? Perhaps. And our only salvation.

Carmine Sarno had arranged to meet me that night. He was accompanying his singer Alessio to various performances around Naples. And I was to be there.

Sarno had discovered Alessio when he was sixteen years old and singing '*Vola cardillo*', the prisoners' hymn to freedom. Now Alessio was the best horse in his stable. Tens of thousands of people cheered him at his concerts in the Teatro Palapartenope, and Alessio couldn't complain about performing as a star guest at family parties and discos. Forty minutes of Alessio cost 1,500 euros, and he could do as many as five performances in a single night.

Carmine Sarno was waiting for me in the car park behind his house. He drove ahead in his silver Mercedes, Alessio followed in a grey van, along with the guitarist, keyboard player, drummer and roadie. Before the tour began, Carmine Sarno distributed Madonnas to his musicians. Keyrings that his wife had brought back from Lourdes. Then he put the lock of the seatbelt into the lock without the belt – so that the alert wouldn't constantly remind him to do himself up. Seatbelts aren't for men like Sarno.

He hurtled through the night at 125 mph, and was in a mind for confessions. About the fact that he was a former gambler, but had overcome that addiction. That after leaving jail he had slept in the car for eight months because he didn't want to go back to his wife at the flat. That apart from his four legitimate children he had two illegitimate ones. That there had only been one turncoat in the Sarno clan – one *infame*, although he wasn't a blood relation. And about the fact that his brother Ciro had got five degrees in jail and was now writing his life story. 'If you see him, you'll think he's a professor,' said Carmine Sarno.

He'd already been offered a transfer fee of 700,000 euros for Alessio, although Sarno had turned it down. Alessio was more than a singer to him, he said.

'It was through me that Alessio was born,' said Carmine Sarno. 'And he will die with me.'

That night Alessio had his first performance as a star guest at Anna Chiara's first communion party, in the Piccolo Paradiso restaurant, where the children had already drunk themselves into a Coca-Cola rush by the time Alessio entered the room. He was twenty-three, wore a retro-style leather jacket, a Rolex on his wrist and a lot of gel in his hair, and said: 'My songs come from my heart.'

The communicant Anna Chiara weighed about twelve and a half stone and wept into her napkin when she saw Alessio. When he started singing, all the females in the room between the ages of eight and eighty started screeching as if the Messiah had suddenly appeared. Twitching ecstatically, they sang along and took photographs with their mobile phones, and the mother of the communicant cried: 'Take him, take him!' – until at last her daughter embraced him with her short, fat arms and kissed him, blushing, on the cheeks. At the end of the concert, Carmine Sarno applauded too, for politeness' sake.

Then we glided on through the night, the moon hung like a bisected disc above a mountain, and Carmine put on his singers' CDs. In the distance you could see the sea, with the moonlight reflected on it. Next stop was the bingo hall in Teverola. Here it was as silent as a church — not a sound apart from the rustle of paper and the creak of the chairs when the winning numbers were read out. It was already midnight when a security man started setting up crowd barriers for Alessio's performance. The security man had mascara on his eyelashes and upper arms like oak trees, and didn't reply when the girls asked him if Alessio had already arrived. The huge hall was completely packed. Fat women, whose bodies spilled like soft mountains over the edges of the chairs, chain-smoked. An orange carpet swallowed the sound of every footstep. Sometimes the women whispered to the moneylenders who ran back and forth like stray dogs between the players' tables.

Bingo halls are Camorra money laundering institutions, although Carmine would never have put it like that — quite the contrary, he felt sorry for the people there, everyone has his feelings after all, he himself had been a gambler, and many of the people who win something here will be robbed when they leave the bingo hall. A woman turned to Carmine, pointed to me and said she knew me off the television. Sarno didn't reply, he just gave a flattered smile. Then Alessio came and a whirlwind swept through the rows of seats, a wave of weeping girls surged against the barriers and it was all the security man with the mascaraed eyelashes could do not to be crushed.

'*Sei bellissimo*,' screamed the girls, 'you're gorgeous,' and Carmine Sarno looked at his watch.

The next morning the sports ground in honour of the late Francesco Paolillo was opened in Ponticelli. When I arrived, there was no sign of Sarno. Presumably he was still sleeping. Or pretending to, because he doesn't like appearing at public events. Listening to politicians' speeches. After all, he knows the politicians better than anyone. He knows how high their price is.

Alessandro, the dead boy's brother, was very excited; he kept running along the seats where his neighbours were all sitting, repeating that the limousines of mayoress Iervolino and the regional president Bassolino would soon be there. The sports ground looked like a cage; it was laid with green artificial lawn and surrounded by high fences. The dead boy's sister delivered a speech inside the cage. 'Francesco, we'll never forget you,' she said, and her mother bit her handkerchief. A single local politician had come; he too delivered a speech in the cage and managed not to use the word Camorra once.

While the speeches were being delivered, Alessandro, the fair-haired, unemployed kid, looked into the street. And then he turned away and said: 'They haven't come again. They'll never come.'

Messina Denaro

When Shobha steps on to the terrace, she's turned herself into a glittering apparition with sparkling earrings, a deep décolleté and coal-black eyes. And pointed shoes. At the end of the day she always needs to get rid of the flat shoes and trousers that she makes herself wear when she's working. Making herself feminine again. Although this time we don't have a sense of having worked at all. It's more as if we'd just taken a walk, like the French and American tourists who walk through Palermo, always slightly anxiously, pressed close to the walls of the houses, in the deluded hope that they won't be recognized as tourists. Whose tour guides do everything they can to ensure that visitors to Sicily think not about fugitive bosses but about the ancient theatre of Segesta, the colonnade of the cathedral of Monreale and the oratory of Santa Cita, where myriads of angels whirr about — the baroque extravagance, the Sicilian excess.

From Shobha's roof terrace you can watch the city getting ready for nightfall. Putting on stars and bathing in moonlight.

The domes of the baroque churches curve triumphantly next
to Palermo's single, rather anorexic-looking skyscraper, and
in the distance the lights gleam from the illegally built
houses on the hill of Mondello. Shobha has uncorked a bottle
of Chardonnay from Planeta; we listen to David Bowie and a
jingling wind chime.

'Trapani,' says Shobha, after she has tasted the wine.
Strange, it tastes like Trapani. The sea and wisteria. The way
it smelled in the morning when we used to go to processions.

I hold the wine under my nose, close my eyes and try to
smell Trapani. I actually smell jasmine, rosemary and oregano. A hint of wisteria. Perhaps some salt in the air, and,
if I put my mind to it, I can also smell a bit of myrrh. For
years we took a pilgrimage to the Good Friday procession of
Trapani, *La processione dei misteri.* We set off from Palermo
at night and drove, drunk with sleep, down the autostrada
to reach Trapani at dawn. We parked the car in the harbour
and walked shivering through the night air, always heading
towards the funeral march. You could hear the music from a
long way away, music that sounded beautiful and skewed and
grabbed our hearts in its clutches.

When we got there, the faithful had already been following the penitential procession for hours. Men in dark suits
carried the enormously heavy stations of the cross: Christ before Pilate, the scourging, the crown of thorns, the raising of
the cross, the entombment, the mother of sorrows. Each time
the bearers set down the bier, lit with incandescent bulbs, for
a few minutes, they passed around bottles wrapped in brown
paper, and the women leaned against a house wall, closed

their eyes and murmured the rosary to keep from falling asleep. '*Santa Maria, Madre di Dio, prega per noi peccatori.*' As day palely dawned, the world stood still for a moment. Just long enough for the music to start again and the sea on the horizon to colour itself pink.

We felt intoxicated. Shobha photographed angels, Roman legionnaires in shimmering gold armour, brides of Christ and little girls carrying the crown of thorns through the streets on purple velvet cushions. She photographed mothers holding their handbags in front of them like protective shields, she photographed the notables in their sashes, all the presidents who take very small, important steps – *president della confraternità dei pescatori, president dell'associazione SS. Crocefisso, president della società sanguinis Christi* – and I walked behind the brass bands with my tape recorder, in search of funeral marches. '*Una lacrima sulla tomba di mia madre*' remains my favourite funeral march, 'A Tear on my Mother's Grave' – Chopin, Op. 32, with the tuba at the beginning, the tremolo clarinet and the trumpets which, when they come in, sound as if the funeral march is about to turn into a piece of dance music.

The climax of the procession was reached when the stations of the cross were carried back into the Chiesa delle Anime del Purgatorio in the early afternoon: a finale like a never-ending act of coitus, the church struggling against it doggedly and without success. With seeming hesitancy, the individual groups of figures were carried in and out through the portal of the church, rocking back and forth, amidst applause, a rain of rose petals and out-of-tune trumpet entries. Inside the church it looked as if a weary travelling circus had collapsed: on the floor, amidst damp sawdust and crushed blossoms, the bearers sat blank-faced, others hugged and wept with exhaustion — whether it was the exertion of carrying things for hours, or the contents of the bottles in their brown-paper wrappings, everything was discharged in a collective crying fit, the men wiped the tears from their eyes with white damask handkerchiefs, and we wept along too.

And just a day later Trapani was as forbidding as ever. With gleaming light and a landscape buried under concrete.

———

'Strange, isn't it?' says Shobha, sniffing the wine again. 'At some point I lost the desire to go there,' she says.

Was it that moment when the part-time photographers and amateur film directors gained the upper hand and kept walking into the picture? Or when, still in Trapani, we went in search of the boss Matteo Messina Denaro? At some point we lost the procession virus. Like a scab under which new skin has formed.

'Trapani,' says Shobha, sticks her nose back in the wine glass and adds: 'Have you heard about the murals?'

'What murals?' I ask, really thinking about art for a moment.

'Murals of Messina Denaro,' says Shobha. In the style of Warhol. With the inscription *You'll be hearing from me.* They appeared in Palermo and in Messina Denaro's place of birth, Castelvetrano, not far from Trapani. 'The police investigated,' Shobha says and smiles ironically. The murals were immediately painted over.

Messina Denaro is a kind of icon among mafiosi. When investigators or public prosecutors talk about Messina Denaro, there's a hint of respect for their opponent. Investigators see Messina Denaro as the boss with the greatest political foresight. In his case the word *latitante*, fugitive, has a different ring: it sounds like a mark of distinction, like an accolade, a higher Mafia qualification.

Certainly it's the case that hunters would rather go after a tiger than a rabbit. Particularly since most bosses are more like rabbits. Powerful rabbits, admittedly, but rabbits nevertheless. So it's all the more striking when a boss like Matteo Messina Denaro moves around the world as if it belonged to him – not least since he has slipped the Mafia's moral straitjacket and consolidated his position as a ladies' man, defying the Sicilian proverb that giving orders is better than fucking. Messina Denaro has proved that you can do both. When he was in hiding he even managed to father an illegitimate daughter, who is now ten years old, has never seen her father and lives in her grandmother's house in Castelvetrano – along with her mother who, as long as she lives, will never look another man in the eye. To keep from damaging the boss's reputation. And to protect her own life. If a mafioso loses face as a result of his wife's infidelity, she is as good as dead.

The Mafia revere Matteo Messina Denaro as a saint: 'I'd love to be able to see him, touch him, just once,' they sigh on the telephone, as if they dreamed of dabbing kisses on the hem of the Madonna's robe with their fingertips. 'Everything good comes from him,' the mafiosi whisper, 'we must worship him.'

His nickname is 'Diabolik', the name of an Italian comic character, an elegant gangster who lives in the grand style from his jewel robberies: a representative of evil who always maintains a certain code of honour. Diabolik basically only robs rich people from the top levels of society — although the similarity to Robin Hood stops there, because you couldn't exactly say that he shares his booty with the poor. It's more that evil triumphs with him in a world of weak supermen, as the mafiosi imagine the world to be in their idle moments — idle moments when they believe the singer Vasco Rossi's hymn to the fearless life, 'the exaggerated life, the life full of troubles'. Idle moments when they manage to fade out reality as if it were a film: the reality in which they smell of fear because they're next on the hit man's list, a hit man who boasts that he's never worn gloves when dissolving corpses in hydro-chloric acid; the reality that consists in throttling a friend, beheading and castrating him, and stuffing his genitals in his mouth. The reality is one in which children can be kept for years in an underground dungeon, like little Giuseppe di Matteo, who was locked up in a cell in San Giuseppe Jato until he was strangled and dissolved in acid.

Giuseppe's father had become a turncoat and the abduction of his son was supposed to keep him quiet. At the end of his imprisonment, the boy had been reduced to nothing but a 'human larva', said the mafioso who had been given the job of strangling him.

All the more important are the miracle stories about

Messina Denaro, of whom the mafiosi couldn't get enough: about how he is supposed to have driven an Alfa 164 armed with machine guns which could be activated by the push of a button from the driver's seat; how he boasted that he could fill a cemetery with his victims; how he guarded the treasure of the arrested boss Totò Riina, a treasure that consisted not only of jewellery but also of the Mafia archive, and how he had hidden with that treasure in an underground flat in a jeweller's shop in Castelvetrano, entered via a strongroom with a lift built into it.

It's a long time since Cosa Nostra produced such a pop star.

———

Matteo Messina Denaro comes from Castelvetrano and in the police files his profession is given as 'farmer'. He is what people here call an 'artist's son': his father Francesco was one of the most powerful bosses of Cosa Nostra, a member of the *cupola*, the Mafia council. Both Matteo Messina Denaro and his brother Salvatore, as well as his father Francesco, were on the payroll of one of the richest families in Trapani, the family of the Forza Italia senator and current president of the province of Trapani, Antonio D'Alì, a large landowner, banker and businessman – Matteo and his father as estate managers, his brother Salvatore as a clerk in the family-owned bank.

'No one had any idea of Messina Denaro's involvement with the Mafia,' the senator said. And he sued anyone who claimed otherwise – like the two Rai journalists who accused the provincial president of being behind the transfer of a prefect who was unacceptable to the Mafia.

At Trapani police headquarters we met the investigator who has been on Messina Denaro's trail for years. The office was papered with newspaper cuttings about arrests, next to it there hung a faded list of the names of mafiosi currently in hiding. Matteo Messina Denaro was the last on the list. There was even a hint of respect in the investigator's voice when he spoke of the boss: 'If you met Messina Denaro, you'd like him,' he said. 'Messina Denaro is generous, he's an effortless conversationalist and he can judge the *perlage* of a fine champagne.'

Finally, a cosmopolitan boss.

Then the investigator called one of his men who did nothing more than listen in on suspicious conversations, using a mobile surveillance device, and record unusual movements, in Messina Denaro's birthplace of Castelvetrano. The investigator was waiting for us in a car park just outside the town, a bearded man in jeans and trainers. What drives these men isn't money, it's a hunting instinct. The thrill when they catch a boss in his sleep after lying in wait for him for months, disguised as an Albanian, as a gypsy, as a grass-mowing peasant. For a long time it didn't occur to any of the men to claim overtime.

When we were driving through Castelvetrano, we had the impression of driving through a town where nothing ever happens; you couldn't even hear a dog barking. The houses with the closed shutters looked like lockers. You avoided people's eyes, as if they could pass on an infectious illness.

'They're all friends here,' said the policeman, and drove past Messina Denaro's parents' house, where his mother, his partner and their daughter live. It was in an alley not far from the church. A run-down-looking, three-storey house, and the policeman cried: 'Whatever you do, don't take a photograph!' Just as he was constantly warning us not to write this and that because Messina Denaro was extremely sensitive where his family was concerned – until finally I wondered how dangerous could it be to write that Francesco Messina Denaro's mausoleum is a high, narrow chapel with a glass mosaic Christ, locked with a cast-iron gate, flanked by two *Ficus benjamina* trees which, as the policeman observed, had recently been watered?

Messina Denaro's mother visited the grave every day, dressed in black even ten years after her husband's death. She often went there with her three daughters. On one occasion, the police had hidden bugs in the grave to listen to the dialogue that she liked to have with her husband. Unfortunately, one of the policemen hadn't put one of the vases back in the right place. Messina Denaro would never forgive those sons of bitches that impious act of eavesdropping.

By the time his father died ten years ago, Matteo Messina Denaro had been underground for a long time. The boss Francesco Messina Denaro had died of a heart attack, presumably the result of the fury unleashed by the recent arrest of his eldest son, Salvatore. Someone had carefully laid the corpse beside a vineyard in Castelvetrano, dressed in a silk dressing gown. When the body was found, it had already rained on the body. His wife tore off her own Persian lamb coat to wrap her dead husband in it. And at the funeral she threw herself on the coffin and cried: 'At least they didn't manage to put handcuffs on you!'

The Messina Denaro family commemorates the day of his death every year, not just with a religious service, but also with an obituary, most recently in Latin: 'There is no time to be born and to die, but only he who wants to can fly. And for ever your flight was the highest.' The investigators assumed that this might be a coded message. But it was only a statement of faith – in blood, in family, in the Mafia.

Of course, it may be that the boss doesn't live in Sicily at all but in Venezuela or Colombia, somewhere in South America – unlike the other Sicilian bosses, who are always tracked down only a few miles from their own territory. But.

But even an icon could drop his guard in his own territory, the investigator said. A young mafioso had to have seen the boss at least once. Otherwise his magic would flee.

To kiss the hem of the Madonna's robe, just once.

———

'You remember how run-down the house of Messina Denaro's family looked?' I say to Shobha, as she serves the *caponata*.

Messina Denaro's house had dirty white walls and frosted glass in the windows. Clearly it was designed to give the lie to any thoughts of a worldwide Mafia organization. As if the Mafia was still controlled by a handful of shepherds. As if the Mafia wasn't a social and political problem, but just an occasional inconvenience to public order.

Would the children of the mafiosi, the ones who have

studied — maybe even at the London School of Economics, as the children of some Catania bosses are said to do — live in rickety-looking houses like that today? Shobha asks.

Again and again, I'm struck by the discrepancy between the pointed frugality and the vast incomes of the Mafia bosses. Mafia families have every interest in not standing out, in being accepted as part of society — that's their shield, and their strength at the same time. Give or take their millions, the foundation of all Mafia power remains their rootedness in social consensus.

Here too, protection money has a fundamental part to play. Above all, it's about a demonstration of power when superglue is squeezed into the greengrocer's lock to make the urgency of the payment quite clear. If a mafioso leaves a bomb outside a shop, it's reported in all the papers. But if he squirts superglue into fifty locks, nobody hears about it. And the Mafia don't want to appear in the papers, they just want to get on with their business in peace.

One of the biggest Mafia bosses of recent years was the doctor Giuseppe Guttadauro, the brother-in-law of Matteo Messina Denaro. He received patients in his surgery from five till seven in the evening, and from seven onwards the *picciotti*, the lowest-ranking mafiosi, and gave them orders about collecting protection money. And this wasn't just about filling the war coffers of Cosa Nostra; more importantly, it was about control, about demonstrating presence, marking territory.

Sometimes in Palermo you see little black-rimmed stickers on waste bins: *Un intero popolo che paga il pizzo è un popolo senza dignità*, A whole people that pays protection

money is a people without dignity. These are the stickers of
the Addiopizzo organization, which developed out of a student
group and now calls for a revolt against paying protection
money to the Mafia. Thanks to this organization, the Italian
business association has finally summoned the courage to exclude those businessmen who pay protection money. Sicilian
public prosecutors, on the other hand, urged the association
to exclude from its ranks those businessmen who had already
been legally punished for supporting the Mafia. Because they
were the real criminals, while a businessman who doesn't report the extortion of protection money is just someone who
lacks moral courage. However, many Sicilian businessmen
had an interest in ensuring that everything stayed as it was:
what's at stake, after all, is millions in European funding, the
benefits of which they want to go on enjoying, thanks to the
Mafia. After all, it is a long time since the Mafia was content
to extort 500 euros in protection money. For ages now it had
been sitting in the businessmen's drawing rooms. In Calabria,
even northern Italian businessmen don't report the extortion
of protection money by the 'Ndrangheta, but take the protection money into account: as a 'security cost'. After all, you don't
want to turn down big public contracts, like the construction
of the Salerno–Reggio motorway. The companies pay 3 per
cent of the contract fee directly to the 'Ndrangheta.

————

Because it's late now, I decide to say a quick goodbye to Letizia
before she gets ready for bed. When I go downstairs to her
flat, I hear that she's watching television. Giulio Andreotti

is a guest on a talk show again. When Letizia notices my footsteps, she turns off the television. Then she picks up a box of household matches and tries to relight her cigarette in the wind from the ceiling fan. It takes her three matches before the cigarette is finally burning. She could have got up and lit it somewhere else. But that wouldn't be her way.

'You know, I'd really love to escape from Palermo. If my grandchildren didn't live here, I'd get out. It's too painful, it's too humiliating, to watch our values being co-opted here. The bad guys have even taken over the anti-Mafia movement. On the anniversaries of Falcone and Borsellino's killings, the whole of Palermo was full of posters saying *Our heroes forever!* Signed by none other than the city administration of Palermo.'

'The bad guys'. I like Letizia's direct way of putting it. The ceiling fan cuts through the smoke, and I'm thinking about the Forza Italia caste which has triumphed in Palermo when Letizia says that even the Italian left won't come to the rescue, because it's sold its soul to Berlusconi.

'In the past, the left-wing ideal was like a warming blanket to me,' she says. 'Now it no longer exists. Or only among a very few young people. The ones in *Antimafia Duemila*, perhaps, the anti-Mafia newspaper. But otherwise? Nothing.'

Letizia bends down to me and asks if I've got enough material for my article about her, urges me to call her if there's anything else I want to know, tells me about the next exhibition that she and Shobha are having together in China – even in China people are interested in the Mafia, just not in Palermo. Then she looks over at the terrace door. The night wind runs through her hair.

'They've thrown our dreams in the sea,' she says, 'and their own as well.'

———

The sky over Palermo shimmers as if the stars were constantly being turned on and off in the firmament. It's still hot and sultry, a warm damp settles on our arms. Because Salvo's off duty, Shobha has called a taxi, but even after half an hour the woman on the switchboard can do nothing but console me. 'Patience, you need to have patience,' she says, until I decide to try my luck on foot. Shobha suggests coming with me. When we step out of the cool entrance hall of the building and into the street, petrol-filled air hits us, air that stings the lungs and would prompt a choking attack in any asthmatic. Although midnight is long past, the traffic is just as solid as it was in the morning. The nighthawks flit from one side of the road to the other like a swarm of mosquitoes. The marble pavement gleams as if it's sweating. We walk towards Via della Libertà, and those posters with the famous photograph of Giovanni Falcone and Paolo Borsellino. *Our heroes*. The city of Palermo.

As we cross the piazza in front of the Teatro Politeama, little purple dots gleam on the marble paving stones and the air suddenly smells of lemon verbena. And cooking fat. On every street corner there are vans selling fried calves' cheeks between two slices of bread, or bread with spleen. Our pace assumes the rhythm of the revellers hurrying towards Piazza Olivella. The flower sellers who tout their wares by day are still standing on the pavement in front of the Teatro

Massimo, and a newspaper vendor has spread out his piles of papers next to them.

We walk on without saying anything, our footsteps hammer on the marble. There are no taxis outside the Teatro Massimo either. So we walk on before turning off at last into one of the twisting alleys near the Piazza Olivella, where the gas-canister filler Nino sits by the door to his shop. Shobha lived opposite him for a while, so Nino greets her particularly warmly. As usual, his whole family has assembled beside him on white plastic chairs: his wife with her toothless mouth, his fat sister, his children, one grandchild and his gaunt brother-in-law who runs a cobbler's shop next door. They all sit there with their hands folded over their bellies, as if watching the performance of a play, while cats poke among the rubbish on the other side of the street.

It's quieter at the end of Via Patania. We walk on, now along the Via Roma, past the Piazza San Domenico, where, as always, a few Nigerian prostitutes lurk, and past the steps that lead to the Vucciria market and which, even at night, smell of fish guts. Here there are no revellers and our footsteps echo. A wind blows up. From the walls and palisades that support the derelict *palazzi*, it tugs at the posters. We walk on.

———

By way of farewell, Salvo puts on Antonacci again, 'Dream of me if it snows'. 'But just for you, Petra, I don't understand what women see in him.'

We drive out of town, past palm trees and box hedges, past the enamelled domes of the churches, past street after street of air-raid-shelter tower blocks which look as if they might harbour life, past the dry leaves of the rubber trees blown by the wind on to the pavements.

At last we drive on to the motorway, towards Trapani, towards the *Aeroporto Falcone e Borsellino*: it's still called that, for how long? On our right the Isola delle Femmine bathes in the morning light. 'They have thrown our dreams in the sea, and their own as well.'

I think of Montalbano — Saverio Montalbano, whom I met on my first assignment, the policeman who was once responsible for tracking down fugitive mafiosi as part of the mobile task force, and who discovered the 'pizza connection'. Recently I met up with him over coffee and biscuits. He looked unchanged, which may have had something to do with the fact that Montalbano, with his bald patch and his silver-grey fringe of hair, had never looked young. The only change was a thin-rimmed pair of reading glasses, over which he looked at me ironically. As always, he asked how I managed to live in a city that consisted only of water. As a respectable Sicilian, he said, he feared the sea.

Montalbano was on the point of retirement. His last job had been as head of the local police of Termini Imerese. Before that, he had been head of the administrative police of Ragusa; he had been kept as far as possible from Mafia investigations. One day he had received an anonymous letter. In it someone expressed his admiration for him: 'I like the real Montalbano better than the one in the film.' The letter was signed 'Diabolik'.

Eventually he had decided no longer to address the subject

of the Mafia, Montalbano said. 'I fell out of love,' he says. He stopped reading the reports about arrests. Now he read books about Indians.

———

Salvo carries my case to the check-in desk, where a long queue has formed as usual. He kisses me goodbye on both cheeks and expresses his regret at not being able to wait with me, but his ladies need to play their first game of the morning. But he hopes to see me again soon in Palermo. Then he hurries across the departure lounge. Before he steps outside he briefly waves to me again. When I turn around, the very same man who sat next to me on the outbound flight is standing right beside me.

'I'll talk to him now,' I say to myself. But he's ahead of me. He smiles at me. And says in an American accent: 'Nice to see you again.'

Dramatis Personæ

Pietro Aglieri – Sicilian Mafia boss, member of the council
of Cosa Nostra; serving a life sentence since 1997 for,
among other things, his involvement in the murders
of the public prosecutors Giovanni Falcone and Paolo
Borsellino.

Giulia Alvaro – Member of the Nirta-Strangio clan, the
clan involved in the Duisburg massacre; arrested in 2007
for membership of the Mafia and involvement in the
international drugs trade.

Giuliano Amato – Italian politician, former Socialist,
several times prime minister, foreign minister and most
recently minister of the interior in the second Prodi
government (2006–08).

Giulio Andreotti – Italian Christian Democrat, seven times
prime minister; indicted for favouring the Mafia and

convicted in May 2003, his support for the Mafia judged to be proven until 1980 and spent thereafter — there was insufficient proof for further conviction.

Giovanna Atria — Mother of Rita Atria, the teenager who spoke out against the Mafia in her village.

Rita Atria — Daughter of a Sicilian Mafia boss, who decided, after the murder of her father and brother, to collaborate with the judicial system, was rejected by her mother and, after the murder of public prosecutor Paolo Borsellino in 1992, threw herself out of a window.

Gaetano 'Don Tano' Badalamenti — Mafia boss from the Sicilian Cinisi clan; built up the 'pizza connection', the heroin trade between Sicily and America; died of heart failure in 2004 in an American prison, at the age of eighty and without ever saying a word about the Mafia.

Antonietta 'Ninetta' Bagarella — Wife of the Sicilian Mafia boss Salvatore 'Totò' Riina, daughter of an old Corleone Mafia family; lived underground with her husband for almost twenty years, bearing him four children with whom she returned to Corleone after his arrest in 1993.

Leoluca Bagarella — Sicilian Mafia boss of the Corleone clan, hit man responsible for the deaths of hundreds of people, brother of Ninetta Bagarella and brother-in-law of the Mafia boss Totò Riina; in prison since 1995.

Agata Barresi – Sicilian mother of five sons murdered by the Mafia, famous for maintaining her silence.

Antonio Bassolino – Democratic Left regional president of Campania until 2010, who fell into disrepute for nepotism and his responsibility for the waste crisis.

Letizia Battaglia – Internationally award-winning Sicilian photographer and publisher, city councillor for quality of life under Leoluca Orlando in Palermo; later, member of the anti-Mafia party La Rete in the Sicilian parliament.

Piersilvio Berlusconi – Son of Silvio Berlusconi, now director of his father's private broadcasting group, Mediaset.

Silvio Berlusconi – Three times Italian prime minister, the wealthiest businessman in Italy, founder of the Forza Italia party, now known as Popolo della Libertà (People of Freedom); variously indicted for tax avoidance, false accounting, collaboration with a Mafia association, bribery of judges, complicity in assassination attempts – accusations that ended in acquittal, cases dropped because of the statute of limitations or lack of evidence, or convictions that were later subject to an amnesty.

Salvatore Boemi – Leading senior public prosecutor in the anti-Mafia investigative authority of Reggio Calabria.

Stefano Bontade – Mafia boss from Corleone, known as the 'Prince of Villagrazia', known to have had connections with notable Italian politicians including Silvio Berlusconi; murdered in 1981.

Paolo Borsellino – Legendary anti-Mafia public prosecutor in the Palermo Anti-Mafia Pool; murdered by the Mafia in 1992.

Tommaso Buscetta – Sicilian Mafia boss and the first significant turncoat in the history of Cosa Nostra, an important witness in the maxi-trials against the Mafia under Giovanni Falcone; died in New York in 2000.

Giuseppe 'Pippo' Calò – Sicilian Mafia boss, also known as the 'Mafia's cashier', thought to have murdered the banker Roberto Calvi but acquitted of the charge in 2007; serving a life sentence.

Roberto Calvi – Italian bank employee, involved not only in money laundering for the Mafia but also in secret financial operations by the Vatican, which won him the nickname 'God's banker'; found murdered in London in 1982.

Diego Cammarata – Mayor of Palermo until 2012, Forza Italia (Popolo della Libertà) MP.

Francesco Campanella – Turncoat Sicilian mafioso, who had as groomsmen at his wedding the former Sicilian prime minister Salvatore 'Totò' Cuffaro and the former Italian justice minister Clemente Mastella – and whose statements seriously incriminated Cuffaro.

Salvatore Cancemi – Turncoat Sicilian Mafia boss; because of his statements, Marcello Dell'Utri and Silvio Berlusconi were accused of complicity in the assassinations of public prosecutors Falcone and Borsellino – the charges were dropped in 2002.

Mario Carabetta – President of Pro Loco (consortium of local tourist offices) in the Calabrian town of San Giovanni di Gerace.

Michele Carabetta – 'Ndranghetista from San Luca, member of the Pelle-Vottari clan, arrested after investigations into the Duisburg massacre.

Sonia Carabetta – Sister of the 'Ndranghetista Michele Carabetta.

Antonio 'Ninni' Cassarà – Deputy leader of the mobile task force of the Palermo police, a close colleague of the public prosecutor Giovanni Falcone; murdered by the Mafia in 1985.

Carlo Alberto Dalla Chiesa – Chief of police in Palermo; he and his wife were murdered by the Mafia in 1982.

Vito Ciancimino – Mafia boss, Christian Democrat and former mayor of Palermo; sentenced to thirteen years' imprisonment for assistance to the Mafia; died in 2002.

Gaetano Cinà – Businessman from Palermo, mafioso from the Malaspina family, co-defendant in the trial against Marcello Dell'Utri; according to the indictment, a bagman between the Mafia and Berlusconi; died 2006.

Bruno Contrada – Formerly the third most senior member of the Italian domestic intelligence agency; arrested in 1992 on suspicion of having passed on to the Mafia the information needed to assassinate the public prosecutor Giovanni Falcone; in jail since 2007.

Don Agostino Coppola – Parish priest from Carini in Sicily, accused of supporting the Mafia; died while under house arrest.

Renato Cortese – Leader of the mobile task force of Reggio Calabria, previously in the mobile task force of Palermo; arrested the boss Bernardo Provenzano in 2006.

Gaetano Costa – Leading public prosecutor of Palermo; murdered by the Mafia in 1980.

Rita Costa – Widow of the murdered public prosecutor Gaetano Costa.

Maurizio Costanzo – Italian journalist and talk-show host; subject to an assassination attempt in 1993 for his commitment against the Mafia.

Carla Cottone – Wife of Aldo Madonia, youngest son of the notorious Madonia Mafia clan.

Bettino Craxi – Former head of the Italian Socialist Party and former Italian prime minister, known as the 'Lord of Bribes'; sentenced to twenty years' imprisonment for deception, corruption and illegal party financing, which he escaped by fleeing to Tunisia where he died in 2000.

Salvatore 'Totò' Cuffaro – Christian Democrat and former Sicilian regional president; sentenced to five years' imprisonment for favouring the Mafia; then a senator, in jail since 2011.

Antonio D'Alì – Forza Italia (Popolo della Libertà) senator and current president of the senate environment commission, Sicilian businessman and owner of the Sicula Bank, former president of the Sicilian province of Trapani and temporary employer of the Mafia bosses Francesco and Matteo Messina Denaro.

Marcello Dell'Utri – Forza Italia (Popolo della Libertà) senator and former MEP, Berlusconi's right-hand man; sentenced to nine years' imprisonment in December 2004 for supporting the Mafia.

Richard Dewes – Former Thuringian interior minister.

Rocco Dicillo – Bodyguard of Giovanni Falcone; murdered by the Mafia in 1992 along with Falcone.

Emanuele Di Filippo – Turncoat Sicilian mafioso.

Pasquale Di Filippo – Brother of Emanuele Di Filippo, also a turncoat.

Rosalba Di Gregorio – Mafia lawyer in Palermo, defender of many Cosa Nostra bosses including Vittorio Mangano, Silvio Berlusconi's so-called 'stable-keeper'.

Baldassare Di Maggio – Turncoat Sicilian Mafia boss, incriminating witness in the Andreotti trial, testified to the kiss between Andreotti and the boss Totò Riina.

Giovanni Falcone – Legendary Sicilian anti-Mafia public prosecutor, led the maxi-trials against Cosa Nostra; murdered by the Mafia in 1992.

Nino Fasullo – Anti-Mafia priest, Redemptorist padre and editor of the journal *Segno*.

Giuseppe Fava – Younger brother of the turncoat Sicilian
mafioso Marcello Fava.

Marcello Fava – Turncoat Sicilian mafioso, formerly a
member of the Porta Nuova clan in Palermo.

Joseph Focoso – Sicilian mafioso and multiple hit man;
arrested in Saarland and handed over to Italy in 2005.

Francesco Fortugno – Calabrian regional politician;
murdered by the 'Ndrangheta in Locri in 2005.

Padre Mario Frittitta – Carmelite monk from Palermo,
temporarily arrested for favouring the Mafia, then
released again.

Calogero Ganci – Turncoat Sicilian mafioso, multiple hit
man and murderer of his own father-in-law.

Madame Gennet – Real name Ganat Tewelde Barhe,
Eritrean people-trafficker.

Elisa Giorgi – Sister of Francesco Giorgi, the youngest
victim of the Duisburg massacre, daughter of Don Pino
Strangio's cousin.

Francesco Giorgi – Youngest victim of the Duisburg
massacre.

Antonino Giuffrè – Turncoat Sicilian mafioso; until his
arrest in 2002, seen as the number two in Cosa Nostra,
after the godfather Bernardo Provenzano.

Boris Giuliano – Leader of the mobile task force of the
Palermo police, discovered the heroin trade between Sicily
and America; murdered by the Mafia in 1979.

Libero Grassi – Sicilian businessman who publicly refused
to pay protection money; murdered by the Mafia in 1991.

Nicola Gratteri – Leading public prosecutor of the Anti-
Mafia investigation unit in Reggio Calabria, in charge of
the investigations surrounding the Duisburg massacre.

Filippo and Giuseppe Graviano – Arrested Sicilian Mafia
bosses from Palermo's suburb of Brancaccio, ordered the
murder of the anti-Mafia priest Padre Puglisi.

Michele Greco – Sicilian Mafia boss, known as 'the Pope'
because of his important role as a mediator between the
individual clans of Cosa Nostra; died in prison in 2008.

Salvatore Grigoli – Sicilian mafioso; shot the anti-Mafia
priest Padre Puglisi in 1993.

Giuseppe Guttadauro – Surgeon and mafioso from Palermo,
who has excellent contacts with Sicilian politicians and
businessmen, one of the 'new' faces of Cosa Nostra.

Rosa Russo Iervolino – Mayor of Naples, notable for introducing a smoking ban in the city's parks.

Enrico Incognito – Mafioso from Bronte, near Catania, who was shot by his brother Marcello to prevent him becoming a turncoat.

Marcello Incognito – Mafioso and murderer of his brother Enrico.

Antonio Ingroia – Leading senior public prosecutor with the anti-Mafia investigating authority in Palermo, amongst other things presided over the trial of Marcello Dell'Utri.

Mario Lavorato – Calabrian pizza-chef in Stuttgart, known as a friend of the former Minister-President Oettinger, accused of being a member of the 'Ndranghetista; since acquitted due to insufficient evidence.

Monsignore Liggio – Parish priest in Corleone, cousin of the legendary Mafia boss Luciano Liggio.

Luciano Liggio – Mafia boss and multiple hit man from Corleone, until his arrest in 1974 head of the Corleone clan; began a painting career in prison and died there in 1993.

Salvo Lima – Christian Democrat and Giulio Andreotti's 'proconsul' in Sicily; murdered by the Mafia in 1992.

Guido Lo Forte – Leading senior public prosecutor with the anti-Mafia investigation unit in Palermo, prosecutor in the Andreotti trial.

Salvatore Lo Piccolo – Sicilian Mafia boss; until his arrest in late 2007, seen as the successor to Bernardo Provenzano.

Pietro Lunardi – Former minister for infrastructure and transport (2001–06).

Aldo Madonia – Youngest son of the Madonia Mafia clan.

Francesco Madonia – Father of Aldo Madonia, boss of Palermo's Madonia Mafia clan, member of the council of Cosa Nostra.

Nino Mandalà – Sicilian Mafia boss from Villabate, well known for his good contacts with businessmen and politicians, the face of Sicily's 'new' Mafia.

Giuseppina Manganaro – Wife of a Sicilian turncoat mafioso.

Cinzia Mangano – Middle daughter of the Mafia boss Vittorio Mangano.

Loredana Mangano – Eldest daughter of the Mafia boss Vittorio Mangano.

Marina Mangano – Youngest daughter of the Mafia boss Vittorio Mangano.

Vittorio Mangano – Sicilian Mafia boss, known as 'Berlusconi's stable-keeper', who lived in the businessman's villa; died in prison in 2000.

Francesco Marino Mannoia – Turncoat Sicilian mafioso of the Santa Maria di Gesù clan, state witness in the Andreotti trial.

Franco Marasà-Di Gregorio – Mafia lawyer in Palermo, husband of Rosalba Di Gregorio, defender of the Mafia boss Bernardo Provenzano.

Vincenzina Marchese – Sister-in-law of the Mafia boss Totò Riina and wife of the boss Leoluca Bagarella.

Marco Marmo – 'Ndranghetista, victim of the Duisburg massacre and killer of Maria Strangio, wife of the 'Ndranghetista Giovanni Nirta.

Clemente Mastella – Justice minister in the second Prodi government (until 2006).

Piersanti Mattarella – Christian Democrat and regional present of Sicily; murdered in 1980 because of his fight against the Mafia.

Leonardo Messina – Turncoat Sicilian mafioso, worked closely with the public prosecutor Paolo Borsellino.

Francesco Messina Denaro – Mafia boss from Castelvetrano, member of the council of Cosa Nostra, father of the fugitive boss Matteo Messina Denaro; died in hiding in 1998.

Matteo Messina Denaro – Mafia boss of the province of Trapani, son of the godfather Francesco Messina Denaro and probable successor to the Mafia boss Provenzano; in hiding since 1993.

Salvatore Messina Denaro – Brother of the Mafia boss Matteo Messina Denaro, son of Francesco Messina Denaro.

Gianfranco Miccichè – Former Forza Italia (Popolo della Libertà) MP and former president of the Sicilian regional assembly.

Rolf Milser – Former German weightlifter.

Saverio Montalbano – Former leader of the mobile task force of Trapani and 'pizza connection' investigator, now retired.

Antonio Montinaro – Bodyguard of Giovanni Falcone; murdered along with Falcone in 1992.

Nino Mormino – Forza Italia (Popolo della Libertà) MP and defender of Marcello Dell'Utri and Salvatore Cuffaro.

Francesca Morvillo – Wife of the anti-Mafia public prosecutor Giovanni Falcone; murdered with her husband in 1992.

Gioacchino Natoli – Leading public prosecutor with the anti-Mafia investigation unit in Palermo.

Michele Navarra – Doctor and Mafia boss in Corleone; murdered in 1958 by his foster-son, Luciano Liggio.

Giovanni Luca 'Gianluca' Nirta – Head of the Calabrian Nirta-Strangio clan from San Luca, widower of Maria Strangio; killed in the Christmas 2006 attack that was intended to kill her husband.

Günther Oettinger – Former minister-president of the German state of Baden-Württemberg. Now Commissioner for Energy in the European Commission.

Leoluca Orlando – Former mayor of Palermo and former leader of the opposition in the Sicilian assembly.

Anna Palma – Anti-Mafia public prosecutor from Palermo, now on the anti-Mafia commission in Rome; she worked for Renato Schifani, President of the Italian senate and Popolo della Libertà MP.

Alessandro Paolillo – Brother of Francesco Paolillo, the boy who died while playing in a derelict building in Ponticelli.

Francesco Paolillo – Boy who died while playing in a derelict building in the Naples suburb of Ponticelli.

Roberto Pannunzi – 'Ndranghetista with strong connections to the Colombian drugs cartel, father of Alessandro Pannunzi, with whom he was arrested in 2004.

Antonio Pelle – Calabrian businessman in Duisburg, originally from San Luca, proprietor of the Landhaus Milser.

Giuseppe Pelle – Head of the Pelle-Vottari clan from San Luca, arrested on charges of Mafia membership.

Spartaco Pitanti – Italian businessman, former proprietor of the Paganini restaurant in Erfurt.

Father Vincenzo Pizzitola – Parish priest in Corleone.

Romano Prodi – President of the Democratic Party, several times Italian prime minister, most recently until 2008.

Angelo Provenzano – Son of the Mafia boss Bernardo Provenzano; imprisoned in 2006.

Bernardo Provenzano — Formerly the most wanted Mafia boss, successor to Totò Riina as head of Cosa Nostra; arrested in Corleone after forty-three years of hide-and-seek.

Padre Giuseppe Puglisi — Anti-Mafia priest in the Brancaccio suburb of Palermo; murdered by the Mafia in 1993.

Rosario 'Saruzzo' Riccobono — Mafia boss of the Partanna-Mondello clan, member of Cosa Nostra council; murdered by his enemy Totò Riina in 1982.

Giovanni Riina — Eldest son of the Sicilian Mafia boss Totò Riina.

Giuseppe Riina — Youngest son of Mafia boss Totò Riina.

Salvatore 'Totò' Riina — Mafia boss from Corleone, for a time sole ruler of Cosa Nostra, responsible for Mafia wars and various series of assassinations in the 1980s and 1990s; serving a life sentence since 1993.

Placido Rizzotto — Trade unionist from Corleone, murdered by Luciano Liggio in 1948 on the orders of the boss Michele Navarra.

Franco Roberti — Former leading senior public prosecutor with the anti-Mafia investigation unit in Naples. Now chief prosecutor in Salerno.

Antonio Romeo – Clan chief of the Calabrian Romeo family, closely associated with the Pelle-Vottari clan.

Ernesto Ruffini – Former Archbishop of Palermo (1945–67).

Salvo – Taxi driver in Palermo.

Ignazio Salvo – Christian Democrat, the richest businessman in Sicily and representative of the bourgeois Mafia of the 1980s.

Benedetto 'Nitto' Santapaola – Sicilian mafioso, clan chief in Catania, member of Cosa Nostra council; in prison since 1993.

Carmine Sarno – Music producer from the Naples suburb of Ponticelli, member of the Sarno Camorra clan.

Ciro Sarno – Imprisoned head of the Sarno Camorra clan.

Vincenzo Scarantino – Temporary Mafia renegade who admitted involvement in the murder of Paolo Borsellino, and later withdrew his statements.

Roberto Scarpinato – Leading senior public prosecutor in the anti-Mafia investigation unit of Palermo, chief prosecutor in the Andreotti trial, now chief prosecutor in Caltanissetta.

Renato Schifani – President of the Italian senate and Forza Italia (Popolo della Libertà) MP.

Rosaria Schifani – Widow of the bodyguard Vito Schifani.

Vito Schifani – Bodyguard of Giovanni Falcone; murdered in the attack on Falcone in 1992.

Antonino Scopelliti – Prosecuting magistrate with the supreme court in Rome; murdered by the Mafia in 1991.

Shobha – Internationally award-winning Sicilian photographer, daughter of the anti-Mafia fighter Letizia Battaglia.

Heinz Sprenger – Detective Chief Superintendent with the criminal police in Duisburg, leader of the investigations into the Duisburg massacre.

Don Stefano Fernando – Priest in San Luca, Calabria.

Maria Strangio – Wife of the 'Ndranghetista Gianluca Nirta; murdered by their enemy clan at Christmas 2006 in an attack intended to kill her husband.

Don Pino Strangio – Parish priest of San Luca and spiritual head of the pilgrimage site of Madonna di Polsi.

Sebastiano Strangio – Owner of the pizzeria Da Bruno in
Duisburg, victim of the Duisburg massacre.

Domenico 'Don Micu' Trimboli – Boss of the Calabrian
Trimboli clan, international drug dealer; arrested in
2008.

Bernhard Vogel – German Christian Democrat and, until
2003, minister-president of Thuringia.

Franco Zecchin – Italian photographer and long-term
partner of Letizia Battaglia.